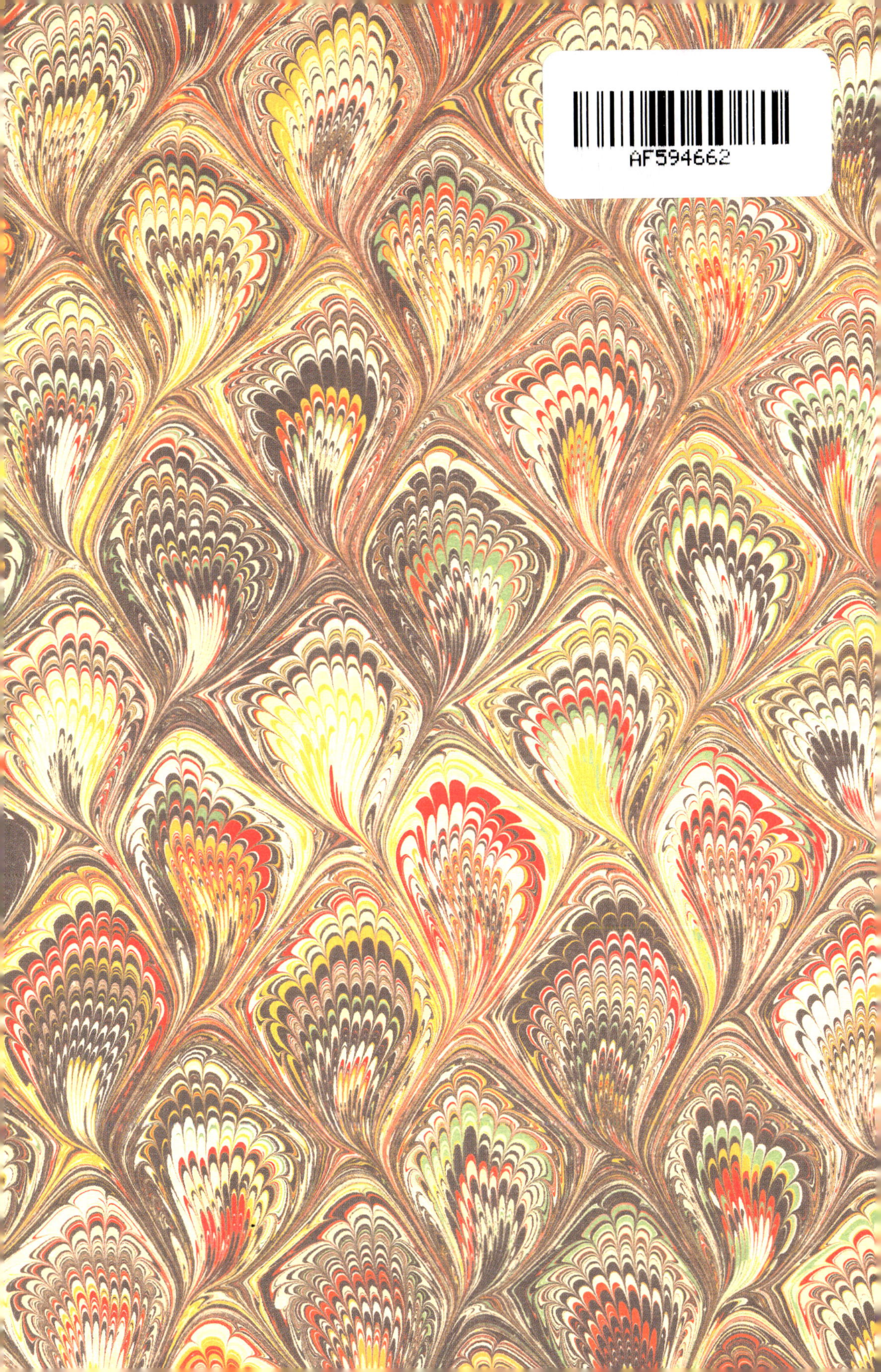
AF594662

IMAGES
of America

NOTABLE WOMEN OF PORTLAND

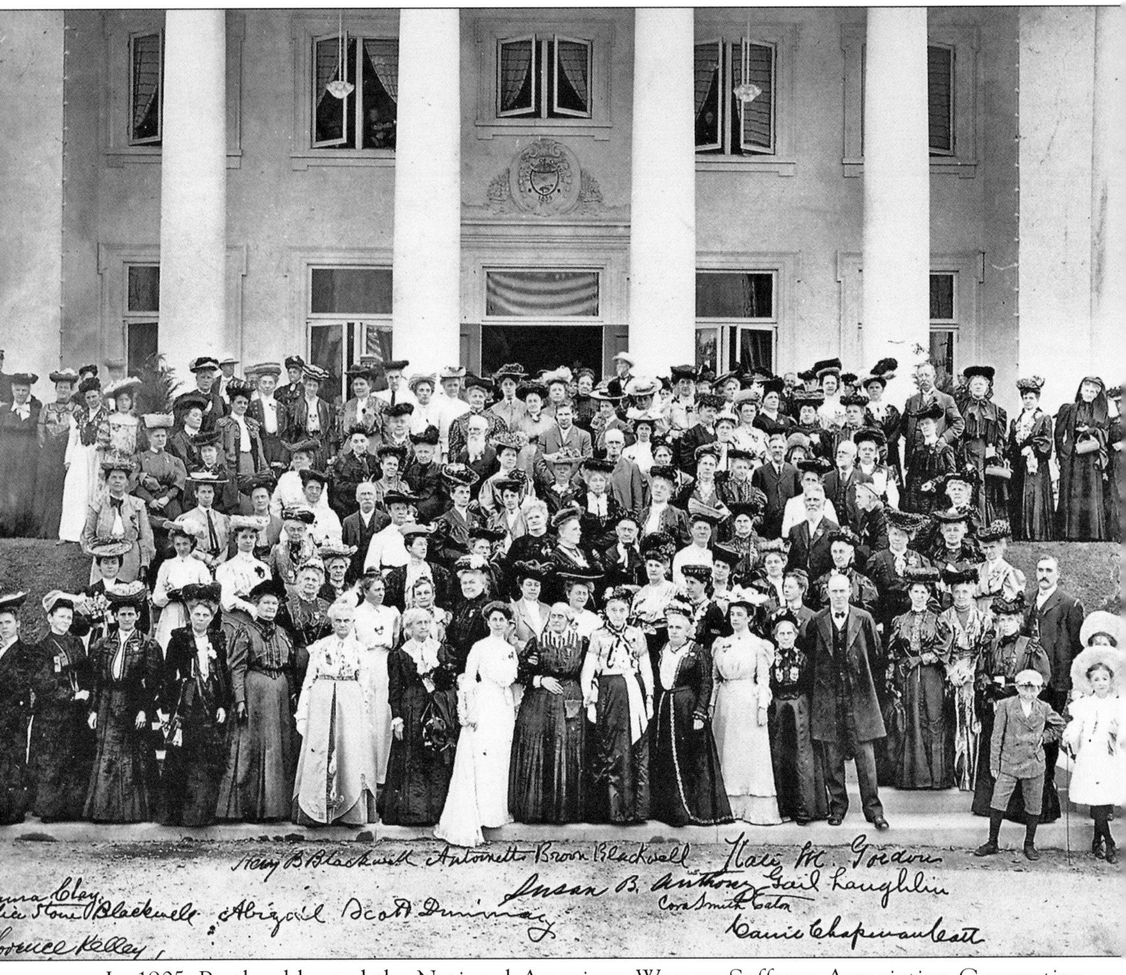

In 1905, Portland hosted the National American Woman Suffrage Association Convention. Attendees are pictured at the Lewis and Clark Exposition's Oregon Building at a reception for Susan B. Anthony (center). Abigail Scott Duniway is to her right (with the crossed scarf), and Dr. Marie Equi is directly behind her on the left. The Oregon suffrage vote failed five times before male voters finally gave women the right to vote in 1912. (OHS 59438.)

On the Cover: Margaret Vale Howe, Pres. Woodrow Wilson's niece, holds the shield representing the Oregon delegation at a 1913 woman's suffrage march in Washington, DC. She was not an Oregonian, but as an actress from a prominent family she was one of the suffrage movement women carrying shields of states that had already won women's suffrage. In 1912, Oregon became the ninth state to approve women's right to vote. (Library of Congress.)

IMAGES
of America

NOTABLE WOMEN OF PORTLAND

Tracy J. Prince and Zadie Schaffer

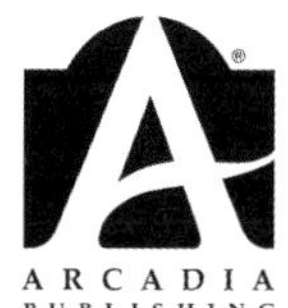

ISBN 978-1-4671-2505-5

Published by Arcadia Publishing
Charleston, South Carolina

Printed in the United States of America

Library of Congress Control Number: 2017935225

For all general information, please contact Arcadia Publishing:
Telephone 843-853-2070
Fax 843-853-0044
E-mail sales@arcadiapublishing.com
For customer service and orders:
Toll-Free 1-888-313-2665

Visit us on the Internet at www.arcadiapublishing.com

Bartlesville, Oklahoma Examiner-Enterprise, Sunday, February 16, 1975

Comments On Using Husband's Name

Dear Sir:

I have never written to any editor before but I am compelled to tonight. As I sat down tonight to read my daily Enterprise, I read an item about some membership meeting and appreciation luncheon given by all these Mrs. John Does, Frank Funkys and Dick Dingdongs. I started smiling to think how silly it is that the husband's names were printed instead of the persons who were really responsible. My smile did not last long when anger filled my being. I am not a libber, and haven't been even though I've been lectured to by many of my friends on the subject. I have always been a placid, let live type of person. But this has just incensed me and I had to write to you. In this day of enlightenment when women are being treated as people, why is it taboo to print their names in public. I wonder if I'm just overreacting. I wonder if anyone else sees the folly in this practice, even though etiquette might dictate this policy. Etiquette changes quite often and I hope to see this nonsense stopped very soon. Maybe the Enterprise can be a forerunner — a leader — of other dailies—by saying, this is nonsense and we will change what we believe to be ridiculous. How do you feel about this sir? Also, I wonder how the men in this community feel about this practice.

Sincerely,
Mrs. Susan Schaffer
1908 S. E. Sheridan Rd.
Bartlesville, OK
333-2554

This book is dedicated to the women who paved the way before us. To Shirley Prince, who read Miss Manners' books with the idea that very good manners (and lots of library time) would give her children a much less chaotic and impoverished life than she had. She was right—excellent manners and a lot of reading go a long way in this world. To Susan Schaffer, who, in 1975, wrote this letter to the editor of her hometown Oklahoma newspaper asking them to stop using only the names of husbands to identify women. When she read a name like Mrs. John Doe, she did not know what the first name was. She was new to town and wanted to know their names. The *Bartlesville Examiner-Enterprise* changed its policy. And to generations of our grandmothers—Lois Prince, Chessie Dale Prince, Lucinda Priest, June Marie McBride, Rosetta Cason, Mattie McBride, Sarah Schaffer, Machna Schaffer, Sprintza Toback, Ruth Kramer, Nettie Singer, and Rachel Kramer—all women who longed for better opportunities for their daughters than the times they lived in.

Contents

ACKNOWLEDGMENTS

We are deeply indebted to our dear friend Norm Gholston, who so graciously allowed the use of many images from his vast private collection.

We appreciate the archivists who helped so much, especially Meg Langford, Oregon Health Sciences University; Julie Yamaka, Oregon Blue Book at Oregon State Archives; and Cris Paschild and Carolee Harrison, Portland State University.

Image credit is abbreviated as follows: City of Portland Archives (CoPA), Gholston Family Collection (Gholston), Library of Congress (LOC), Doug Magedanz (Magedanz), New York Public Library (NYPL), Oregon Cultural Heritage Commission (OCHC), Oregon Health Sciences University Historical Collections and Archives (OHSU), Oregon Historical Society (OHS), Oregon Jewish Museum and Center for Holocaust Education (OJM), Oregon State Archives (OSA), Oregon State University Archives (OSU), Portland Art Museum (PAM), Portland State University Archives (PSU), Reed College Special Collections, Eric V. Hauser Library (Reed), San Francisco Bay Area Television Archives (SFBATA), Archives of the Sisters of the Holy Names of Jesus and Mary, U.S.–Ontario Province (Sisters), Triangle Productions for Gracie Hansen books (trianglepro.org), University of Oregon Archives (UofO), University of Portland Athletics (UP), Wikimedia Commons (W), and Willamette University's Ruth Dennis Grover Papers_III_4_8, Pacific Northwest Artists Archive (WU). All images not cited are photographs in our collection.

We most appreciate support from our family, Scott Schaffer and Price Schaffer, who cheered us on, posed for pictures, and were very patient with the enormous amount of time involved in writing this book.

All proceeds will benefit women in crisis at the Safety Off the Streets and Jean's Place shelters, part of Transition Projects.

INTRODUCTION

The story of Portland, Oregon, like much of history, is usually told with a focus on men's stories. This book tells about some of the women who made Portland what it is today. Their stories inspire us, make us want to understand the social norms they were living in, and help to more accurately reframe Portland's history. An example of how women's erased history needs to be restored is that many historians wrote about William Johnson, a British sailor who settled in what became the South Waterfront and Lair Hill neighborhoods. He was described as having an Indian wife, but historians never mentioned her name. It took incredible sleuthing by researcher Ginny Mapes to uncover records showing that her name was Polly. Then there is Etienne Lucier, who is described as the first white resident of what became East Portland; but his Native wife, Josette Nouette, who lived there too, is rarely mentioned. Portland pioneers whose surnames are on land records and street names, Charlotte Terwilliger and Minerva Carter, have been mostly lost to history though they were prominent in their time.

For millennia, thousands of Native American women lived in and passed through what became Portland. Several Chinook Indian bands (including the Multnomah, Cascade, and Clackamas) had permanent villages at the site of what is now Portland. But other tribes passed through and lived here seasonally, including the Tualatin, Kalapuya, Molalla, and Klickitat. Glimpses of this long history of Native American women are shown in chapter 1 with illustrations by explorers, pioneer stories, and stone implements used by Native women. Page 112 shows a berry basket made by a Native American woman that was collected by Lewis and Clark in 1805. Before Portland was incorporated in 1851, passing Native Americans and Hudson's Bay Company traders camped in The Clearing, surrounded by a dense forest. The February 4, 1911, *Oregonian* identifies The Clearing as being between Washington and Jefferson Streets along the Willamette River (see page 14). A seal carving on page 11 disproves historian assumptions that what became Old Portland (originally just the inner west side along the Willamette) did not have a pre-1840s history of Native Americans other than occasional stops at The Clearing. The carved seal found on the South Park Blocks indicates a larger habitation area for earlier Native people.

Historians also depict post-1840s Portland as being devoid of Native Americans. This is incorrect. This book works to more accurately tell the history of early Portland's Native American women. The reality is that pioneers and Native Americans interacted frequently, often living next to each other (see page 16). According to a Work Projects Administration (WPA) interview of a pioneer ("Oregon Oddities," December 15, 1940), Portland's 1850 population was 275 white people and 1,000 Native Americans. These 1,000 Native people came from many different Oregon and Washington tribes, drawn to the new city by trade opportunities. Native Americans and pioneers used Chinook Jargon to communicate in the prolific commerce between them. Pioneer families prided themselves on being fluent in Jargon. Even in the 1910s, Pioneer's Association gatherings were often conducted in Jargon. In 1914, when Henrietta Failing (see page 25) went to New York's Vassar College, she and her father wrote to each other in the Jargon. He called her "hertenas kloochman"—little woman. Until the 1930s, Portland had annual encampments of Native Americans who stayed for months while trading (see page 27).

Progressive Era women in chapter 2 worked for suffrage, temperance, prohibition, sanitation, free libraries, and protecting women and children's labor. Known as Portland's first woman physician, Mary Anna Cooke Thompson came to Oregon in 1866 with her husband and children via the Panama Canal. She spoke to the National Woman Suffrage Association Convention in Washington, DC, and before the US Senate and lobbied Pres. Rutherford B. Hayes on suffrage. The first female lawyer in Oregon, Mary Gysin Leonard, was known for courtroom expertise, hard drinking, and giving free legal advice to ladies of the night. Women working in the suffrage movement such as Abigail Scott Duniway, Dr. Marie Equi, Lizzie Weeks, Sarah Bard Field, and many others worked tirelessly for women's right to vote.

Chapter 3 shows Portland women from World War I to II, with nurses, the Red Cross, Women's Service League, Uncle Sam's Kanning Kitchen, Women Airforce Service Pilots, Women's Army Auxiliary Corps, Rosie the Riveters, Wendy the Welders, and women in war housing. Dr. Harriet Lawrence developed a Spanish flu serum to treat the World War I pandemic. Dr. Esther Pohl Lovejoy was the first woman to serve on the American Red Cross Commission in France. To show how it felt in Portland during both wars, all photographs depict Portland women, except for page 56, with Yeomanettes marching in Washington, DC.

Chapter 4 tells of women in postwar to contemporary Portland, with Vanport and Guild's Lake women, Dorothea Lensch (Portland's first recreation director who made sports accessible to women), Verdell Rutherford (a civil rights leader who helped Oregon pass civil rights laws a decade ahead of the nation), Dr. Lena Nemerovsky Kenin (an early researcher on postpartum depression), and quirky gals like Grace Wick and Gracie Hansen (who marched to the beat of their own drummer and kept Portland weird before that was a thing).

Chapter 5 features Portland's women in the arts, with dancers, singers, actors, musicians, painters, photographers, and writers. Two women were honored as a "Living Legend" by the Library of Congress: world-famous authors Beverly Cleary and Ursula Le Guin. Some writers are featured in other chapters to more fully tell that era's story: Frances Fuller Victor (see page 20) did much of her important work as a ghostwriter for H.H. Bancroft; Esther Pohl Lovejoy (see pages 22, 41, 44, and 55) wrote four histories of women in medicine; Eva Emery Dye (see page 28) popularized Sacajawea's story as an icon for suffragists; Louise Bryant (see page 37) was the first woman reporter for the *Oregonian*; and Beatrice Morrow Cannady (see page 116) was editor and publisher of the *Advocate*. Chapter 6 includes some Portland women who have been elected or appointed to political office or ran for office though they were not elected. Nan Wood Honeyman was Oregon's first congresswoman. Beatrice Morrow Cannady was the first African American to run for office in Oregon. "No Sin" Dorothy Lee, the first woman mayor of Portland, cracked down on Portland's notorious vice industry of gambling, brothels, and organized crime, and Barbara Roberts was the first woman elected governor of Oregon. Esther Pohl Lovejoy, who ran for Congress, is featured in earlier chapters.

Because space is limited, this book is not an encyclopedic listing of Portland's notable women; many are not included. As a pictorial history, the publisher's format requires brief captions. This is only a small snapshot of women's lives in Portland. The book focuses on women from history—rarely on contemporary women. Many famous women are included, but it is also important to include women whose names are less known or even unknown. Images of unnamed Native American women, women in war housing, 1940s exercise classes, or at protests offer views into many eras and walks of life that collectively tell a history of women in Portland. We wrote this book to do our part to mend the telling of Portland's history.

One

Native American and Pioneer Women Pre-1851 to 1870s

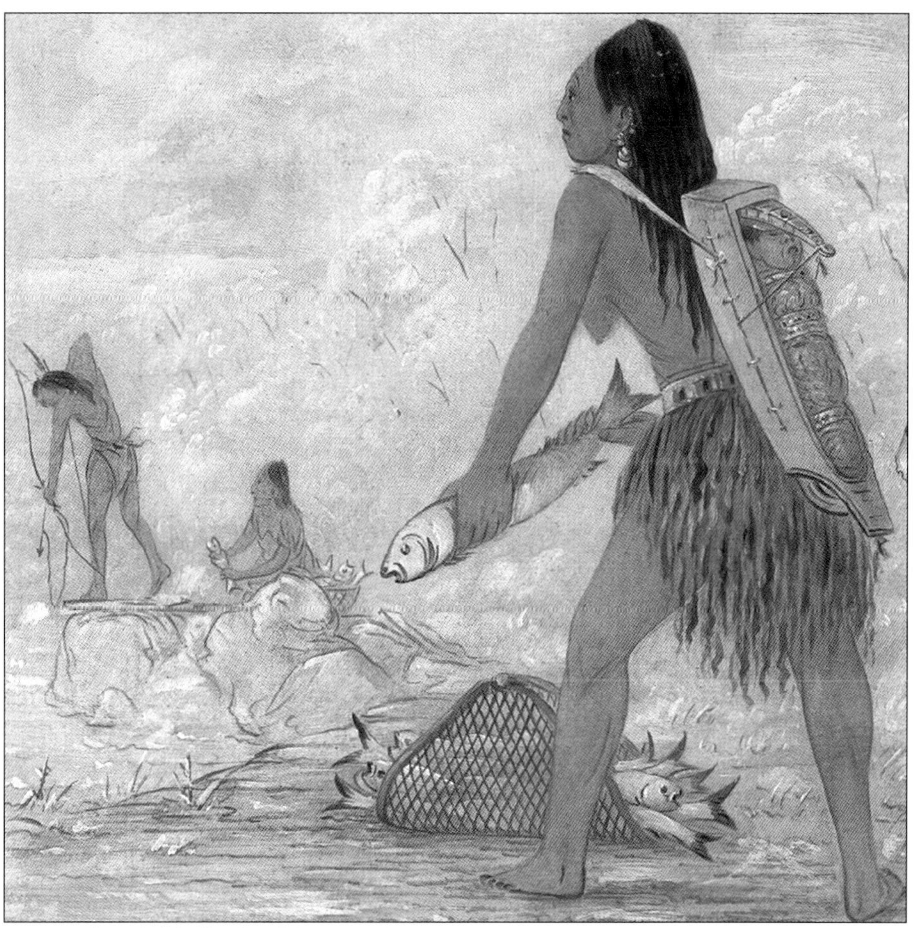

Incorporated in 1851, Portland has much forgotten history, including that there was a strong presence of Native Americans before and after pioneers arrived in Portland in the 1840s. This George Catlin 1841 illustration shows Chinook people fishing and a Native woman carrying a baby in a cradleboard designed to flatten foreheads in the local custom. Native people in what is now Portland were largely Chinookan bands of Multnomah, Cascade, and Clackamas people who fished and lived in this manner for thousands of years. (NYPL.)

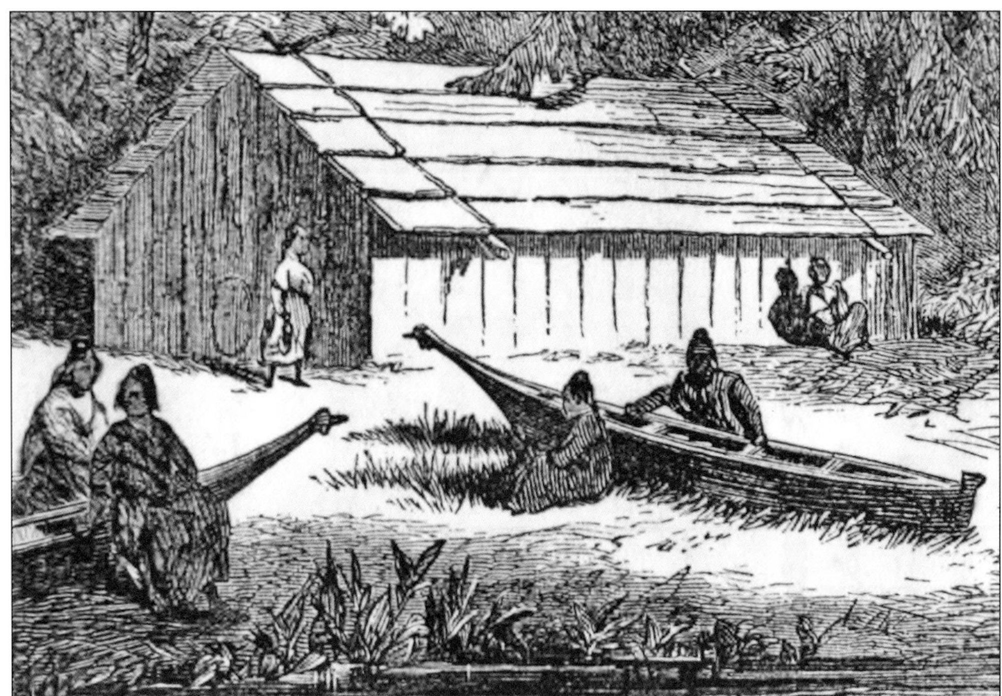

In the 1850s, James Swan lived for three years among Chinook Indians, chronicled in his book *The Northwest Coast*. His illustrations give a rare look at Chinook women's lives in their plank houses. In the interior scene, women are cooking and caring for children, and they put fish on cross-beams to dry. In 1806, Lewis and Clark described such plank houses at what is now Portland. The exterior scene shows Chinook women and children and what pioneers and Indians called "Chinook canoes" with animal effigy prows. Used by many Northwest tribes, Chinook canoes were numerous along the Oregon coast and Columbia and Willamette Rivers. Some Canadian historians claim that these canoes were made exclusively by Vancouver Island's Nootka. However, Swan describes watching Chinook people make this exact type of canoe, so this theory is incorrect. (Both, PSU.)

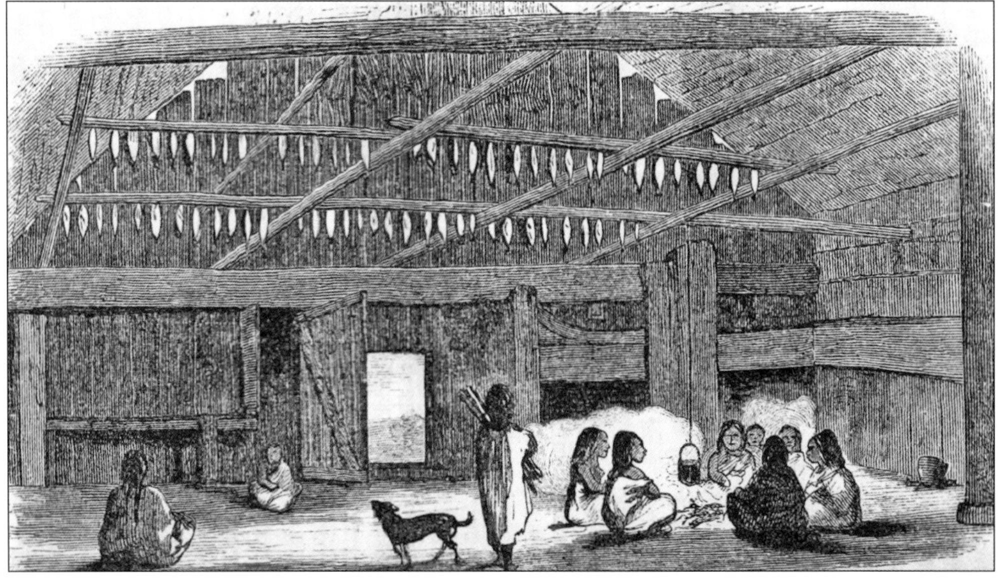

An 1837 Alfred Jacob Miller illustration shows a Chinook woman. Miller was commissioned to sketch on a William Drummond Stewart expedition. Chinookan territory ranged from the Pacific Ocean down the Columbia to The Dalles and along parts of the Willamette River. Below right, Portland Art Museum displays stone carvings found on Portland's Sauvie Island. These were used by Native women to cook in or to pound salmon, wapato, or camas as foods that were dried, stored, and traded. In the 1850s, such "Indian relics" were stacked outside of pioneer houses—turned up by plowing and available to anyone who would haul them away. On the left is a 22-pound Native American carved basalt seal discovered in 1963. It was eight inches underground on the South Park Blocks (1400 block), kicked up when a backhoe was digging out parking spaces. This area was likely never ploughed, since it was dedicated parkland early in Portland's history. (Right, Yale.)

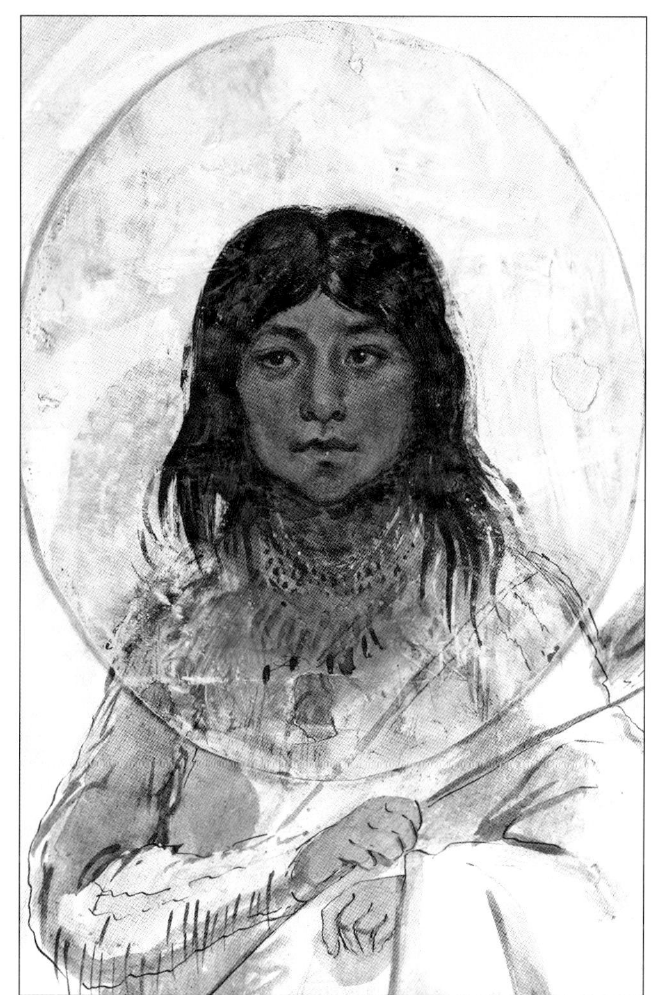

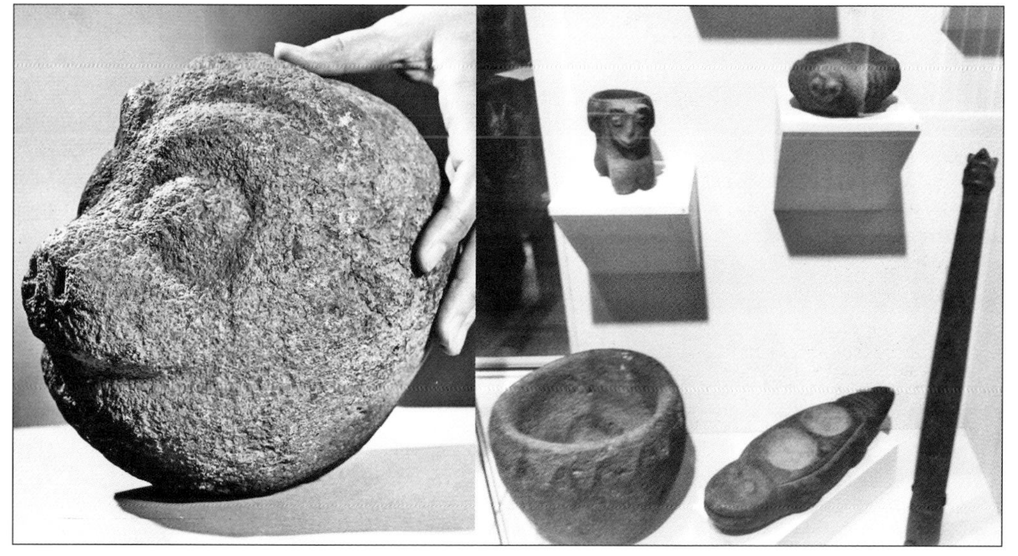

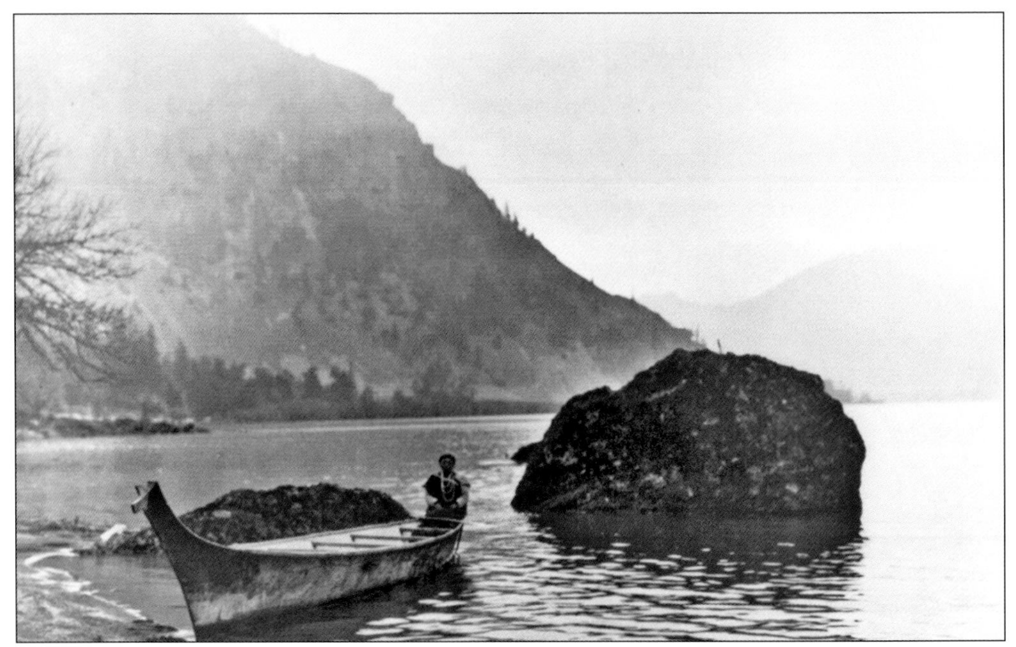

A 1910 Edward Curtis photograph of the Columbia River near Portland shows a Native American woman with a Chinook canoe. Her name is Virginia Miller (Why-lick-Quiuck), from the Cascade band of the Chinook. Her nephew was Curtis's Columbia Gorge guide. This image is a reminder that the Native presence did not end when pioneers arrived. Even in 1910, Native Americans and Chinook canoes were frequently in Portland and along local rivers. (LOC.)

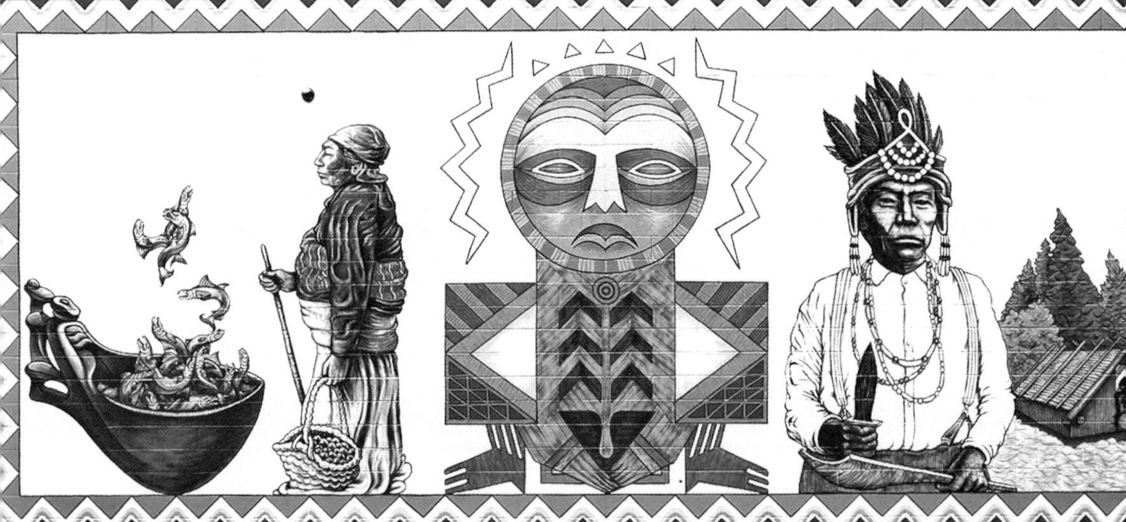

Tribal histories overlap between Portland and Vancouver, Washington. Perhaps because of the Hudson's Bay Company's history with Native Americans at Fort Vancouver, the Vancouver area does a better job of teaching about local Native history via public art. Vancouver's 2012 mural at Washington and Sixth Streets, *Chinook Indians*, depicts Catherine George—an eyewitness to life along the Columbia River as Native Americans dealt with the impacts of traders and pioneers coming into their land.

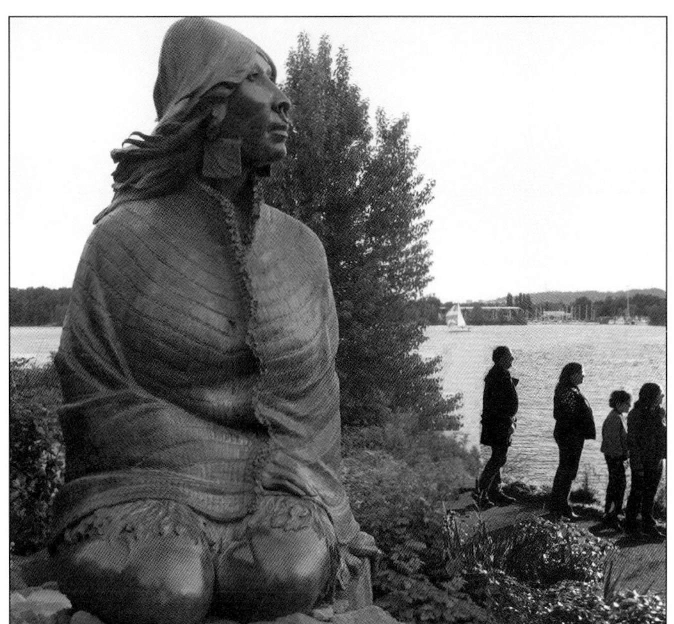

This 1994 bronze statue of Ilchee, daughter of Chinookan Chief Concomly, overlooks the Columbia River at Vancouver's Waterfront Renaissance Park. Ilchee was married to Duncan McDougall, chief factor of John Jacob Astor's Pacific Fur Company, and later married Chief Casino, a high-ranking Chinookan chief in the Portland/Vancouver area. Native women wove cedar bark to make baskets and such water-resistant capes as Ilchee is wearing.

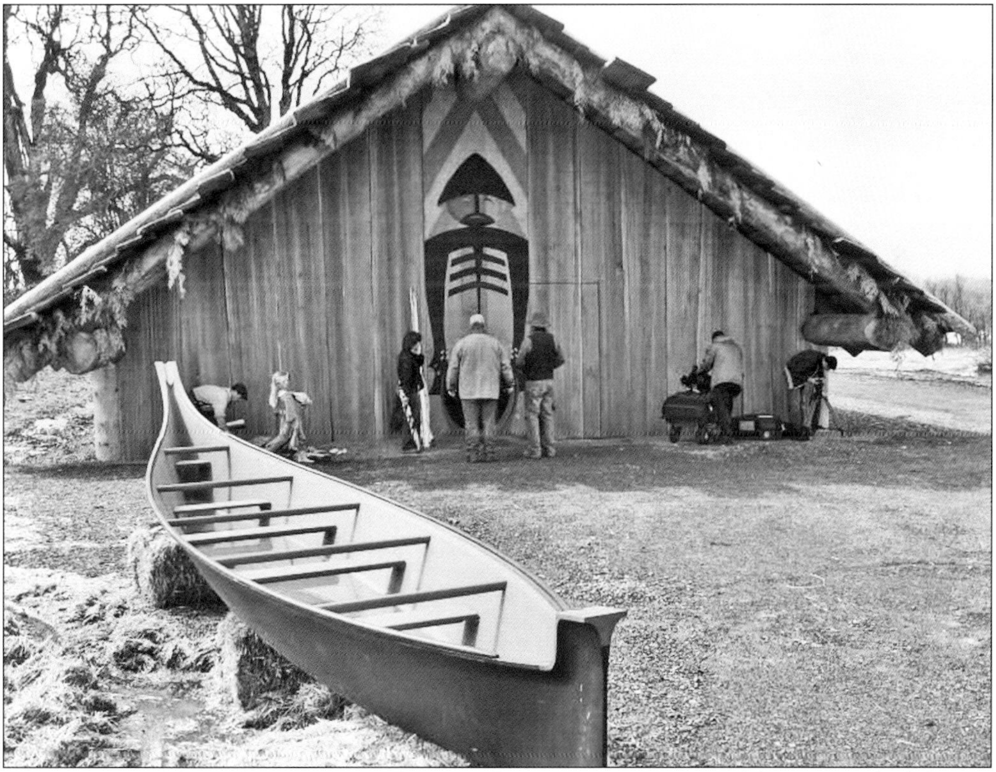

Nearby Ridgefield, Washington, has an historically accurate re-creation of the type of plank houses that once occupied Portland. Justifiably proud of the Cathlapotle Plankhouse, the town boasts in its slogan to "Visit Ridgefield. Lewis & Clark did—twice!" The village Lewis and Clark visited has been verified by archaeological evidence. The Chinook village is described in great detail in their journals. The journals describe similar plank houses in what is now Portland.

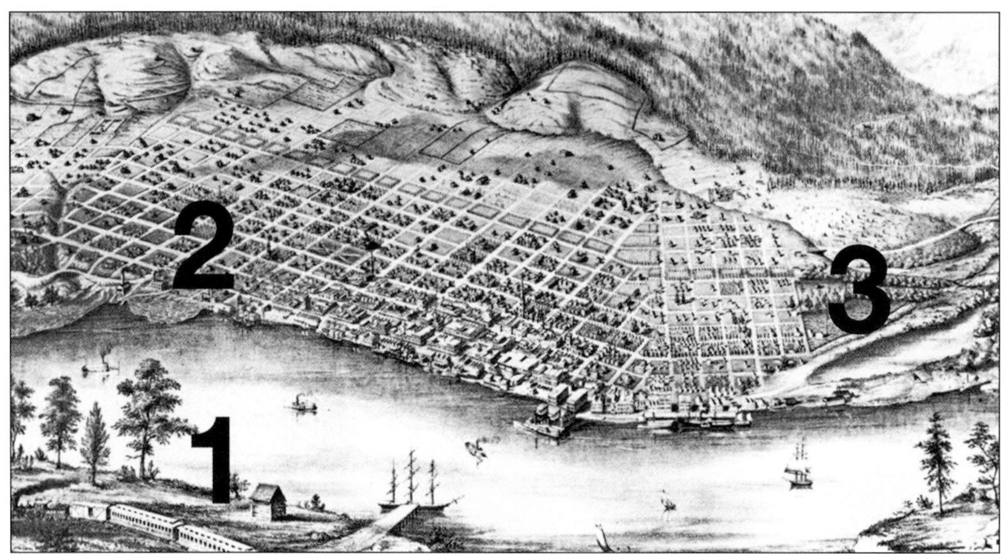

Etienne Lucier (1) was the first white resident of what became East Portland, where he and his Native wife, Josette (or Josephte) Nouette, briefly lived around 1828, possibly near the foot of today's Southeast Morrison (sources vary). Sources also vary on her tribal origins—she was either Chinook or from Canada's Vancouver Island. Later, in 1850, around 1,000 Native Americans lived in Portland where The Clearing (2) once was and around Couch Lake (3).

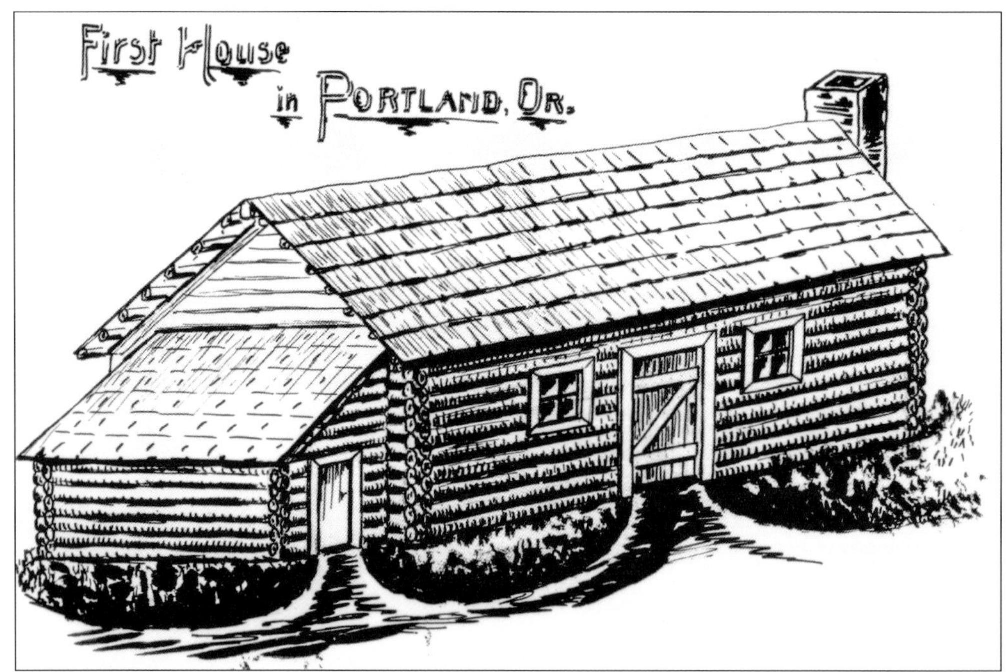

In 1841, William Johnson was the first white settler in what became Portland. Little is known about his Native American wife, Polly. Their house was bounded by Macadam, Curry, Hood, and Whitaker Streets (now bisected by Interstate 5). Johnson descendants were edged out of their claim by Elizabeth and Finice Caruthers, mother and son, under suspect legal circumstances. A park was named after Elizabeth, though many decry a park named after a claim jumper. (OHS.)

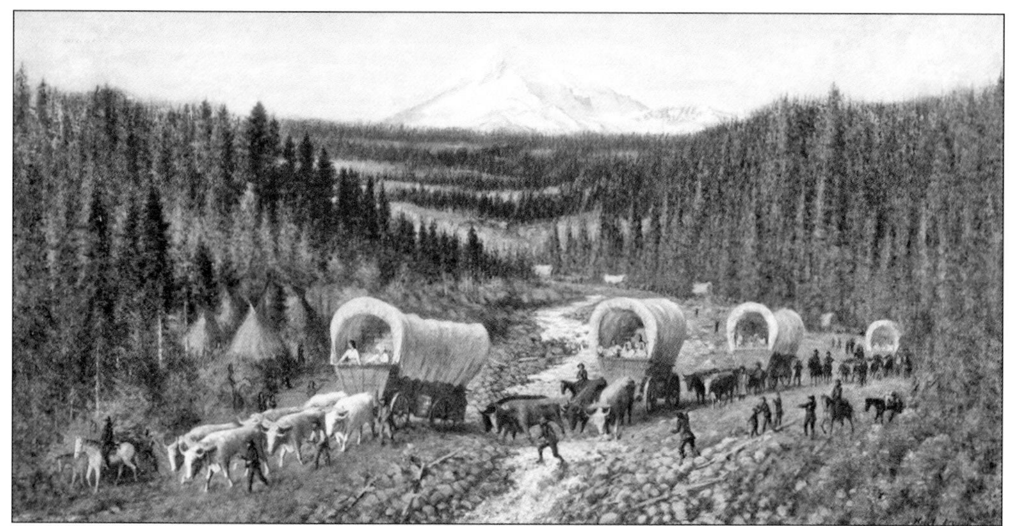

The Oregon Trail was laid out by Native Americans, trappers, traders, and explorers from 1811 to 1840. During the "Great Migration," 400,000 people crossed the Oregon Trail seeking new lives in Oregon Territory, often leaving from Independence, Missouri. The largest wave of pioneers on the trail occurred from 1846 to 1869. This 1920s painting is of a pioneer wagon train on the Barlow Road. Mount Hood is in the background. A Native American encampment is in on the left. The painting is by Karl Feurer, from the pioneer family of Louis Feurer, owner of Gambrinus Brewery, which once stood at Northwest Twenty-Fourth Place and Burnside Street. Below are two stories from pioneer women about life and hardships along the Oregon Trail. These stories appear in the 1905 book *The Souvenir of Western Women*. (Above, O'Gallerie.)

* **Reminiscence of Mrs. Julia A. Wilcox (a pioneer of 1845), widow of Ralph Wilcox, who was the first school-teacher in Portland, Oregon: "In crossing the plains on Meek's cut-off we were without water for thirty-six hours. The cattle had disappeared; they were found by a spring where they had found the water. A great many of the company were taken sick and died from eating the cattle that had been driven so far. Food was scarce and the cattle had to be killed and eaten. In some places the mountains were so steep that the wagons nearly stood on ends; the oxen were taken off the wagons and the men had to hold on to the back of the wagons to keep them from tipping. An Indian swam the Deschutes River and carried a rope across. The wagon beds were fastened to the rope, and the people and provisions were carried across this way."**

* **Mrs. Jane Gage Goodhue Thomas contributes this interesting incident of crossing the plains: "The road was strewn for hundreds of miles with discarded things from overloaded wagons—food, bedding, wearing apparel, even trunks full of ball dresses, books, furniture, machinery—everything, in fact, that could be mentioned. On the Platte River, where we camped one evening, we noticed a white tent in the bushes near by. Upon examination there was found pinned to the tent a note which read, 'Died of cholera.' Inside was a neatly-made bed and a trunk full of woman's clothing. Beside the tent was the grave. The dead were buried by putting in a layer of earth and then a layer of prickly pear, alternately, to prevent wild animals from digging the bodies up. At Fort Laramie the wagons were searched and all liquors confiscated."**

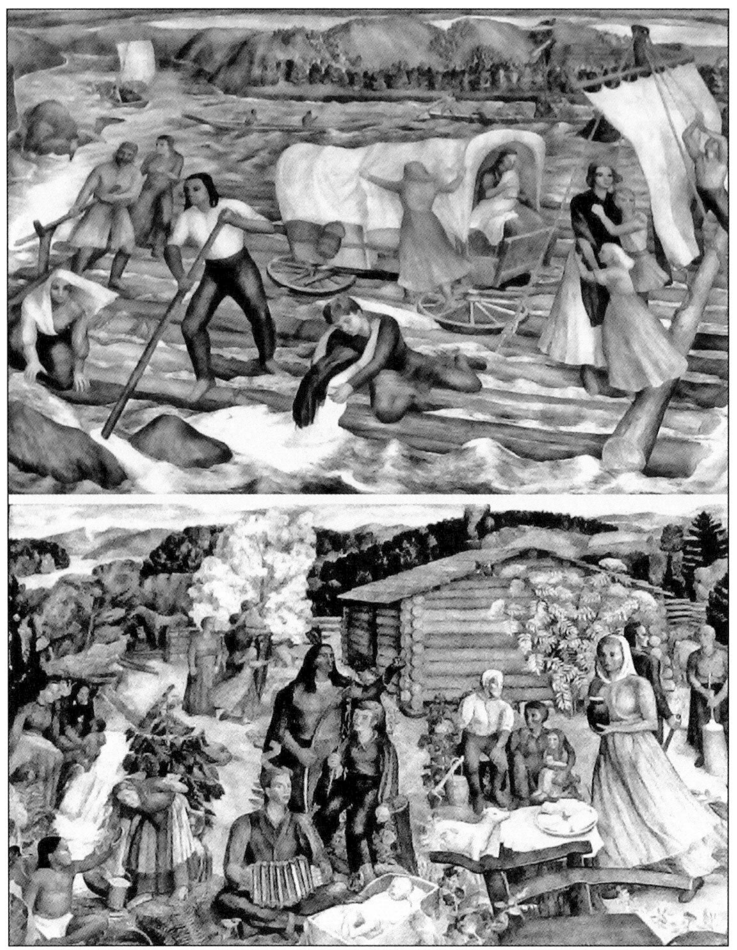

WPA artist Martina Gangle Curl (see page 105) painted these 1940 murals: *The Columbia River Pioneer Migration—The Raft* and *The Homesteaders*. First at Rose City Park Elementary, they were moved to Madison High School Auditorium.

Charlotte Terwilliger Moffatt Cartwright (1842–1915) was a member of the Pioneer's Association, State Equal Suffrage Association, Sacajawea Statue Association, and Portland Woman's Club. In 1845, she traveled the Oregon Trail at age three. Her mother died of camp fever as they portaged around the Columbia River cascades. Her father, James, built a house and blacksmith shop at First Avenue and Morrison Street, later staking a claim in Southwest Portland. In 1909, his heirs gave land to the city for Terwilliger Boulevard, designed by the Olmsted brothers. According to the October 8, 1915, *Oregonian*, her brother Hiram described their childhood as growing up with only Indian playmates, with no white neighbors closer than the next claim, learning Chinook Jargon better than English, and seeing Indians use sweat lodges along the Willamette River near their home. (Gholston.)

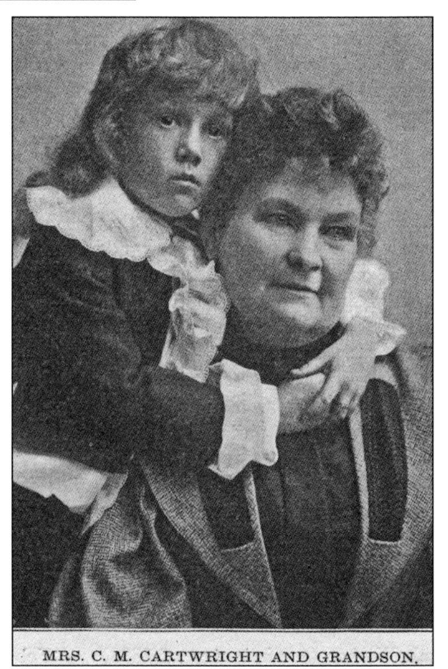

MRS. C. M. CARTWRIGHT AND GRANDSON.

This story from *Touching incidents in the life and labors of a pioneer on the Pacific coast since 1853* describes Oregon Trail miseries. This is what is was like in 1853, as bedraggled waves of pioneers rolled into Portland, including "a number of orphans, children to be cared for by strangers or wander without care, ragged and destitute and forsaken." Pioneer John Talbot's daughter described 1850s Portland as a wild place—the outskirts of the city were "forest land, with cougar and panther waiting to drop down out of the dark firs."

About the first of August, the emigrants began to arrive from the plains, wearied and sometimes sick, and many of them disheartened on account of the loss of teams and wagons during the journey, and the worst of all the death and burial of friends in the desert. Sometimes it was a husband, sometimes a wife, a son or a daughter; sometimes both husband and wife, leaving a number of orphans children to be cared for by strangers, or wander without care, ragged and destitute and forsaken, themselves to perish in the wilderness. No pen has ever been able to adequately describe the terrible sufferings of those early emigrants during the ten years succeeding 1850. Having crossed the Isthmus of Panama, I had a few weeks to spare before the bulk of the emigrants began to arrive, and nothing could exceed the terrible sufferings I witnessed amongst the first arrivals from the plains. Frequently a solitary horseman would arrive, bringing news of some special disaster, and the settlers would pack several horses and mules with provisions and clothing and hasten to their relief.

When I arrived at Portland in the Autumn of 1853, I found myself confronted with an unusual number of such scenes, and I soon exhausted all my surplus means, in efforts for their relief,

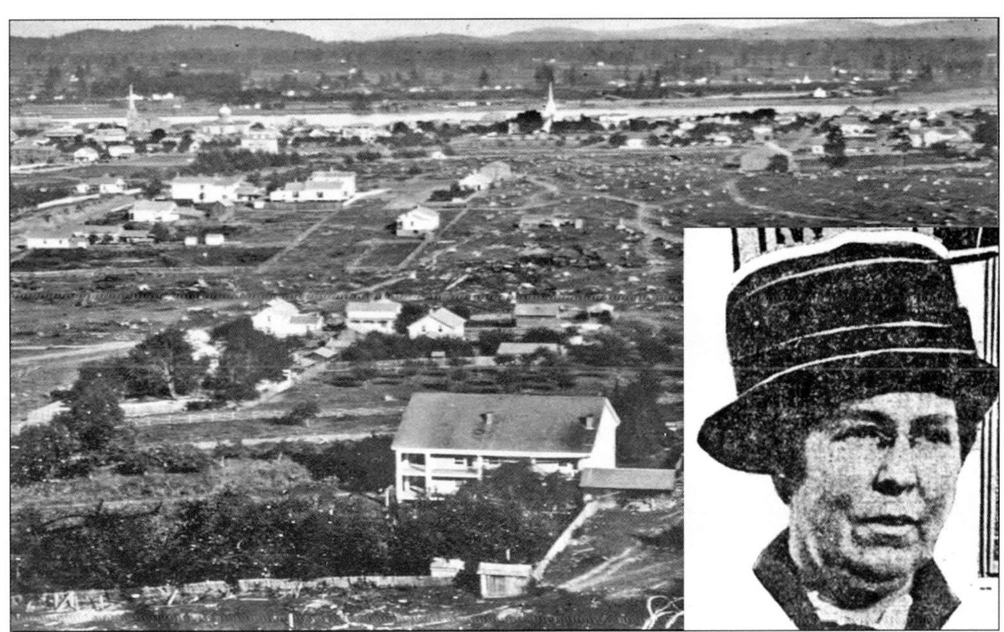

Minerva Feltch Carter (1808–1895), an early Portland pioneer, arrived in 1847 with her husband, Thomas Carter. Their Donation Land Claims covered huge sections of what is now Goose Hollow, downtown, and Portland Heights, and their names are on many land records. They raised five children in this mansion on the edge of town (what is now Southwest Eighteenth Avenue and Columbia Street). (OHS 7116.)

A. H. FRANCIS,

Pioneer Merchant of Oregon ! !

NEW FALL AND WINTER GOODS! !

NOW OPENING, A LARGE AND SPLENDID ASsortment of

Staple and Fancy Dry Goods,

Boots and Shoes,

Clothing,

Carpets,

Oilcloths, &c.

SOLD LOW for Cash or Country Produce.

Receiving by every Steamer,

Ladies' Fine Dress Goods,

English and French Merinos,

Sicilian Cloths,

Wool and Half-Wool Plaids,

Silks, De Laines, Cashmeres, Prints,

New Style Zephyr Shawls, with Hoods,

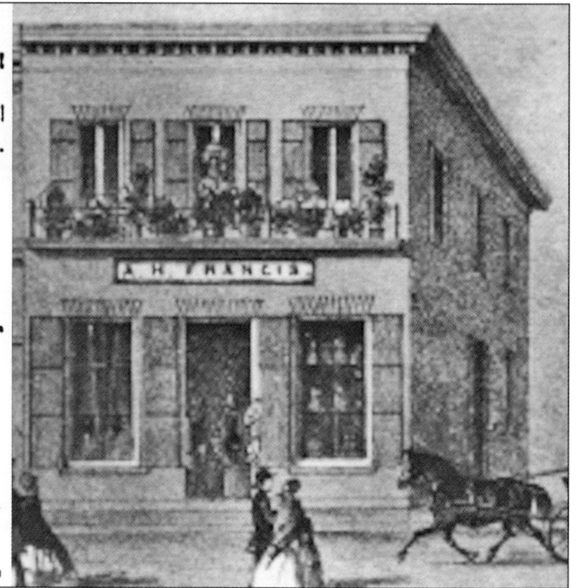

Black pioneers Sydna Edmonia Robella Dandrich Francis (1815–1889) and her husband, Abner Hunt Francis, were some of Portland's earliest residents—living in the city from 1851 to 1860. From 1854 to 1860, they ran A.H. Francis mercantile and a boardinghouse at Front and Stark Streets, living upstairs. Back in New York, they were prominent leaders for women's rights and the abolition of slavery. Both worked closely with Frederick Douglass—organizing abolitionist conventions and writing for his newspaper. Sydna Francis was secretary of the Female Dorcas Society and president of the Ladies' Literary and Progressive Improvement Society of Buffalo. After moving to Oregon, the Francises were threatened with expulsion because of Oregon's 1849 black exclusion law. Sydna's family collected over 200 signatures to overturn the law, which was rescinded in 1854. Bankruptcy forced a move to San Francisco, then to Victoria, British Columbia, where they are buried. (Above, *Oregonian*, February 16, 1861; below, *Oregonian*, August 28, 1852.)

LOOK HERE!

GREAT CHANCES AT THE STORE OF

I. B. FRANCIS,

Front street, under the Columbian Hotel, Portland, O. T.

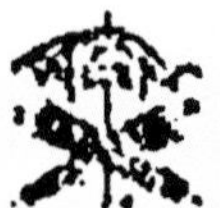

A MOST MAGNIFICENT ASSORTMENT of fashionable **Coats, Pants, Vests, Shirts, Cravats, Pocket Handkerchiefs, Silk Bands, Half Hose, &c., &c.**

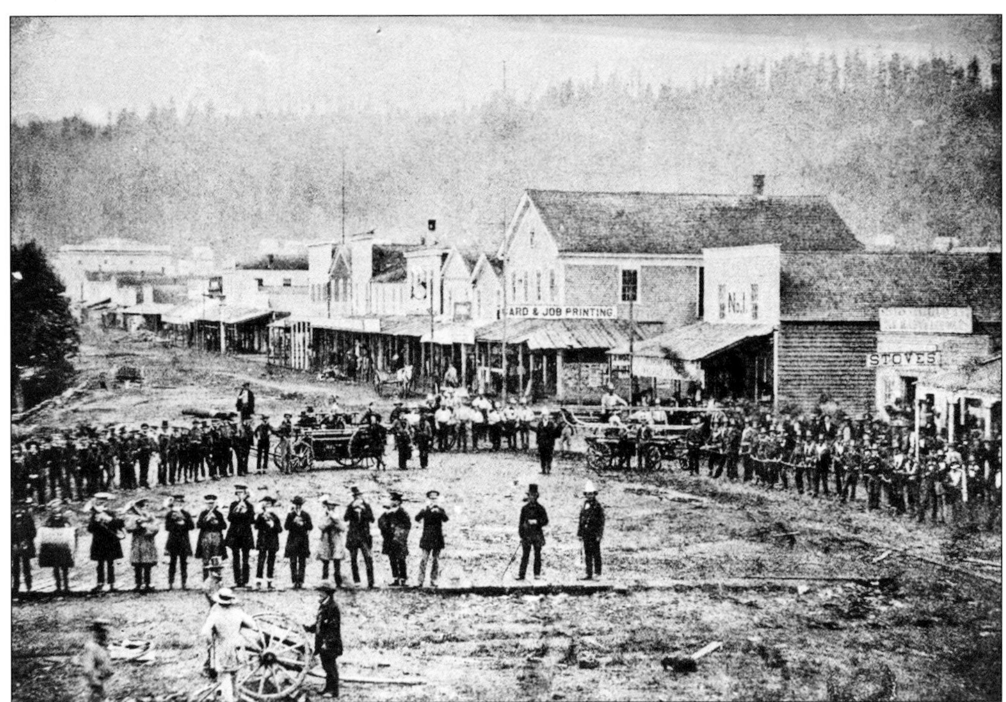

Front Street is pictured in 1858, in a view looking south from Alder Street. Sydna and Abner Francis helped run his brother I.B. Francis's store from 1851 to 1854, then they opened the A.H. Francis store. Most publications on Oregon history list black pioneer I.B. Francis's name incorrectly as O.B. Francis. From 1852 to 1854, Issac B. Francis paid for many *Oregonian* advertisements for his store, such as the one on page 18 from August 28, 1852. Thus, it is irrefutable that his name was I.B. (Gholston.)

A. H. Francis	38	m	M	Agent			N. Jersey
Sydna	35	f	M			150	Va
John Dandrich	48	m	M	Waiter		250	Va
Charlotte	55	f	M				Va

A. H. Francis	45	"	B	Merchant	16000	20000	N. Jersey
Sydna "	44	f	B				Virginia

Abner H Francis	46	M	M	Merchant	12000	1200	New Jersey
Sydna E. R. "	44	F	M		1000		Va

Most publications on Oregon history list Sydna's name incorrectly as Lynda. Her name is indisputable, since she published as "Sydna E. R. Francis" in Frederick Douglass's newspaper, the *North Star*. Also, census records from 1850s Buffalo (top, living next to her parents John and Charlotte Dandrich), 1860s Portland (middle), and 1860s San Francisco (bottom) list her as Sydna. She and Abner are listed as "mulatto" in New York and California and "black" in Oregon.

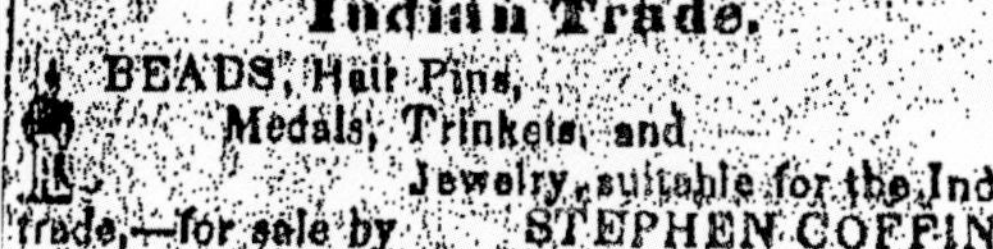

Indian Trade.
BEADS, Hair Pins, Medals, Trinkets, and Jewelry, suitable for the Indian trade,—for sale by STEPHEN COFFIN.

1850 ad in Portland

Indian Beads.

BY recent arrivals of clipper ships, we have received in additions to our former large stock, 20,000 ps. Indian beads, comprising every variety. A large part of which are especially adapted to the OREGON TRADE.
E. FITZGERALD & CO.

1854 ad in Portland

Mosier, Oregon, __________ 191__

To **G. H. ORR,** Dr.

Manufacturer of All Grades of Wampum Beads

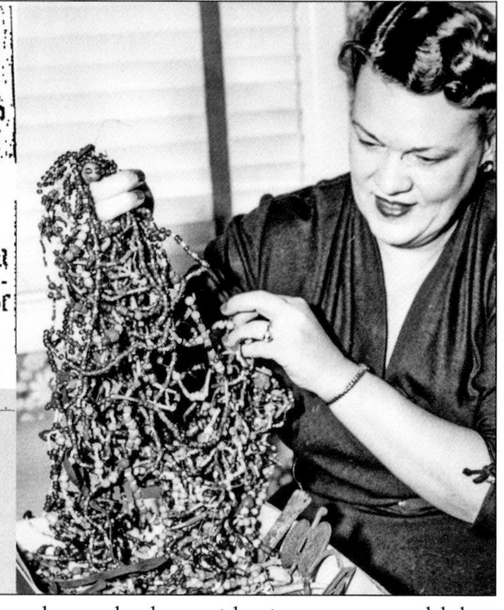

In early Portland, Native Americans traded berries, salmon, baskets, rides in canoes, and labor (to clear trees, farm, and hunt). Pioneers traded clothing, beads, metal trinkets, tools, pans, and blankets. In 1956, Mrs. Fosberg found a box of beads used in such trades in her parent's attic, in a house once owned by "Indian Dave." (Left, *Oregonian* advertisements December 4, 1850, and February 18, 1854; bill of sale, Gholston; right, OHS 010925.)

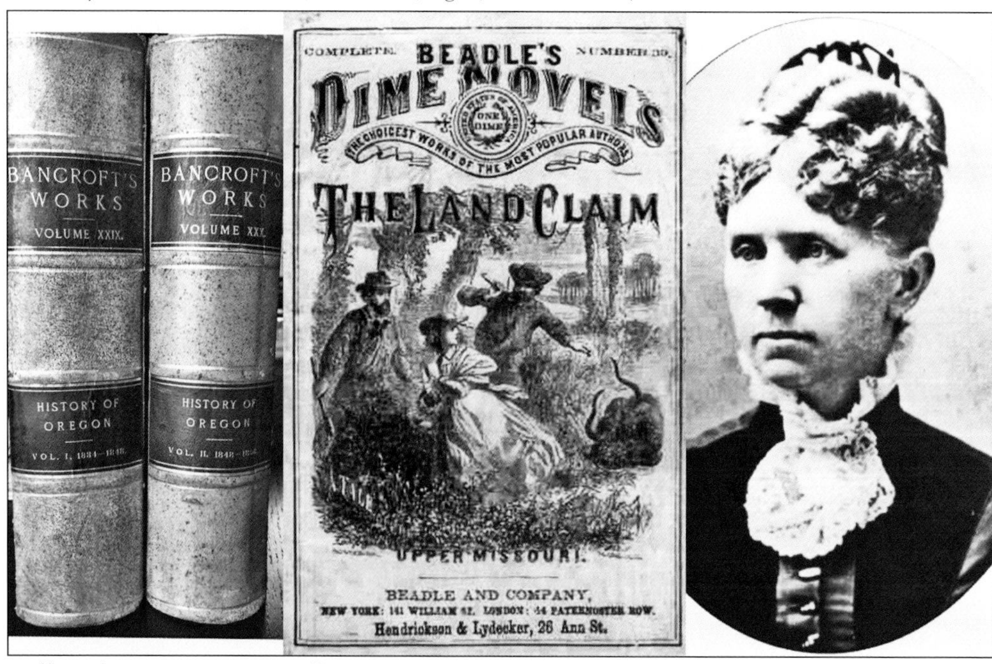

Brilliant historian Frances Fuller Victor (1826–1902) authored dime novels like *The Land Claim* before she moved to Portland in 1864 and documented Oregon history. She wrote about women's rights in Abigail Scott Duniway's newspaper and published *The River of the West* (1870), *All Over Oregon and Washington* (1872), and *The Early Indian Wars of Oregon* (1894). She was a mostly unacknowledged ghostwriter for Hubert Howe Bancroft on *History of Oregon I and II* and other volumes.

Two

Progressive Era Women
1870s to 1920s

WOMEN HAVE FULL SUFFRAGE IN

AUSTRALIA NORWAY ISLE OF MAN
NEW ZEALAND FINLAND TASMANIA

WOMEN HAVE MUNICIPAL SUFFRAGE IN

ENGLAND ICELAND DENMARK
SCOTLAND CANADA SWEDEN
WALES NATAL, SOUTH AFRICA

In the United States Women Vote in twenty-eight states on Municipal and School affairs

WOMEN VOTE
ON EQUAL TERMS WITH MEN
IN

WYOMING COLORADO
UTAH WASHINGTON
IDAHO CALIFORNIA

WHY NOT IN OREGON?

VOTE | 300 X 'YES' | AMENDMENT NO. 1, NOV. 5, 1912

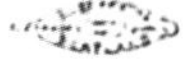

From the 1870s to 1920s, many Portland women fought for Progressive Era campaigns on labor issues, reproductive rights, sanitation, free libraries, temperance, prohibition, and woman's suffrage (the right to vote). However, some women were opposed to suffrage. This suffrage handbill was distributed by Oregon's College Equal Suffrage League. Oregon defeated suffrage more times than any other state, with male voters rejecting it in 1884, 1900, 1906, 1908, and 1910. In 1912, Oregon became the ninth state to grant suffrage. The term *suffragette* was more common in Britain, while *suffragist* was in wider use in America. (UofO.)

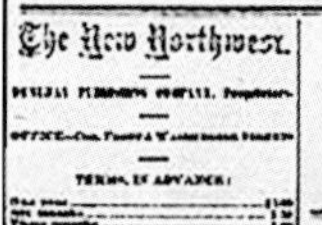

The New Northwest.

VOLUME IX. PORTLAND, OREGON, THURSDAY, NOVEMBER 27, 1870. NUMBER 11.

LECTURE!

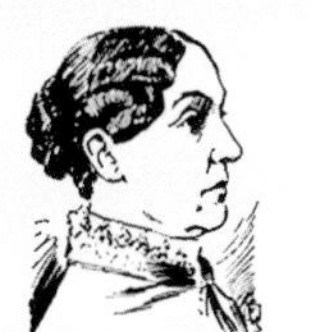

Abigail Scott Duniway

The Veteran Equal Suffrage Leader

OF THE PACIFIC NORTHWEST

WILL LECTURE

TO-NIGHT

BRINGING GLAD TIDINGS, AT

Abigail Scott Duniway

FORDHAM APARTMENTS

170 FORD ST.

PORTLAND, OREGON

WOMEN VOTE IN OREGON, WASHINGTON, CALIFORNIA, ARIZONA, WYOMING, UTAH, COLORADO, IDAHO, KANSAS, ILLINOIS. WHY NOT IN ALL THE STATES?

An 1852 pioneer and Oregon's "Mother of Equal Suffrage," Abigail Scott Duniway (1834-1915) was editor/publisher of the *New Northwest* newspaper, author of 22 novels on improving "woman's condition" and other social ills, and a frequent lecturer and public face for Oregon's suffrage movement. Her brother, Harvey Scott, the *Oregonian* owner, used his influence to defeat women's suffrage five times. She lived in Goose Hollow's Fordham Apartments, at 742 Southwest Vista Avenue (formerly 170 Vista Avenue). (UofO.)

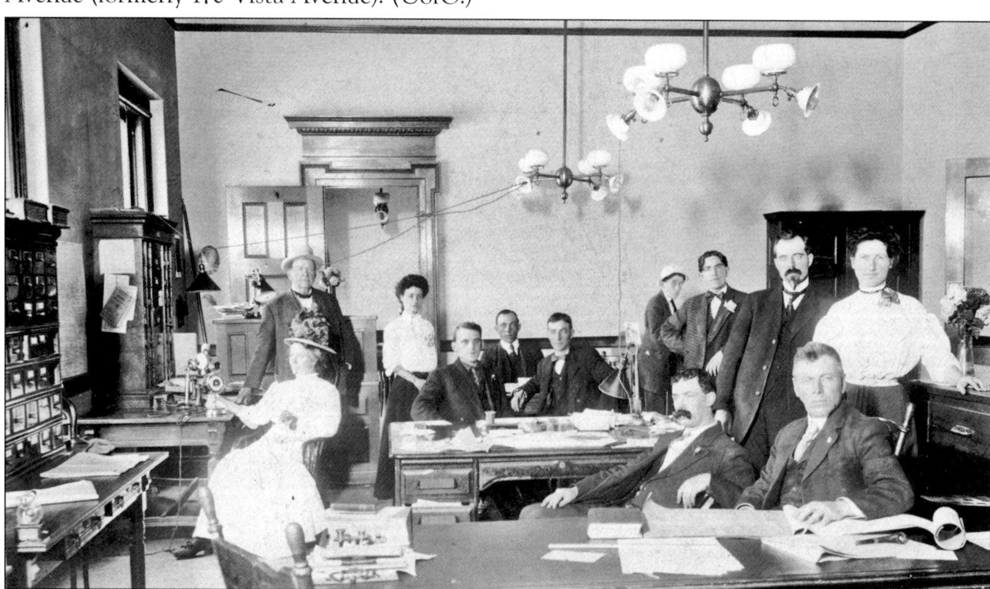

Dr. Esther Clayson Pohl Lovejoy (1869–1967), National American Woman Suffrage Association representative, was a leader in many suffrage groups. In 1894, she was the first woman graduate of the University of Oregon Medical School to practice medicine; she was also the first woman head of a major city's health department. Dr. Lovejoy is seated left with her staff in 1907 in this image. She proposed that suffrage would help women advocate for healthier and safer cities. She ran, unsuccessfully, for Congress in 1920 and wrote four histories of women in medicine. (OHSU.)

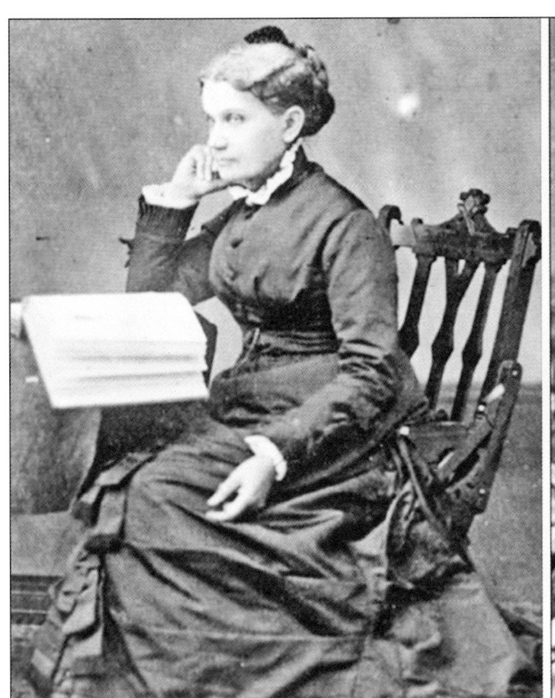

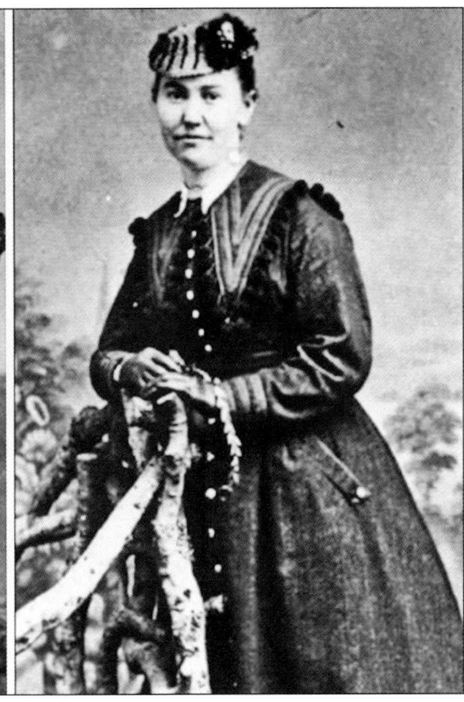

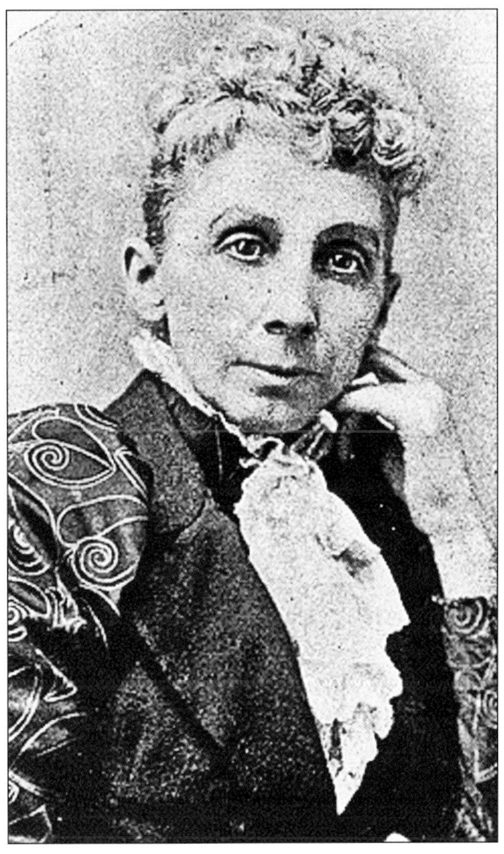

At upper left, Mary Anna Cooke Thompson (1825 1919), an 1866 pioneer, was one of Oregon's first doctors. In Illinois, she studied with two physicians because medical schools did not allow women. Though she had no degree, she practiced medicine in Portland for 40 years. Thompson advocated nationally on women's suffrage, temperance, and prohibition. At upper right, Dr. Bethenia Owens-Adair (1840–1926), an 1843 pioneer, was one of the first women doctors in Oregon with a medical degree. An advocate for women's suffrage, temperance, labor rights, and health, Owens-Adair was also a eugenics crusader advocating to sterilize the "unfit." Though horrifying now, this was a typical sentiment at the time. At right, Dr. Mary Priscilla Avery Sawtelle (1835–1894), an 1848 pioneer and women's rights advocate, was among the first Oregon women to earn a medical degree. In 1869, she was Willamette Institute's first woman medical student, and then she graduated from New York Medical College Hospital for Women in 1872. She practiced medicine in Portland and organized the Women's Medical College of the Pacific Coast in 1881. (Above left, OHS ba000009; above right, OHSU; right, *The Heroine of '49*.)

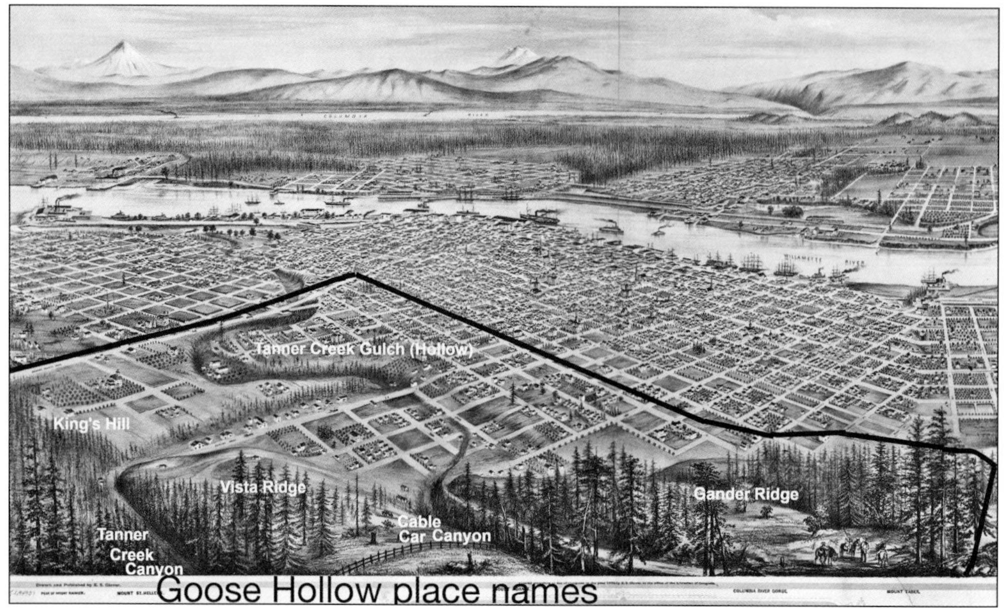

This 1879 map shows Goose Hollow neighborhood place-names. The August 17, 1875, *Oregonian* described "A War About Geese" incident that led to its name. Neighborhood women—mostly German, Irish, and Jewish immigrants—let geese run wild, causing fights over ownership. A police officer responded, trying to divide them. The women assaulted him, outraged over his decisions. Portland chief of police James Lappeus coined the name *Goose Hollow* as a tongue-in-cheek reference to that Tanner Creek Gulch area where those ladies fought over geese.

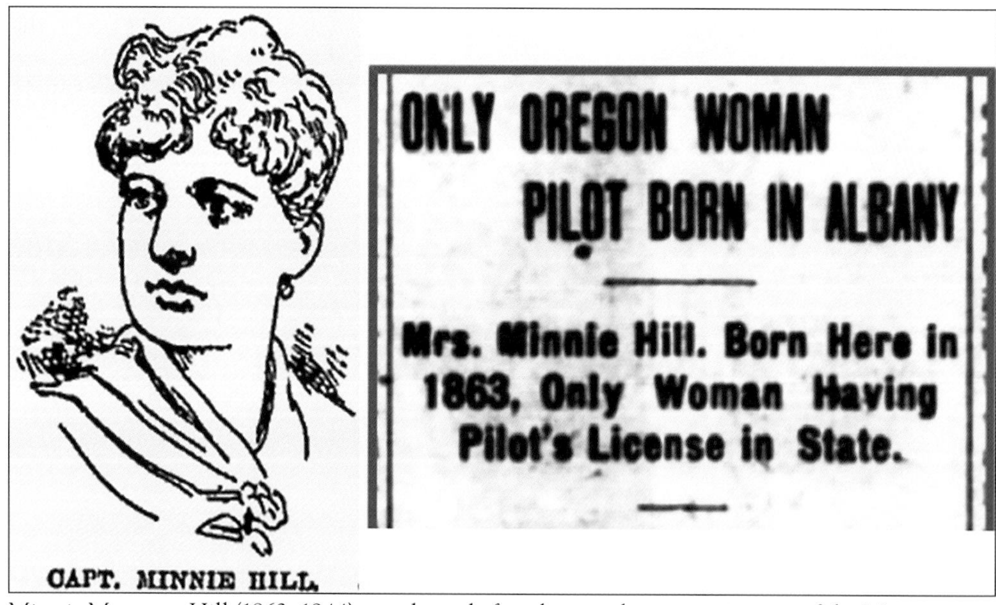

CAPT. MINNIE HILL.

ONLY OREGON WOMAN PILOT BORN IN ALBANY

Mrs. Minnie Hill. Born Here in 1863, Only Woman Having Pilot's License in State.

Minnie Mossman Hill (1863–1944) was the only female steamboat captain west of the Mississippi—licensed in 1886 and boat pilot for 14 years. Hill, with her husband as engineer, purchased supplies in Portland and traded at landings along the Willamette and Columbia Rivers. Since there were no stores near these small towns, farmers would come from up to 15 miles away, bringing butter, eggs, and other trade items to be brought back to Portland. (*Oregonian*.)

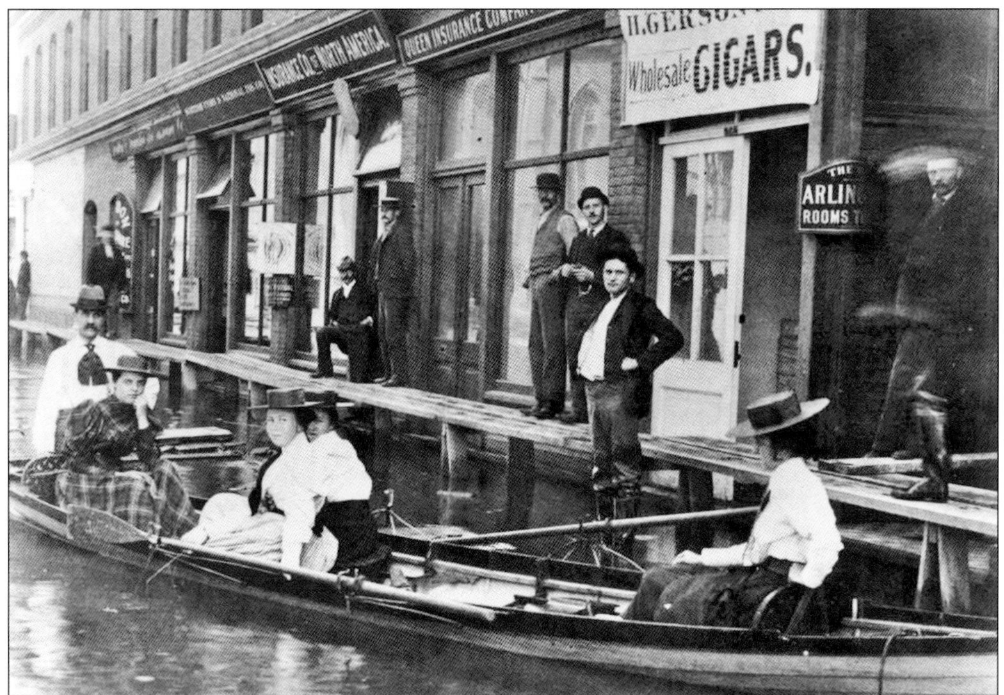

Some Portland women were anti-suffrage, including Henrietta Henderson Failing (1868–1953). One of the first curators of the Portland Art Museum, founded 1892, she taught art history (1910–1940) and was museum director in 1939. She was from an influential pioneer Portland family. Her father arrived in 1852 on a ship around Cape Horn. Her mother arrived in Oregon on a covered wagon in 1846. Henrietta taught art history at Reed College and was active in the League of Women Voters. Henrietta is pictured above at far left during the 1894 flood. Her sister Elsie Failing is at far right. Below, another anti-suffrage leader, Emily Loveridge (center, pictured in 1898) founded the Good Samaritan's Nurses School in 1890, the first nurse training school in the Pacific Northwest. The school still operates as a collaboration with Linfield College. Loveridge Hall dormitory is named in Emily's honor. (Above, OHS 88102; below, Linfield College.)

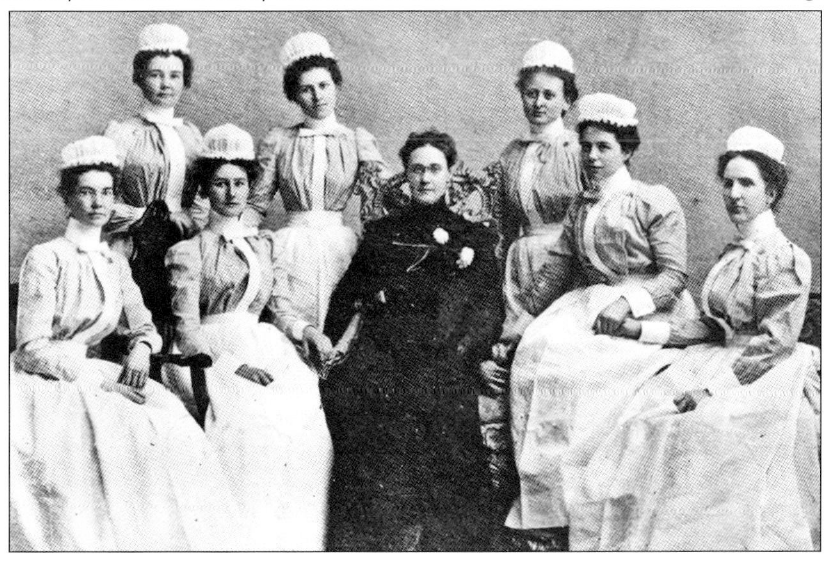

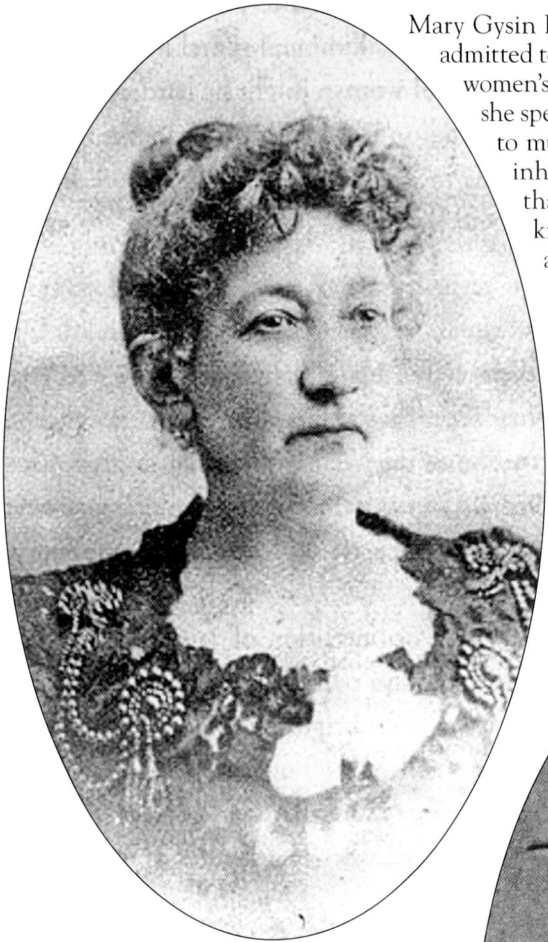

Mary Gysin Leonard (1845–1912) was the first woman admitted to the bar in Oregon. In 1886, she fought for women's right to practice law in the state. In 1878, she spent 11 months in jail, accused of attempting to murder her husband. She was acquitted and inherited his estate. Running a boardinghouse that reputedly catered to prostitutes, she was known for her courtroom skills, hard drinking, and offering free legal advice to ladies of the streets. (OHS 72693.)

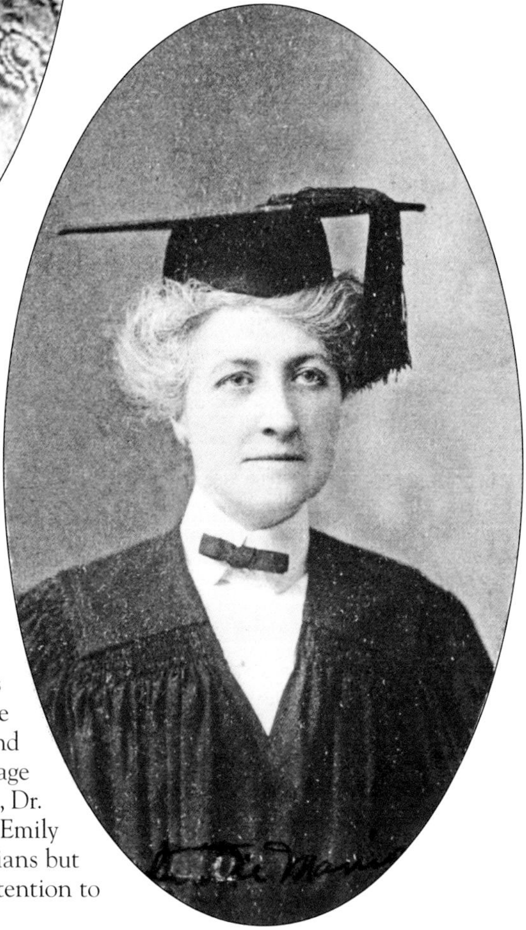

Suffragist Dr. Katherine C. Galbraith Manion (1867–1956) is pictured at her 1903 University of Oregon Medical School graduation. She was a president of the Medical Club of Portland (the first women's medical society in the West) and on the board of Portland's College Equal Suffrage Association. During World War I, Dr. Manion, Dr. Mae Cardwell, Dr. Mary MacLachlan, and Dr. Emily Balcom tried to enlist in the Army as physicians but were rejected as women, drawing national attention to an inequitable policy. (OHSU.)

A Native American woman sells baskets in Northwest Portland around 1900. Native American women were an important part of early Portland's daily life. After many Native people were forced onto reservations in the 1850s, numerous 1860s–1930s *Oregonian* articles told of Indians coming to town to trade, as shown below (which include what is now considered an offensive term). Native American women often set up seasonal encampments in and around Northwest Portland's Wallace Park. Native women sold wild berries called "olallas" in local Chinook Jargon, sold pitchwood called "lagoomstick," and sold baskets they made. They traded these items for clothing, beads, eggs, milk, vegetables, and money. Until at least the 1890s, many Portland residents spoke Jargon (a necessity for pioneers), and these trade transactions were often conducted in Jargon. These spectacularly beautiful Klickitat baskets required great weaving skills and were made by women from many tribes along the Columbia River. (Right, Gholston.)

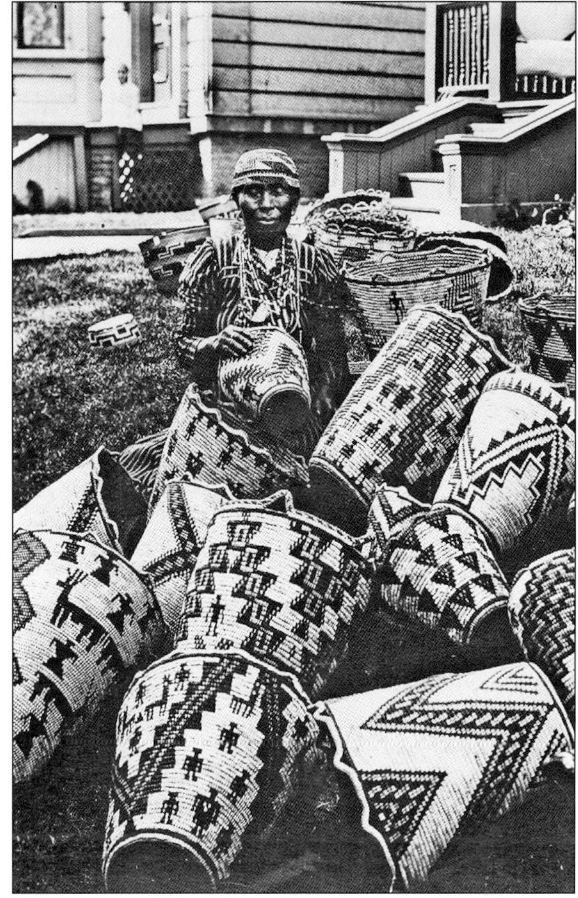

DO YOU REMEMBER?

When squaws peddled wild berries—"Olallas"—from house to house?

When thrifty squaws sold pitchwood kindlings—"lagoomstick"—to provident housewives for fire lighters? O. C. W.

• • •

Five Indian tents are pitched in a grove near Savier street, which has been used by the same Indians for many years. They come from the Siletz reservation and every year journey to Portland to dispose of the baskets and nicknacks which the squaws have made during the Winter.

EARLY DAYS HERE RECALLED

Indians Used to Ride Ponies to City to Sell Berries.

PORTLAND, Feb. 19.—(To the Editor.)—We moved in from the country in 1864.

In those times Indians came to Portland to trade. The squaws rode in on their ponies, carrying great loads of huckleberries in baskets. They traded for old clothing. This was the time for my mother to dispose of the dresses and sunbonnets we wore on the "plains." Before we started west she bought the heaviest ginghams to wear on the long journey and she was keeping them for relics of our journey. They were faded to a dingy brown.

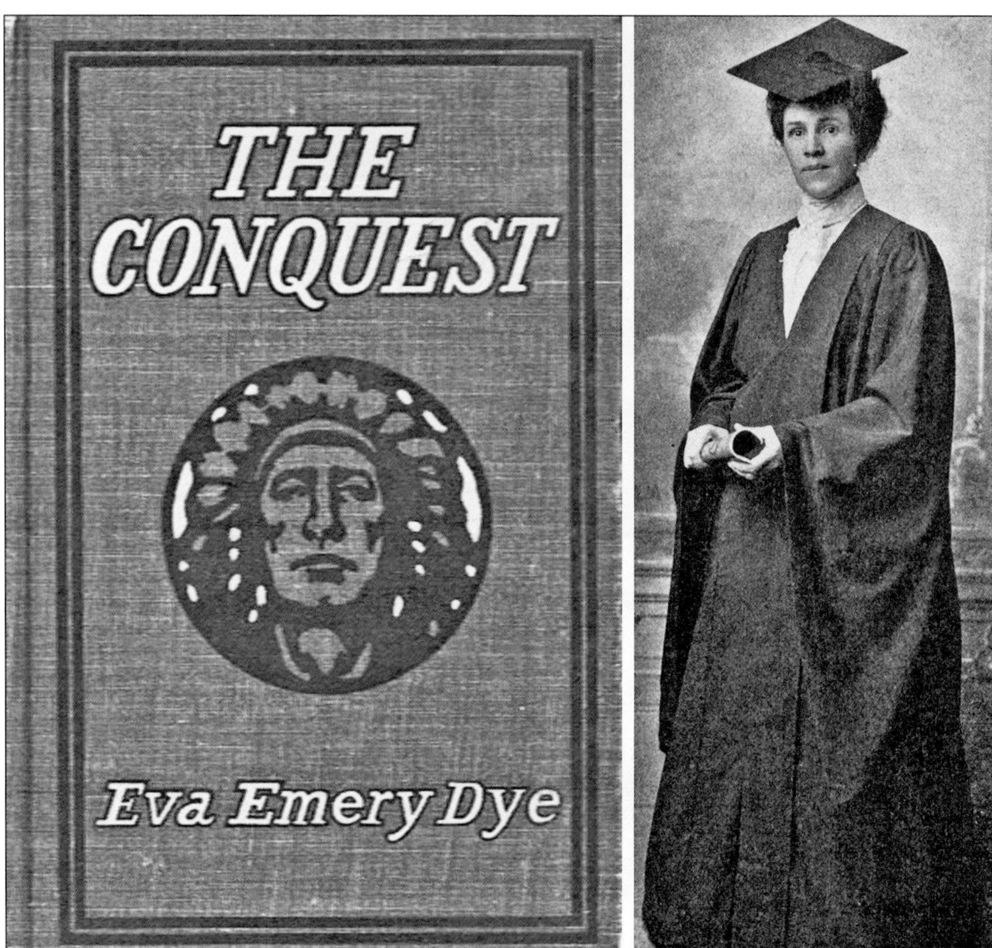

Suffragist and historian Eva Emery Dye (1855–1947) moved to Oregon in 1890. Her father objected to her attending college, so she paid her own way to Oberlin College by teaching (graduated 1882, master's degree 1887). She wrote fictionalized historical novels: *Stories of Oregon* (1900), *McLoughlin and Old Oregon* (1900), *McDonald of Oregon: A Tale of Two Shores* (1906), and *The Soul of America: An Oregon Iliad* (1934). She was an occasional journalist for Oregon newspapers, and her 1901 Oregon Press Association credential is below. Sacajawea became a rallying point for suffragists nationwide because of Dye's 1902 novel *The Conquest: The True Story of Lewis and Clark* romanticizing Sacajawea as an unsung heroine and pointing out that she voted on the 1805 expedition. Suffragists were drawn to this symbolism. Dye was an Oregon Woman's Suffrage Association member and Sacajawea Statue Association president. Though Dye lived in Oregon City, Portland's Sacajawea statue in Washington Park would not exist without her advocacy. (Both, Gholston.)

Membership Certificate

This Certifies that Eva Emery Dye

is a member in good standing of the

Oregon Press Association

Issued for the Year Ending Dec. 31, 1901

Albert Tozier, Secretary. A. L. Fisher, President.

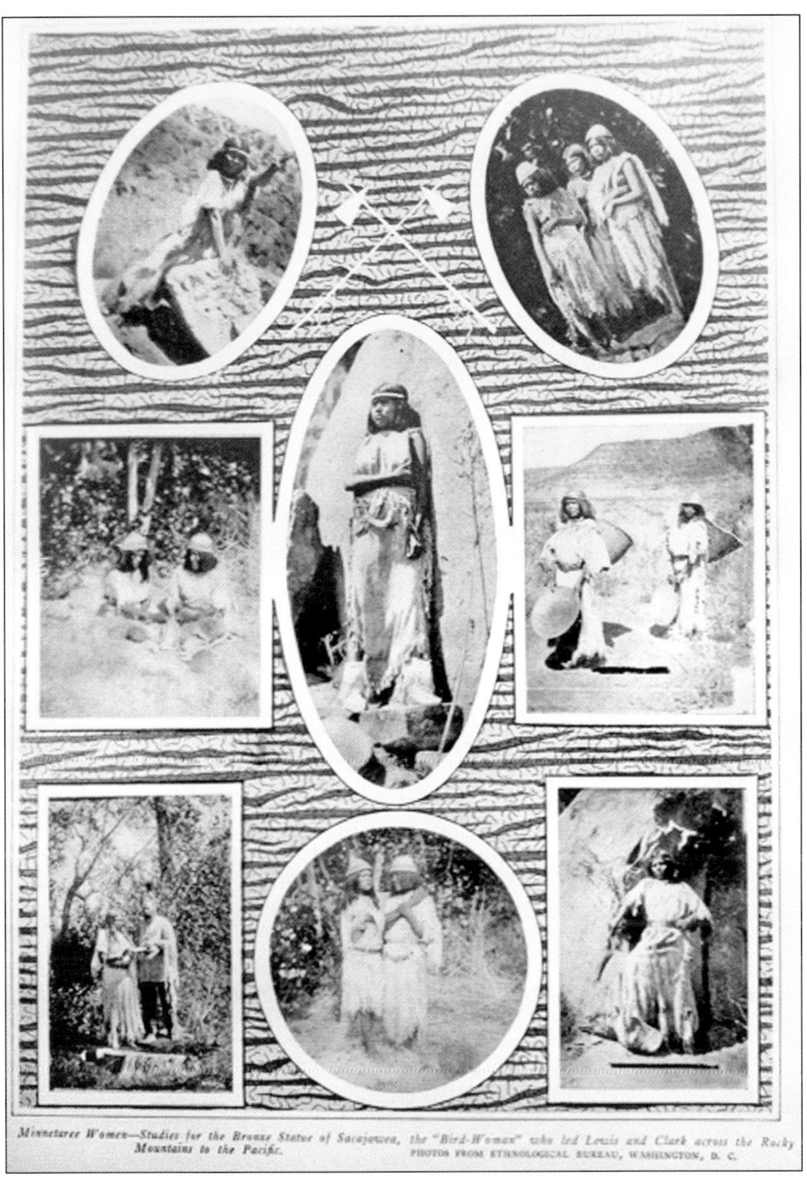
Minnetaree Women—Studies for the Bronze Statue of Sacajawea, the "Bird-Woman" who led Lewis and Clark across the Rocky Mountains to the Pacific.

PHOTOS FROM ETHNOLOGICAL BUREAU, WASHINGTON, D. C.

Inspired by Eva Emery Dye's book *The Conquest*, Portland Woman's Club created the Sacajawea Statue Association. Led by Dye (also Lewis and Clark Exposition Woman's Club president) and with Sarah Evans as secretary, the association advocated for a Sacajawea statue, selling commemorative spoons and buttons nationwide to raise funds. The January 1904 *Lewis and Clark Journal* includes these Smithsonian photographs that the association sent as models to sculptor Alice Cooper. The caption incorrectly identifies the Native American women as Minnetaree (Hidatsa). Sacajawea was Shoshone, from what is now Idaho, and was captured by Hidatsa as a child. The photographs are actually Paiute and Ute women from vastly different terrain and tribes than Sacajawea. The photographs were taken by John K. Hillers on John Wesley Powell's 1860s–1870s Colorado River expeditions. Sacajawea was an important symbol, especially to western states, where pioneer women still remembered the Oregon Trail's hardships and Sacajawea's tenacity as a mother resonated. To this day, western states tend to spell Sacajawea with Dye's spelling, while in the east, the Sacagewea spelling is common.

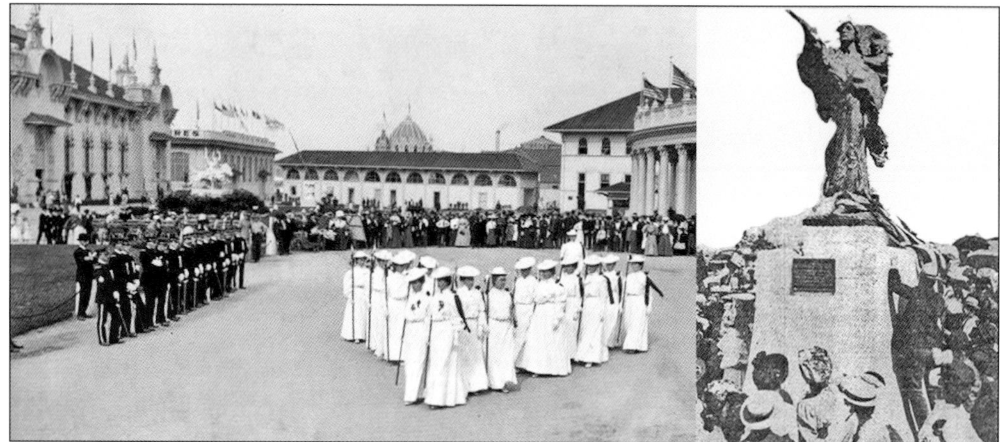

Erecting a Sacajawea statue was a socially acceptable way of saying that Sacajawea endured the same hardships as Lewis and Clark—but did it all with a baby on her back—and she was allowed to vote. In a brilliant marketing tactic, suffragists wrapped the statue in an American flag and framed the story as patriotism. At the Lewis and Clark Expo unveiling, seen above, Susan B. Anthony said, "We pay homage to thousands of uncrowned heroines . . . This is the first time in history that a statue has been erected in memory of a woman who accomplished patriotic deeds . . . This recognition of the assistance rendered by a woman in the discovery of this great section of the country is but the beginning of what is due." A medal for the 1905 National American Woman Suffrage Association convention in Portland uses a Lee Moorhouse photograph of an Oregon Indian woman and baby to symbolize Sacajawea and her son Jean Baptiste. Suffrage opponents argued that women would shirk home responsibilities if given voting freedoms. Sacajawea symbolized maintaining mothering responsibilities while leading and voting. (Above, Gholston; below, Harvard.)

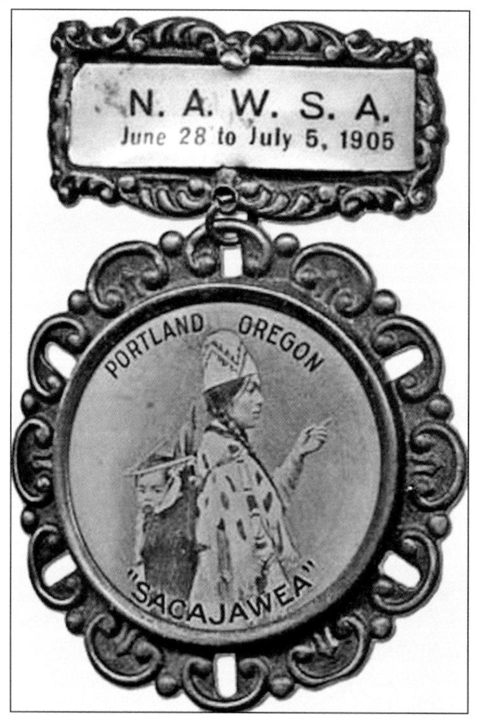

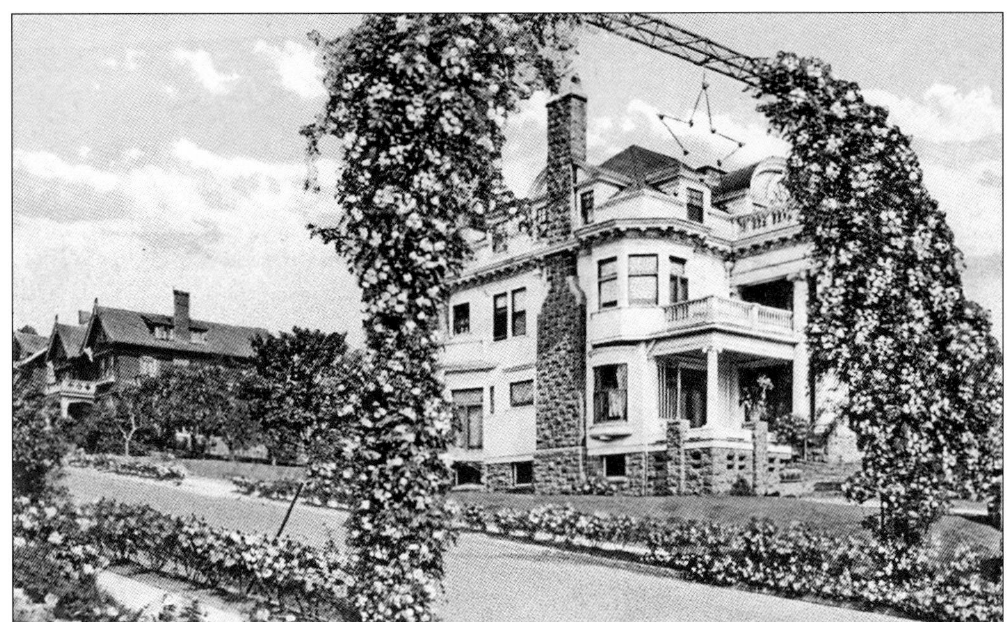

About 2.5 million expo visitors saw 200 miles of rose-lined streets, leading to Portland's "City of Roses" nickname. Important suffragist Dr. Viola Boley Coe (1863–1943) lived here at Northwest Twenty-Fifth Avenue and Lovejoy Street, running Coe Maternity Home here from 1916 to 1925. Dr. Coe (pictured on page 44) was co-founder of the Women's Medical Club and president of Portland's College Equal Suffrage Association, organizing rallies, galas, and trains of speakers throughout Oregon to rally suffrage voters. (Gholston.)

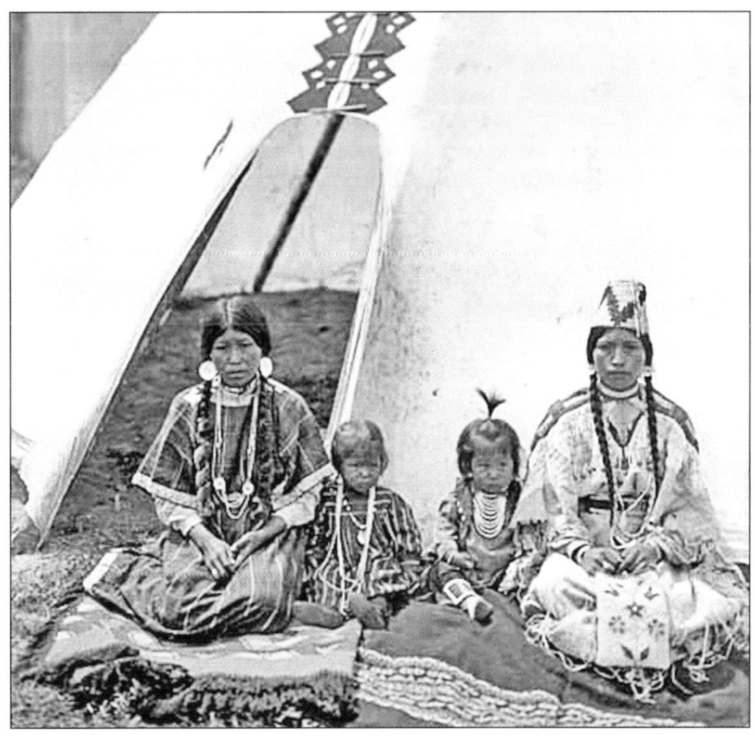

During the expo, Native American women were paid to wear regalia to demonstrate the "Wild West." This was typical for many decades and common throughout all of Oregon. Parades of tribes in their regalia were thought to spruce up a festival and lend an air of authenticity and nostalgia. The Umatilla woman on the right is wearing a woven basketry hat and holding a cornhusk bag. (UW.)

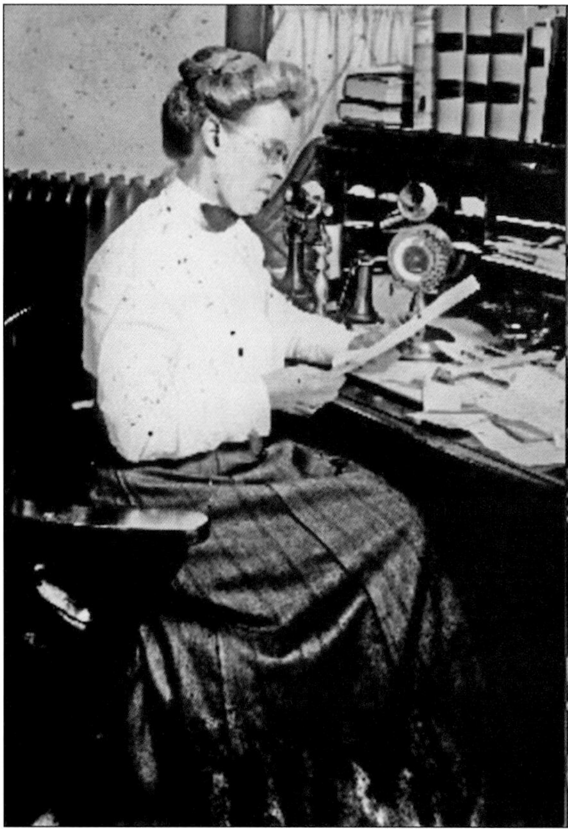

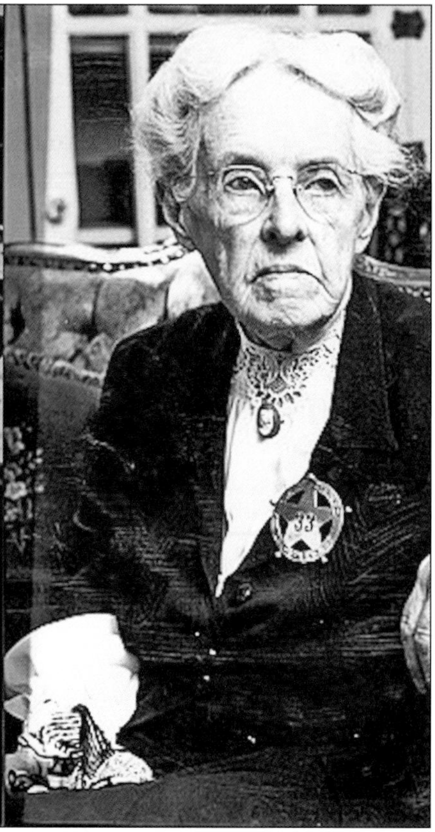

A suffragist and activist, Lola Greene Baldwin (1860–1957) became the first policewoman in the nation in 1908. Baldwin was concerned about women and children's welfare and volunteered at institutions for unwed mothers and troubled children. She was a part of the efforts of the Young Women's Christian Association (YWCA) to make the 1904–1905 Lewis and Clark Expo, pictured below, safe for young women. The idea was that young women would be more easily enticed into vice during such a large event, with so many out-of-towners. Baldwin was a charter member of the Oregon Social Hygiene Society, which distributed information about sex education and venereal disease prevention. After the exposition ended, Baldwin persuaded the city and YWCA to continue with the Travelers Aid movement. Detective Lola Baldwin oversaw the Women's Protective Division, advised the Portland Vice Commission, and served as Oregon special agent for vice control. (Above, W and OHS bb003191; below, Gholston.)

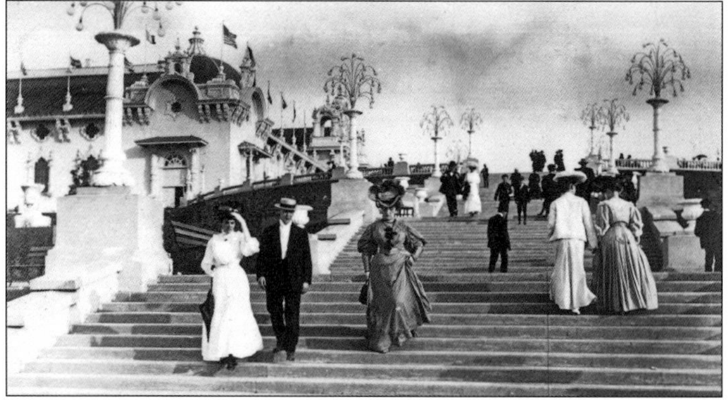

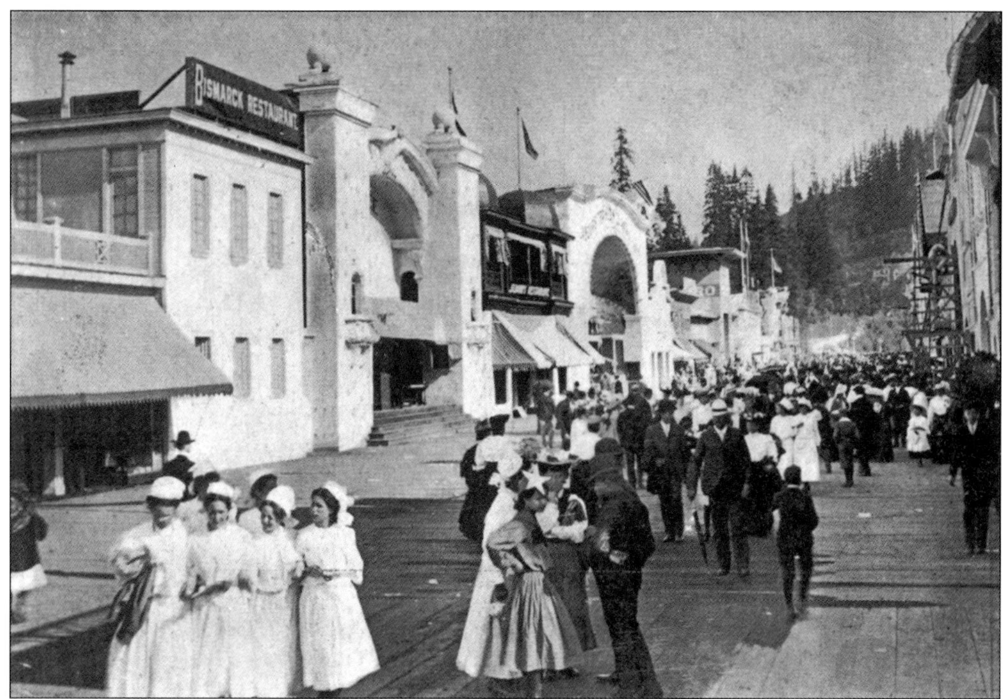

During the 1905 Lewis and Clark Exposition, pictured here, the YWCA partnered with the National Travelers Aid Association, with Lola Baldwin as director, to protect women from pimps and criminals. Baldwin policed vice by keeping a close eye on women and offering housing or employment to keep them from falling into the wrong hands. Suffragists advocated for a living wage to keep young women workers from lives of prostitution or crime. (Gholston.)

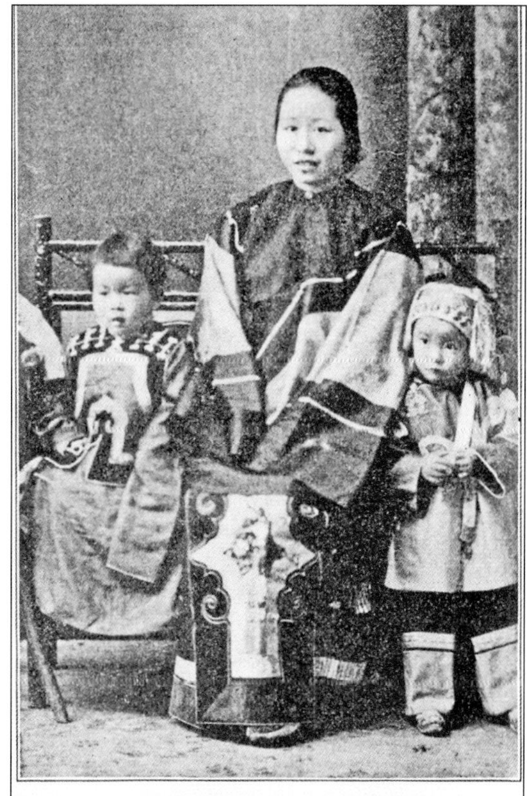

CHINESE MOTHER AND CHILDREN
PORTLAND, OREGON

This Chinese American mother and her children appear in Mary Osborn Douthit's 1905 book *The Souvenir of Western Women*, printed to coincide with the Lewis and Clark Exposition. Many women's groups were catalyzed by the expo to make sure women's stories were told too. Chinese women were prohibited from immigrating, with the exception of merchants' wives. The Chinese Exclusion Act was not repealed until 1943. So, it is meaningful that this book promoting women's history includes a Chinese woman as part of Portland's history. (Gholston.)

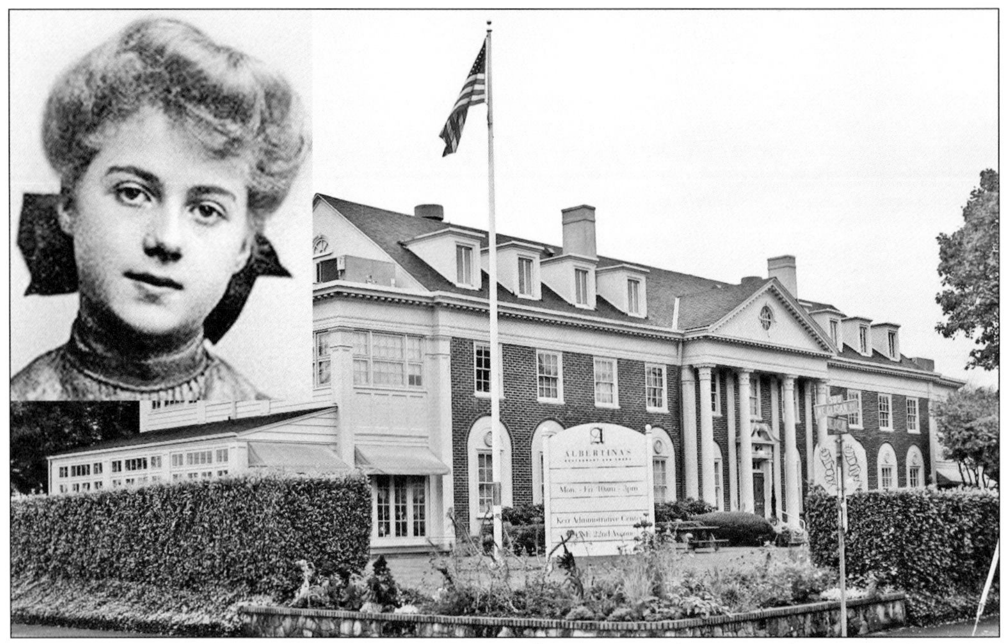

Albertina Kerr (1890–1911) was a mother who cared for children's' health issues and for parentless children. She told her husband on her deathbed, "Look after other motherless babies, too." Her husband donated their house to the Pacific Coast Rescue Society as a home for orphans. The home quickly became too small, so Albertina's husband and his third wife raised enough money to open the Albertina Kerr Nursery. The Albertina Kerr Center, pictured above, still benefits many children.

TOLSTOI PAYS TRIBUTE

APPRECIATED THE WRITINGS OF LUCY A. MALLORY, OF PORTLAND, IN HER ADVANCE THOUGHT.

(Portland Journal.)

Probably no one in Oregon more sincerely deplored the passing of Leo Tolstoi than Mrs. Lucy A. Rose Mallory, a native Oregonian and resident of Portland, whose writings were greatly admired by Count Tolstoi and given prominence in a number of his works.

For many years the distinguished Russian had been a reader of the World's Advance Thought, a weekly published by Mrs. Mallory in this city. He had taken a number of steps to make popular her writings in Russia and Germany, and had printed several volumes of her "key thoughts" in the Russian and German language. Mrs. Mallory's writings are also given positions of honor in a volume entitled "Fuer Alle Tage" (For Every Day), in which some thought of Tolstoi, with several aphorisms by the world's noted writers' are given for each day in the year.

Lucy A. Rose Mallory (1856–1920) was the daughter of Aaron Rose (Roseburg founder) and Minerva Kellogg. Her husband, Congressman Rufus Mallory, ran the Mallory Hotel (now Hotel deLuxe). Lucy was a suffragist, vegetarian, devotee of metaphysical experiences (believing her soul could communicate with faraway people), and an "anarchist creative" with her cultural club, the Association of Artists and Authors. Her newspaper, the *World's Advance Thought*, was so influential that Leo Tolstoy called her the "greatest woman in America." This November 27, 1910, *Portland Journal* article discussed his admiration.

Sophronia "Fronia" Wallace Giltner (1865–1951) worked tirelessly to bring culture to Portland. At her 1729 Northeast Siskiyou Street home in the Irvington neighborhood, she hosted Stradivarius violinists from Europe and nationally acclaimed singers and plays. She supported the Oregon Symphony, was a member of the Monday Musical Club, and introduced Portland to exotic foods and cultures from around the world. A garden club leader, she helped start the Washington Park Zoo and the East Moreland Rhododendron Gardens. (*Oregon Daily Journal*, December 29, 1914.)

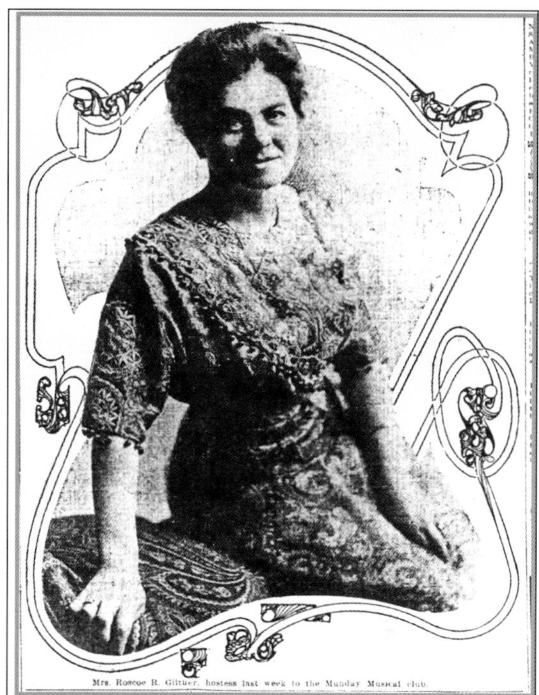

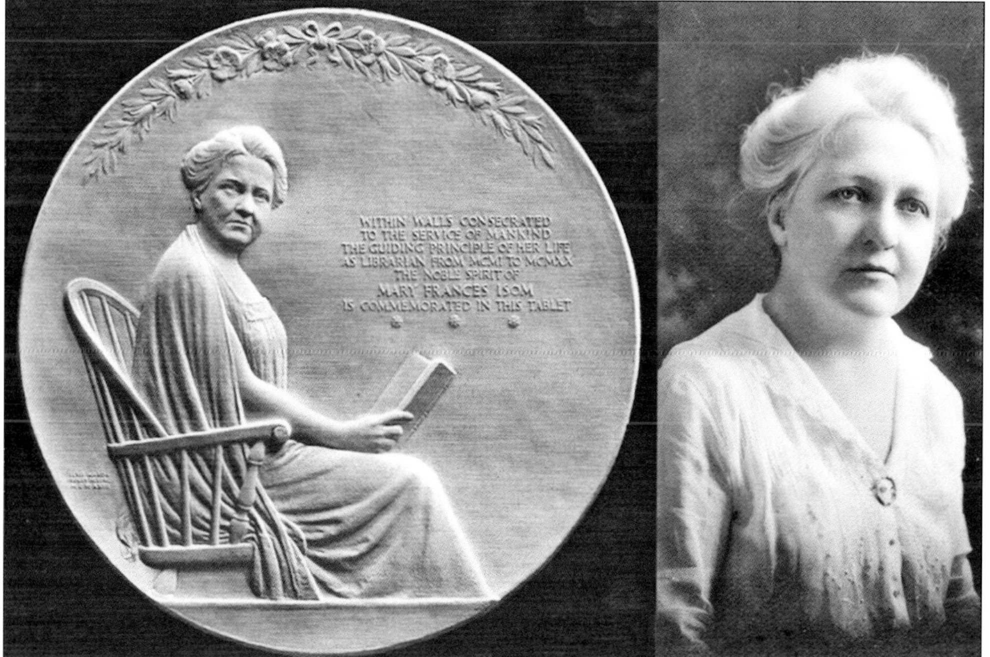

Founder of the Oregon Library Commission, Oregon Library Association, and Pacific Northwest Library Association, Mary Frances Isom (1865–1920) promoted and oversaw Oregon's first tax-supported, free public library. She drafted legislation for Oregon's public libraries, opened many Carnegie-funded branches, and was especially proud of Central Library (opened in 1913), which has this plaque honoring her. In World War I, Isom served troops overseas, visiting 93 American hospitals during a five-month stay in France.

TEN HOURS LAW FOR WORKING WOMEN

Supreme Court Has Established Principle for Whole Country

By Florence Kelley, Secretary National Consumers' Leagues.
(Exclusive Service From Charities and the Commons Press Bureau.)

THE publication of the full text of the unanimous decision by the United States supreme court in the case of the Oregon 10-hour law for workingwomen handed down on February 24, shows that it is more far reaching than at first appeared.

Nominally it applied only to laundries, mechanical establishments and factories in Oregon. In fact, however, it establishes for the whole country the prinicple that a statute limiting women's working hours is, in general, to be regarded as a measure in the interests of the public health. The right of the states thus to legislate is not confined to the working day of 10 hours, or to any group of industries.

The Oregon statute thus become famous was enacted in 1903. It permits women to work at night, or partly by day and partly by night, as well as to work 10 hours by day. It merely forbids employing them more than 10 hours in any one period of 24 hours. Under it a factory or a laundry could be kept running 24 hours a day, seven days a week, provided only that no one woman worked longer than 10 hours in any 24.

On September 18, 1905, suit was begun in the county of Multnomah because Joe Haselbock, manager of Curt Muller's laundry in the city of Portland, had required Mrs. E. Gotcher to work more than 10 hours on the fourth day of that month. Curt Muller, being convicted and fined $10 for this act of his agent, appealed the case. The supreme court of Oregon sustained the law as constitutional and Curt Muller then appealed to the supreme court of the United States at Washington.

Case Reviewed.

The deputy district attorney for the county of Multnomah, Oregon, appeared for the state, and William C. Fenton for the laundryman. Louis D. Brandeis of Boston generously gave his services as counsel for the state of Oregon.

in factories. This virtually deprives women and girls over the age of 16, in New York state, of protection against all-night work and against a working day and working' week of unlimited length, since a woring week of 60 hours is non-enforcable without a closing hour or day limit.

In Colorado the supreme court has decided the same question in opposite ways. In 1903 the legislature asked the supreme court of the state whether a law would be constitutional which should provide that women and children must not be employed longer than eight hours in one day at any occupation requiring continuous standing. The court replied that such a statute would be constitutional. The legislature thereupon enacted a law forbidding the employment of any child or woman longer than eight hours in one day in any occupation which involved continuous standing while at work. During the past summer, however, a laundryman who had violated the statute and appealed has case to the supreme court of Colorado succeeded in inducing the court to reverse in its decision the opinion which it had unanimously expressed five years earlier. The Colorado eight-

In 1905, Emma Gotcher was a laundry worker and member of the Shirt, Waist, and Laundry Workers Union. Oregon had recently passed laws on child labor, workers' rights to join unions, and 10-hour per day limits for women factory and laundry workers. Prior to that, women who worked in factories had to work long hours doing dangerous work and were only paid 45¢ a day. Yet Gotcher's boss demanded that she work more than 10 hours. Her boss was fined, so he contested the 1905 law. An article in the April 19, 1908, *Oregon Daily Journal* described the resulting Supreme Court decision—*Muller v. Oregon*—that impacted work conditions nationwide. (Below, OHS 1131-B.)

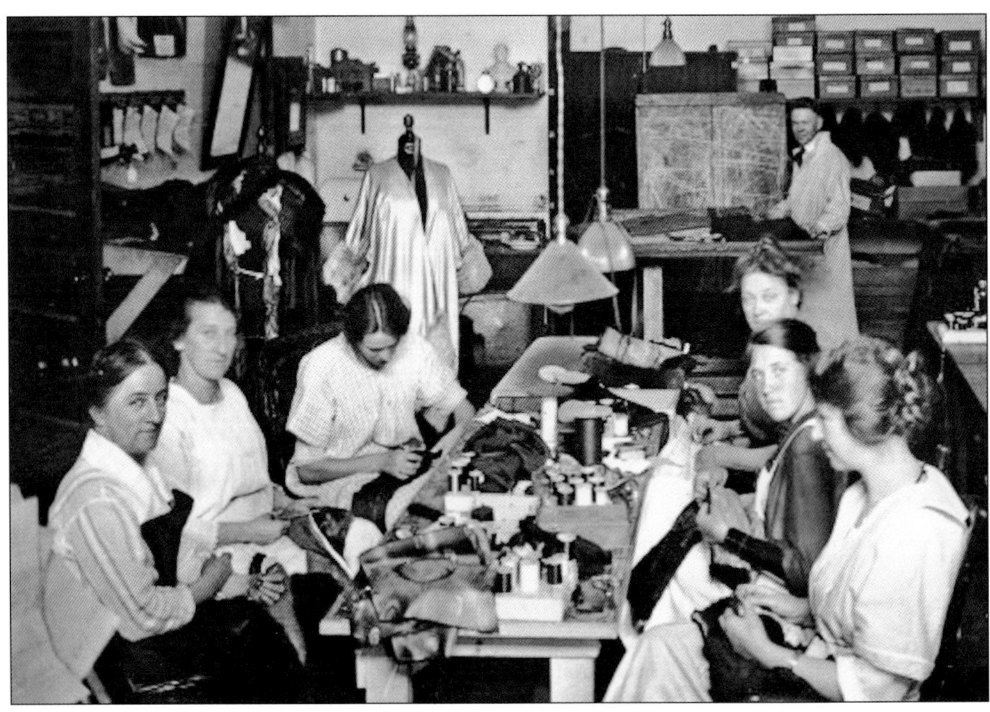

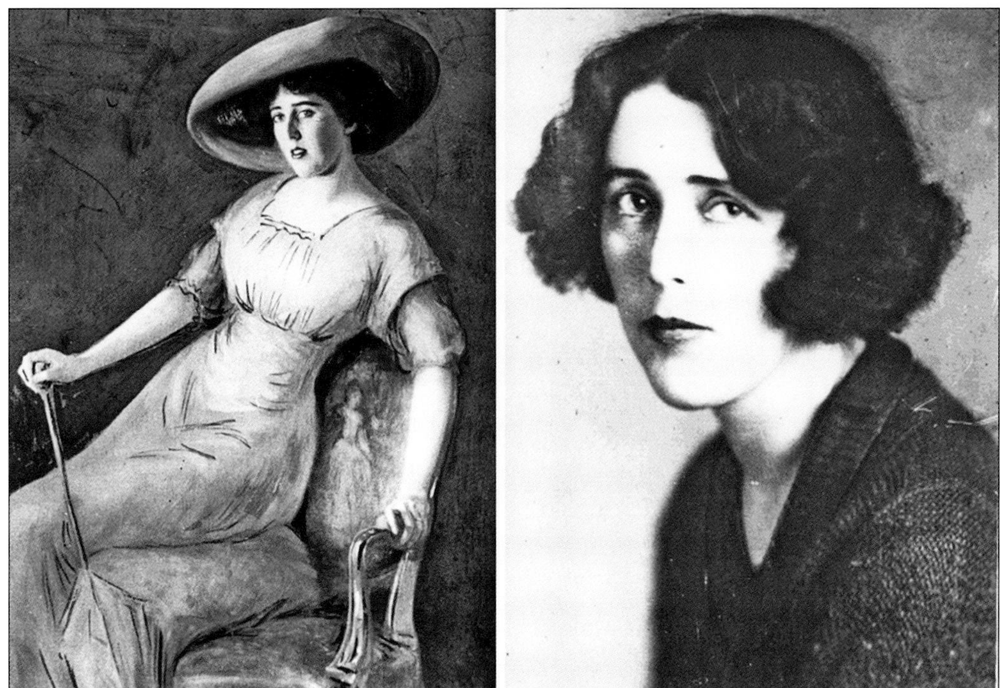

A suffragist and journalist known for her approving depiction of Russia's Bolshevik Revolution, Louise Bryant (1885–1936) was the *Oregonian*'s first woman journalist in 1909. Also a society editor at the *Spectator*, she wrote about leading Russian men and women, with stories in newspapers across North America. Bryant left her first husband and later married John Reed, a labor activist. Both spent time in Russia. Bryant was an international correspondent for Hearst and wrote books such as *Six Red Months in Russia* (1918) and *Mirrors in Moscow* (1923). The 1981 movie *Reds* portrays the love and heartbreak Bryant and Reed felt for each other and for the Bolshevik Revolution, with Diane Keaton playing Bryant. (OHS ba020209.)

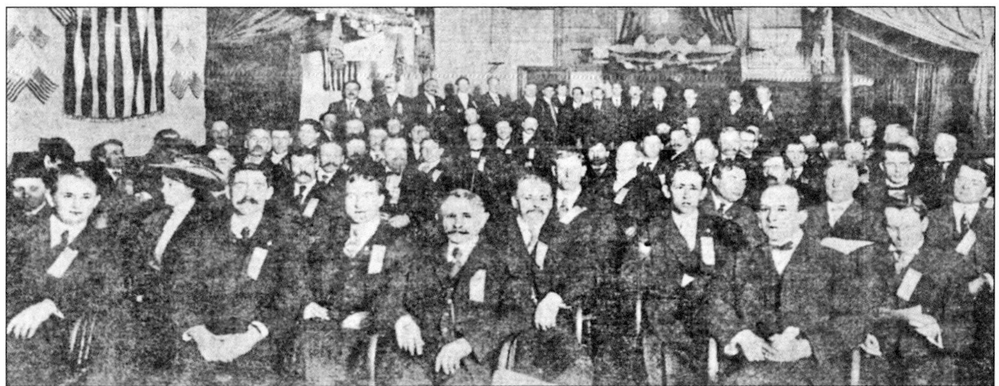

Lucy White, a Ladies' Garment Workers' Union president, is likely the only woman pictured (left), since she attended this Oregon Federation of Labor session as an officer, specifically secretary-treasurer. LGWU members were often recent immigrants, including many South Portland Jewish immigrants. White is quoted in the September 21, 1920, *East Oregonian*: "During the days of long hours, I can remember the girls fainting at their work. Now with improved conditions, we seldom find use for the hospital rooms which are provided." (*Oregonian*, January 11, 1910.)

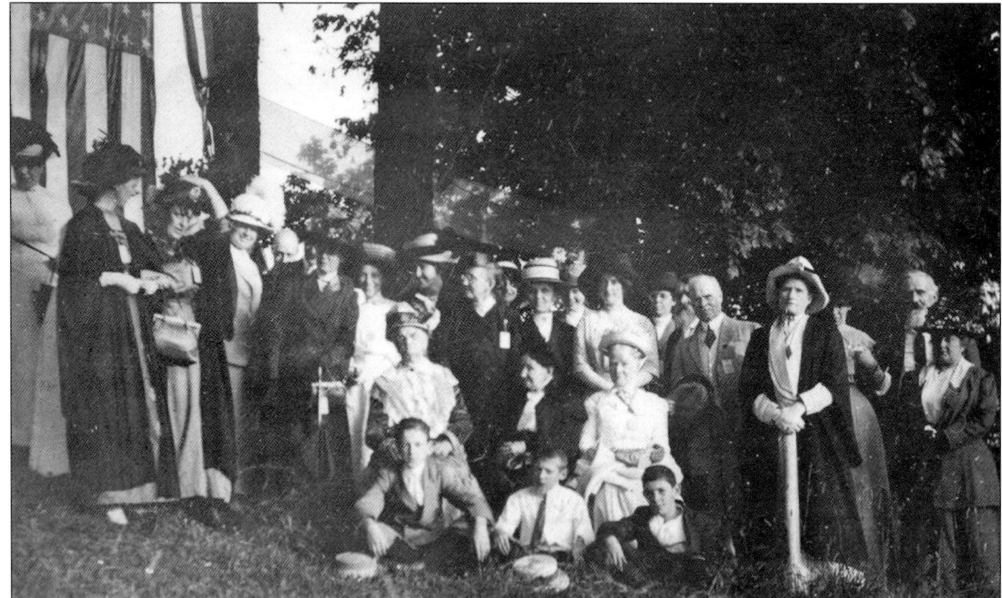

In 1905 suffragists gather for speeches in Portland's Laurelhurst Park, above. Below, national suffrage speaker Margaret Whittemore (standing left on the platform, in a white dress) speaks to Oregon suffragists. Whittemore was of Quaker heritage and the daughter of a leading United States patent attorney. She started her suffrage work in Michigan and became a Congressional Union organizer for Washington State in 1914. In 1917, she was arrested for picketing and jailed for three days. In 1919, she was jailed one day for applauding in court. Suffrage leaders campaigned throughout Oregon to keep energy high for the push for full political franchise nationwide. (Above, OHS, ba019208; below, LOC.)

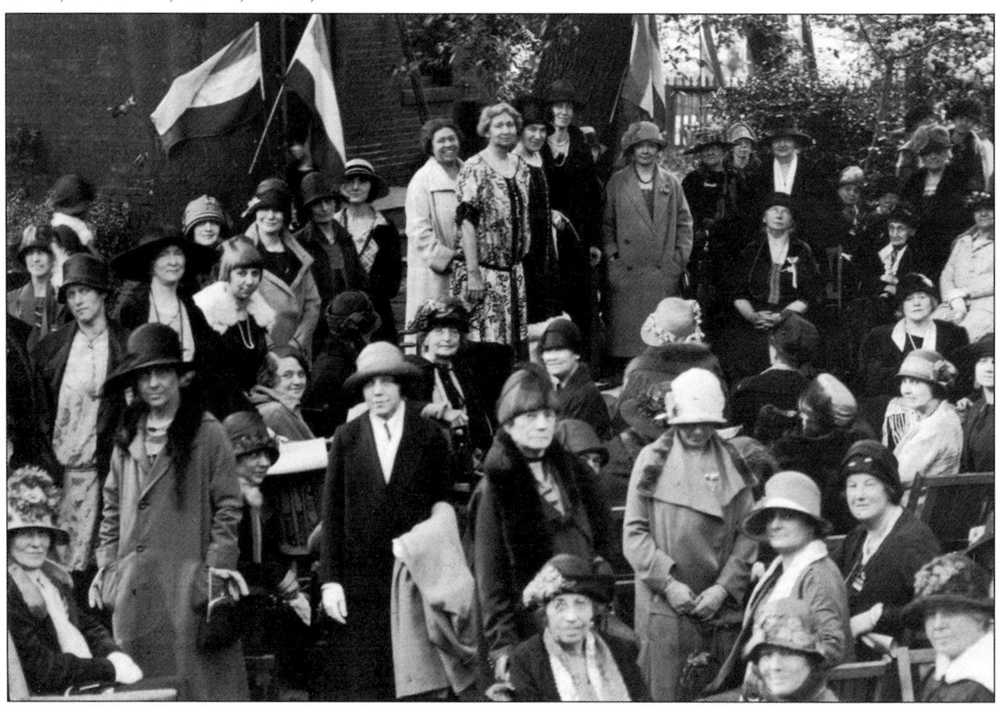

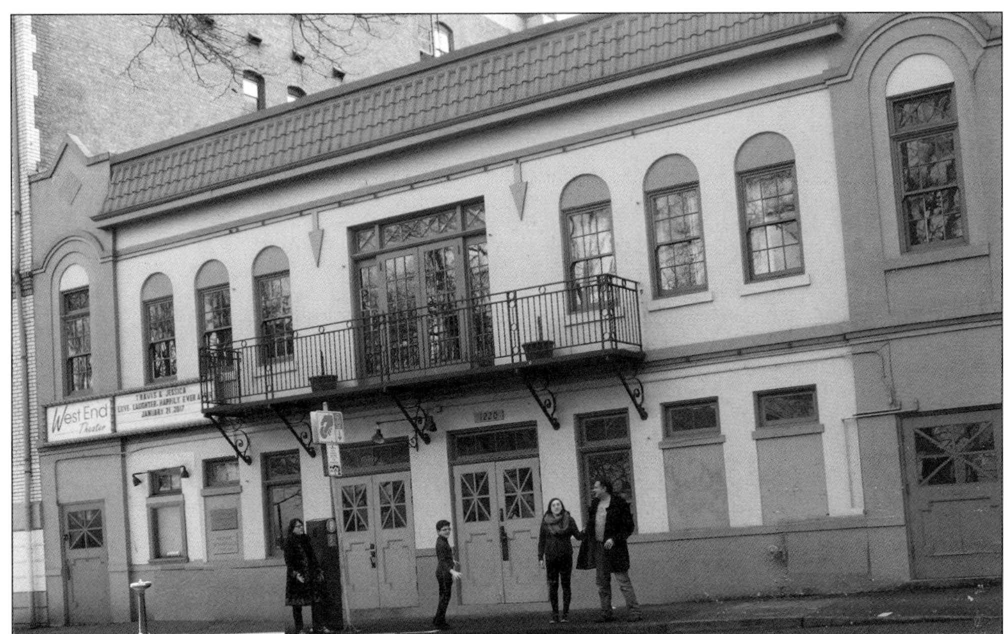

This elegant building at 1220 Southwest Taylor was the 1922–2001 home to Portland Woman's Club, formed in 1876. Abigail Scott Duniway and Esther Pohl Lovejoy were prominent members. The club advocated for many things to make life better for Oregonians—women's suffrage, free libraries, food inspections, better teacher salaries, kindergarten, first citywide trash collection, Red Cross war sewing efforts, scholarships, and helping Vanport flood survivors and the homeless.

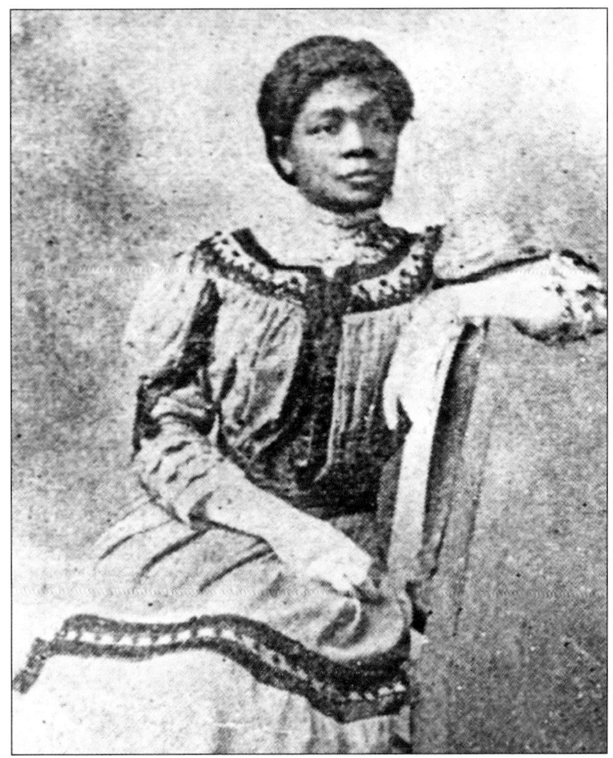

A leader in Oregon's woman's suffrage movement, Harriet "Hattie" Crawford Redmond (1862–1952) moved to Portland in 1880. Her family was prominent in the African American community, especially at Mt. Olivet Baptist Church, where she organized lectures on suffrage. Hattie Redmond was co-founder and president of the Colored Women's Equal Suffrage League and active in the Oregon Colored Women's Council and Portland's YWCA. (OHS bb009628.)

College Equal Suffragists, Chinese Women Dine Together

Celestial Speaker Thanks Her American Sisters Heartily

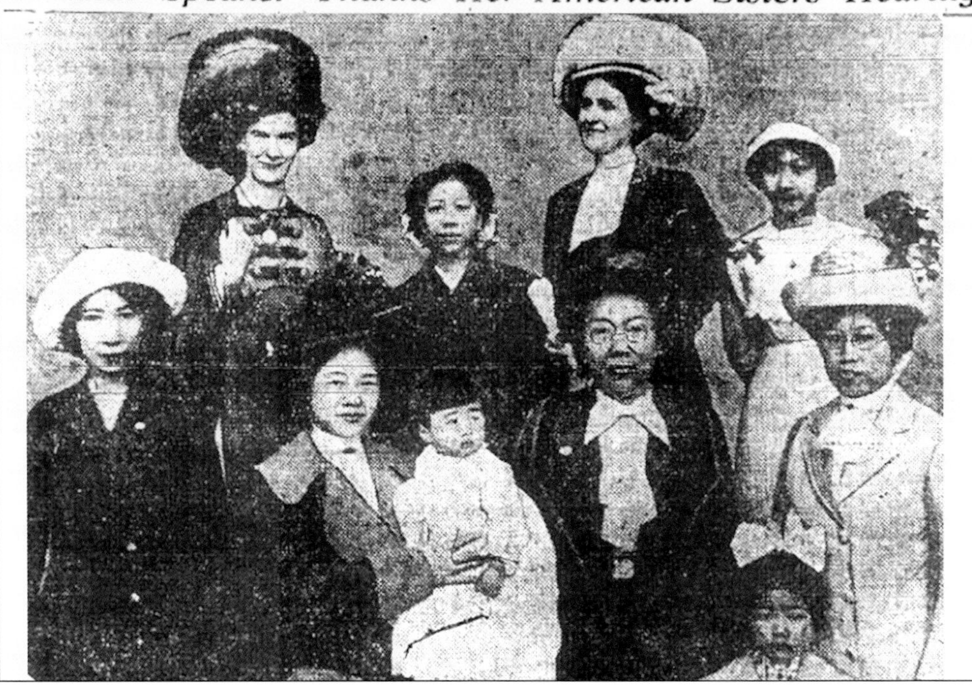

CHINESE WOMEN DINE WITH WHITE

Race Lines Not Drawn at Suffrage Banquet in Honor of La Reine Helen Baker.

ORIENTAL TWITS SISTERS

Mrs. Chan Declares Oregon Is Behind Neighboring States and Nations

Dr. S.K. Chan was a physician and president of the Chinese American Equal Suffrage Society of Portland. The April 12, 1912, *Oregon Journal* detailed Portland's Chinese American women working in the suffrage movement "side by side with their Caucasian sisters." Dr. Chan spoke about China being more progressive than the United States and about surrounding states where women already had the right to vote—Idaho, Washington, and California. She hoped Oregon would follow their lead and grant women the right to vote. From left to right are (first row) Bertie G. Chan, Mrs. Herbert Low, Edna Low, Dr. S.K. Chan, Ida Tong, and Mrs. Ng Tong; (second row) La Reine Helen Baker, Buehlah Tong, Sarah Commerford, and Fannie Chan.

Women of Woodcraft was the women's auxiliary of the Woodmen of the World—a mutual aid society to protect members from lost income because of a husband's illness or death. The name later changed to Neighbors of Woodcraft when more men became involved. It was headquartered in Portland from 1905 to the 1970s at what is now Goose Hollow's Tiffany Center at 1410 Southwest Morrison Street. Below, during the 1912 Rose Festival, the Portland Woman's Club made sandwiches in the Women of Woodcraft kitchen and handed them out during the parade along with flyers promoting changing the law to allow women to vote. In the suffrage lunch wagon, Dr. Esther Pohl Lovejoy holds the "Votes for Women" umbrella. (Right, Gholston; below, OSA.)

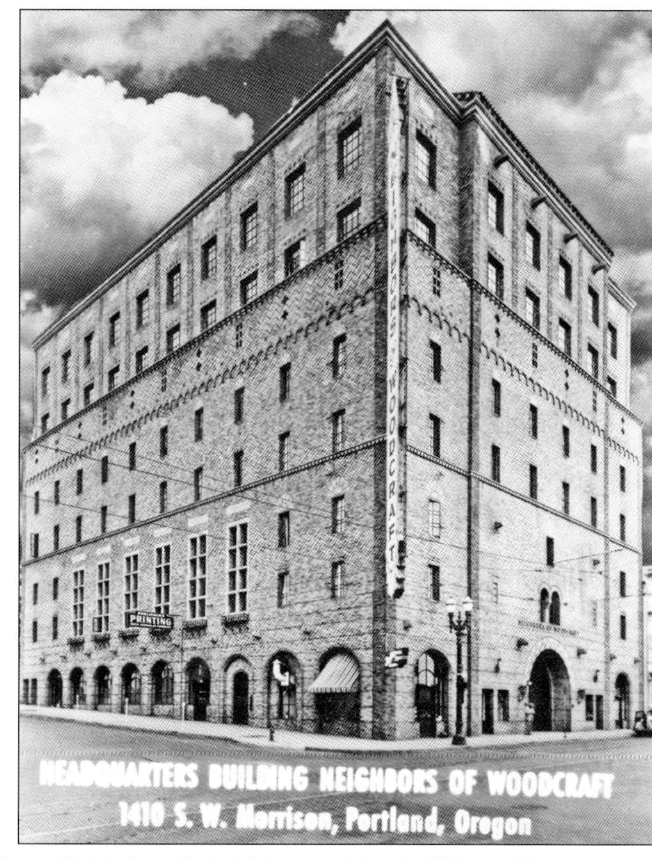

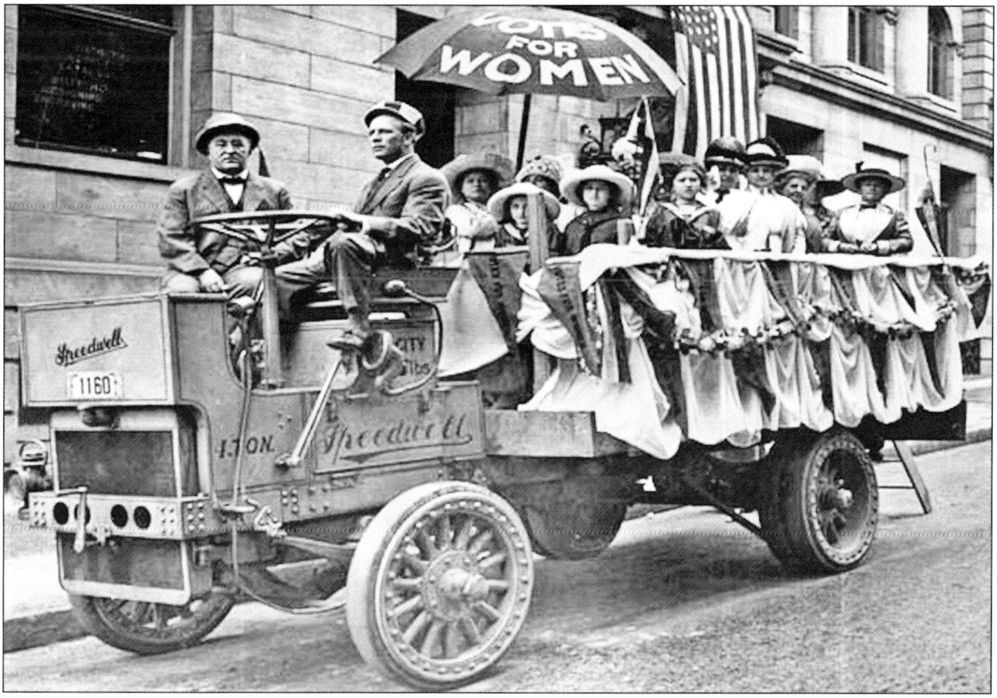

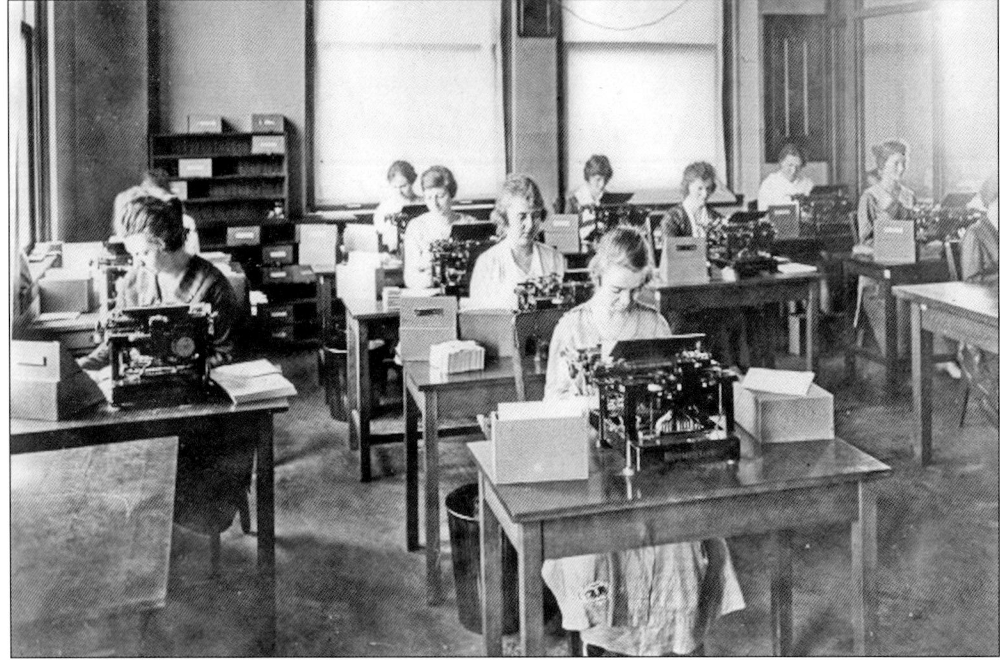

Above is a typing pool of women working. At this time, married women could be beaten by their husbands and could not own property (even their own clothing). Below, Sarah A. Shannon Evans (1854–1940) arrived in Portland in 1894 and was active in the suffrage movement, the Sacajawea Statue Association, promoting public libraries, and sanitation in food and milk. She was co-founder and president of the Portland Woman's Club and the Oregon Federation of Women's Clubs. She edited *Oregon Journal's* weekly "Women's Club" column. In 1905, she was appointed the first market inspector in America and was one of the earliest members of the League of Women Voters. This December 27, 1950, *Oregonian* article is part of the "100 Men of the Oregonian Century," with Sarah Evans named a prominent Oregonian along with those men. (Above, OHS 9077.)

Sarah A. Evans (1854-1940), Who Led Clean-Food Fight, Served Public Long

PORTLAND'S FIRST public market inspector, ten years president of the Oregon Federation of Women's Clubs, Sarah A. Evans (nee Shannon) had a useful career of nearly half a

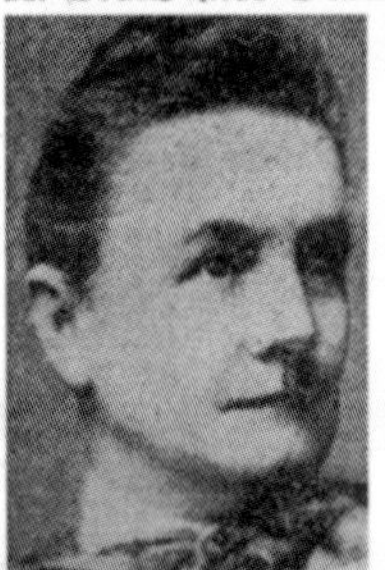

century in Oregon. Born in Bedford, Pa., she attended Lutherville college (now Maryland Women's college), married, came west to Portland in 1894. She was active in the woman's suffrage movement, influential in putting through legislation for free public libraries and for restriction of child labor. As a member of the YWCA domestic science committee she uncovered filthy handling of food in Portland markets, was appointed by Mayor Lane (1905) as market inspector, holding the post 30 years; she was the first woman to receive a commission from the police. She handled the first Liberty Loan drive in Oregon (1917). Mrs. Evans was a charter member of the YW, member League of Women Voters, Forestry association (conservation body); owned one of the best collection of Indian relics in the world. Contemporary evaluation: "farsighted, sincere, constructive . . . there's only one Sarah Evans."

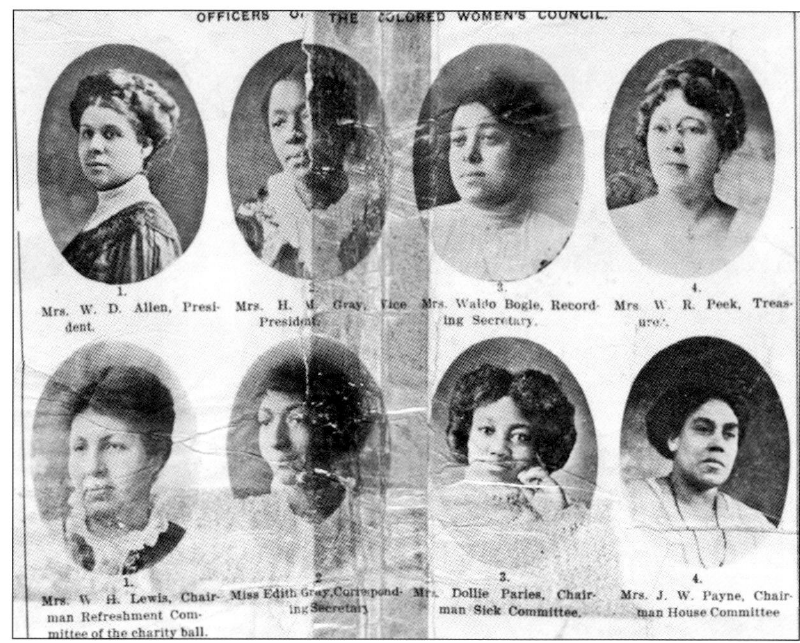

OFFICERS OF THE COLORED WOMEN'S COUNCIL.

1. Mrs. W. D. Allen, President.

2. Mrs. H. M. Gray, Vice President.

3. Mrs. Waldo Bogle, Recording Secretary.

4. Mrs. W. R. Peek, Treasurer.

1. Mrs. W. H. Lewis, Chairman Refreshment Committee of the charity ball.

2. Miss Edith Gray, Corresponding Secretary.

3. Mrs. Dollie Paries, Chairman Sick Committee.

4. Mrs. J. W. Payne, Chairman House Committee

Formed in 1912, when black women were excluded from white women's clubs, the Colored Women's Council (later the Oregon Association of Colored Women's Clubs) worked for women's suffrage, health, and employment issues; talked about arts and culture; and raised money for benevolence projects, with the slogan "Lifting as We Climb." Its college scholarship was named after the first president, Katherine Gray. Pictured in 1913 are, from left to right, (top) Linda Allen, Katherine Gray, Bonnie Bogle, and Anna Peek; (bottom) Mrs. W.H. Lewis, Edith Gray, Dollie Paries, and Anna Payne. (PSU.)

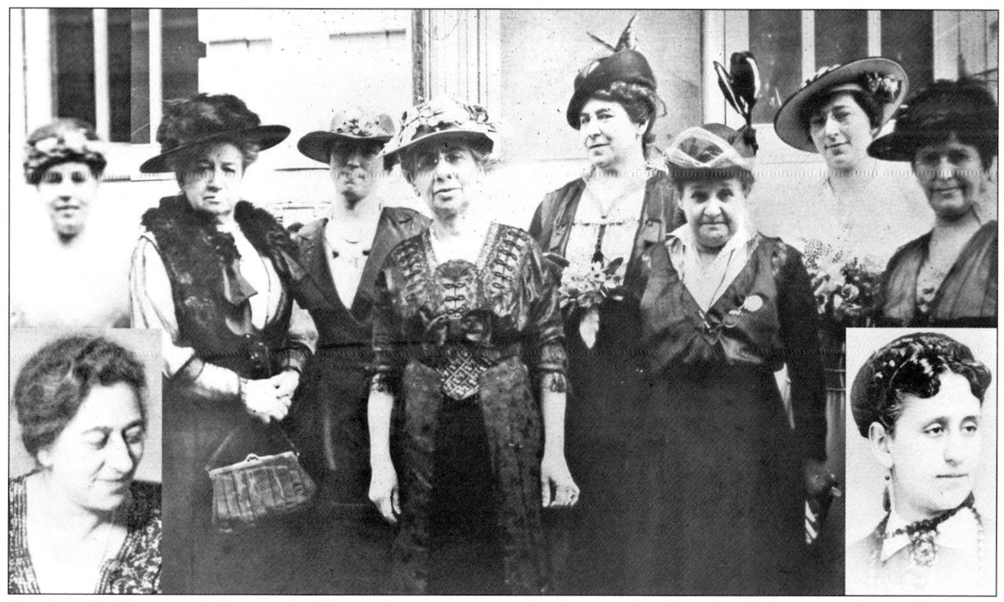

Portland's National Council of Jewish Women worked with the Portland Equal Suffrage League. Founded in 1896, the group also supported Neighborhood House, educating and helping immigrants from many countries. In this 1910 group picture, past presidents are, from left to right, Eugenia Altman, Matilda Selling, Salome Bernstein, Flora Lippitt, Rose Selling, Fannie Blumauer, Clementine Hirsch, Julia Swett. Ida Loewenberg, inset left, and Josephine Hirsch, inset right, were also prominent Jewish women involved in the suffrage movement. (OJM 01582, 03671, 02213.)

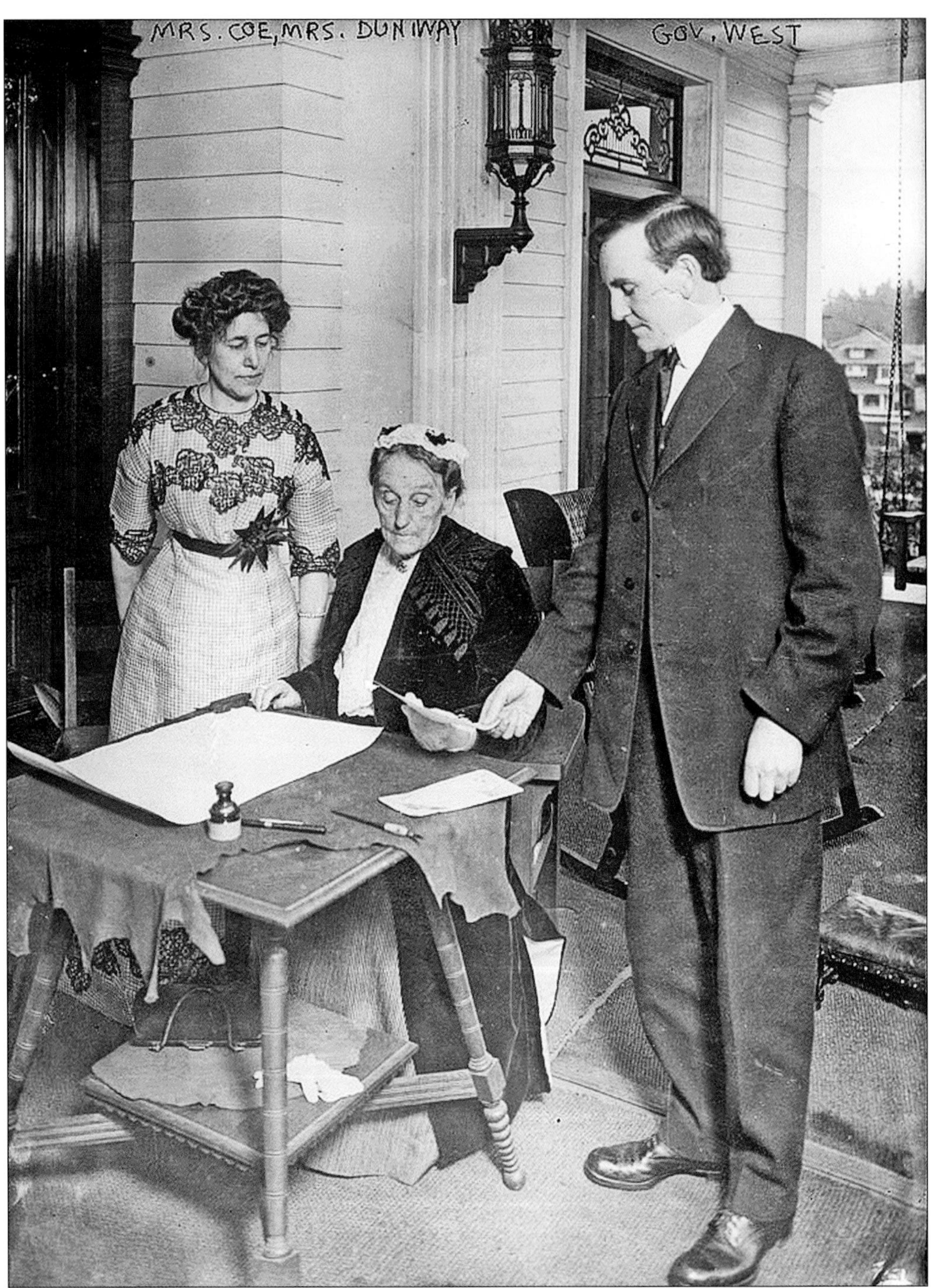

Founder and leader of the Oregon State Woman Suffrage Association and the State Equal Suffrage Association, Abigail Scott Duniway was given the honor of signing the Equal Suffrage Proclamation in 1912 with Gov. Oswald West and Dr. Viola M. Coe (State Equal Suffrage Association chair). Mentored by Susan B. Anthony, Duniway was a National Woman Suffrage Association vice president. She died five years before the Nineteenth Amendment granting suffrage to most American women was ratified on August 26, 1920. (LOC.)

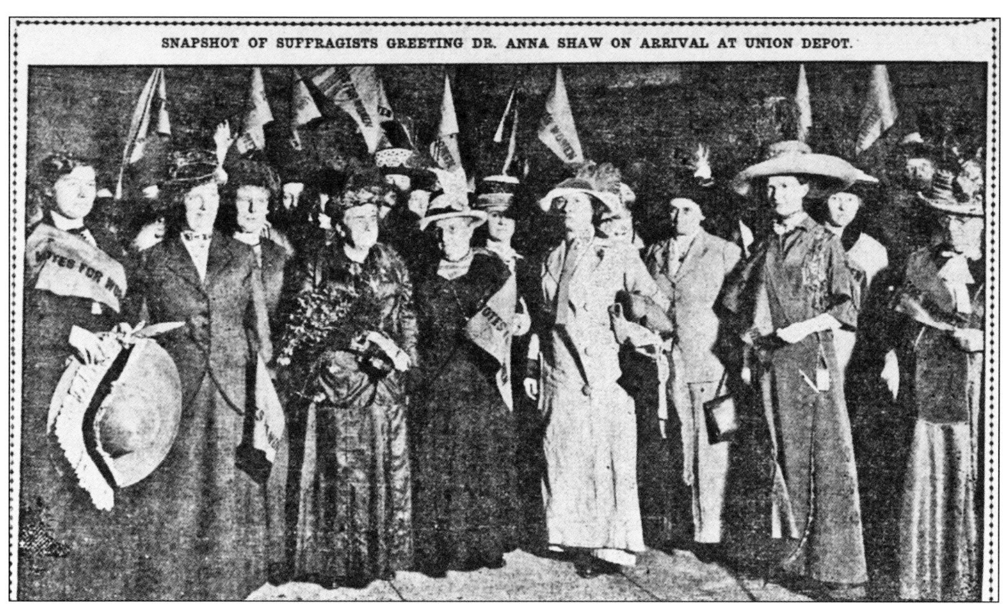

After Oregon women gained the right to vote in 1912, they participated in eight more years of activism for women's suffrage nationwide, such as this September 29, 1912, meeting with national suffrage leader Dr. Anna Shaw in Portland, above. Pictured, from left to right, are two unidentified, Elizabeth Avery Eggert, Rev. Anna Howard Shaw, Sarah A. Evans, Dr. Esther C. Pohl Lovejoy, Lucy Anthony (niece of Susan B. Anthony, who accompanied Dr. Shaw), La Reine Helen Baker, and Dr. Mary Thompson. In a 1913 suffrage march in Washington, DC, below, a Woman's Club delegate holds an Oregon banner. (Above, *Oregonian*; below, LOC.)

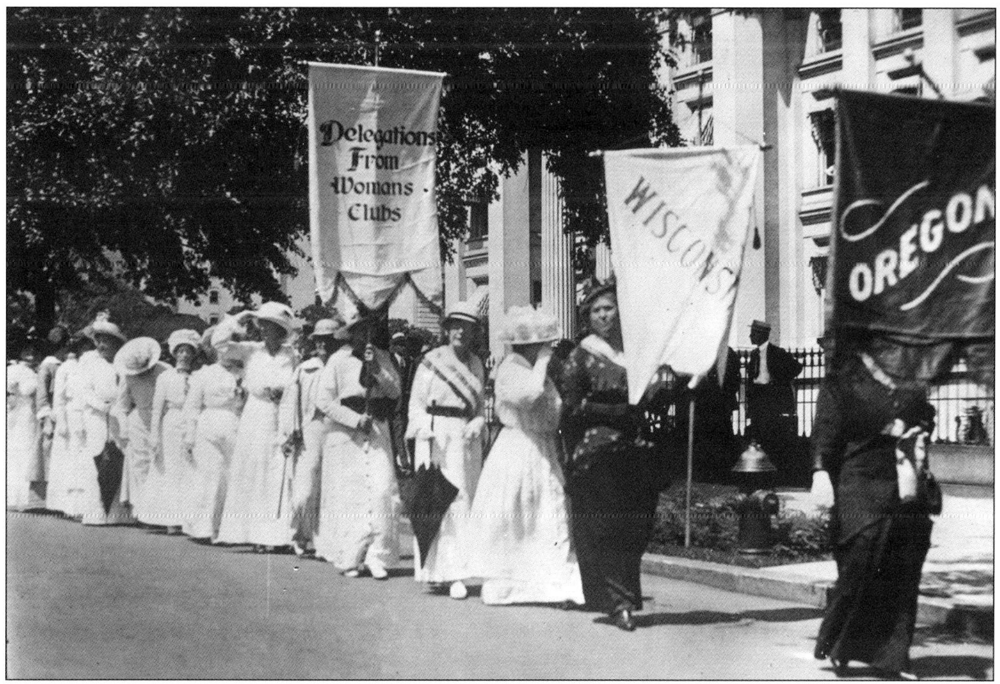

FIRST WOMEN JURY HAS WOMAN'S CASE

Others Eager to Take Responsibilities of Ballot Right When a Few Balk.

HUSBAND'S CONSENT VITAL

Some Ask "Who Else Will Serve?" as Panel Unlike Any Ever Drawn in Oregon Is Summoned Over Phone by Judge's Order.

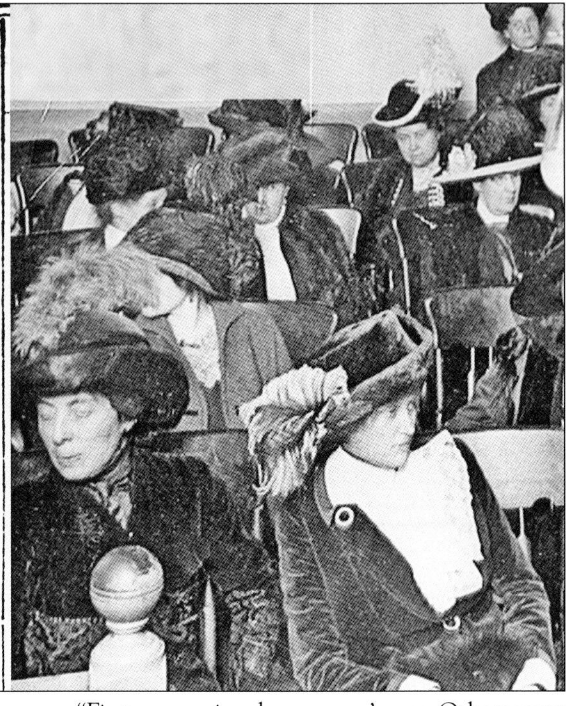

A December 1, 1912, *Oregonian* article announces, "First women jury has woman's case. Others eager to take responsibility of ballot right, when a few balk. Husband's consent vital." Above and below are photographs from the December 5, 1912, *Oregonian* showing women eagerly crowding into the courthouse for the right to register for jury duty. Above on the first row to the left is suffragist Dr. Mary Cachot Therkelsen (1844–1937), a member of the Portland Woman's Club, Portland Equal Suffrage League, and the Oregon State Equal Suffrage Central Campaign Committee and a board member of College Equal Suffrage League of Portland; she was also on the National Advisory Council for the Congressional Union. Below, important suffragist Dr. Viola Coe (see pages 31 and 44) sits under the lightbulb. Labor leader and women's reproductive health and rights activist Dr. Marie Equi is on the left in the second row, looking over the shoulder of attorney W.E. Farrell.

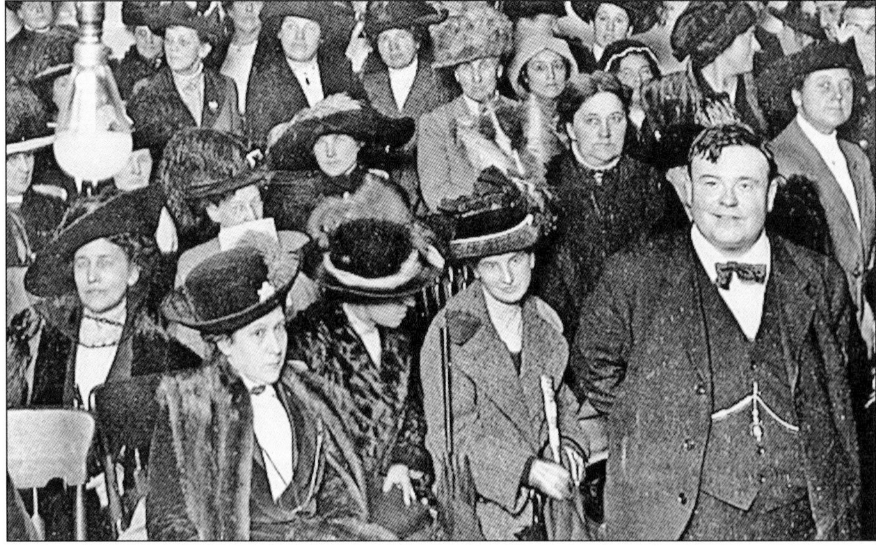

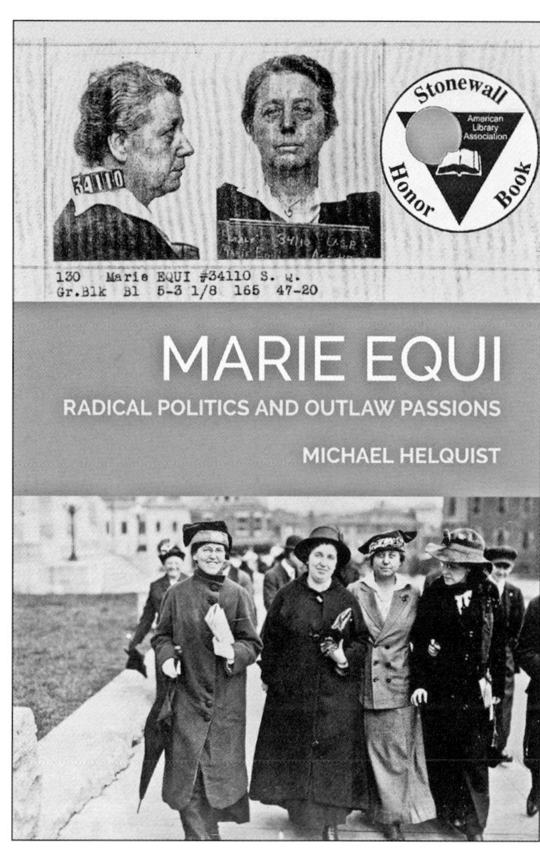

Dr. Marie Equi (1872–1952) was a suffragist, a birth control advocate who spent a night in jail with Margaret Sanger, an abortionist, a labor advocate, a lesbian in a "Boston marriage," and a pacifist who served 10 months in San Quentin prison for giving an antiwar speech at Portland's Industrial Workers of the World (IWW) Hall in 1918. She lived in the Goose Hollow neighborhood with Elizabeth Gurley Flynn (1890–1964) from 1926 to 1936. Michael Helquist's book on Equi is the first in-depth study of her life. Flynn (below) was a suffragist, birth control advocate, labor leader with the IWW—the Wobblies—and founding member of the American Civil Liberties Union in 1920. She and Dr. Equi lived at 1423 Southwest Hall Street. Flynn was arrested after joining the Communists and spent two years in federal prison. She was the inspiration for Joe Hill's 1915 song "Rebel Girl," sung at Wobblies' labor halls and marches. (Below, W.)

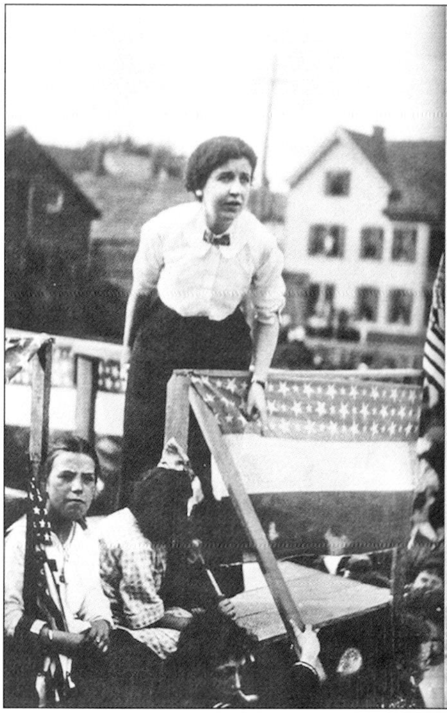

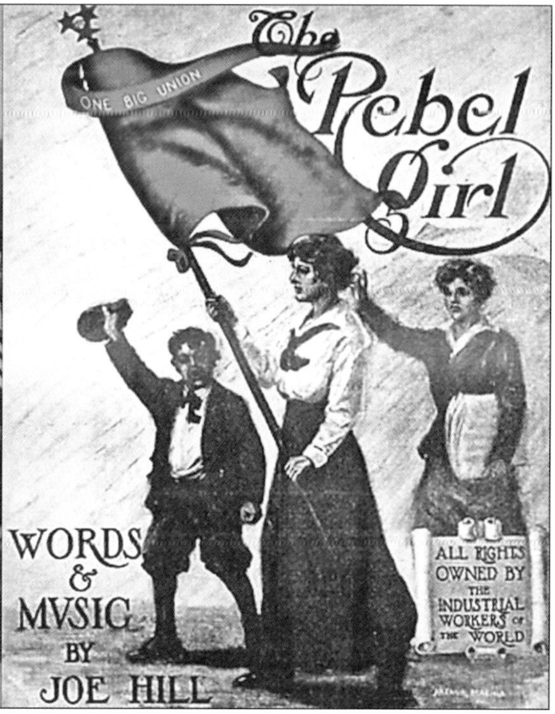

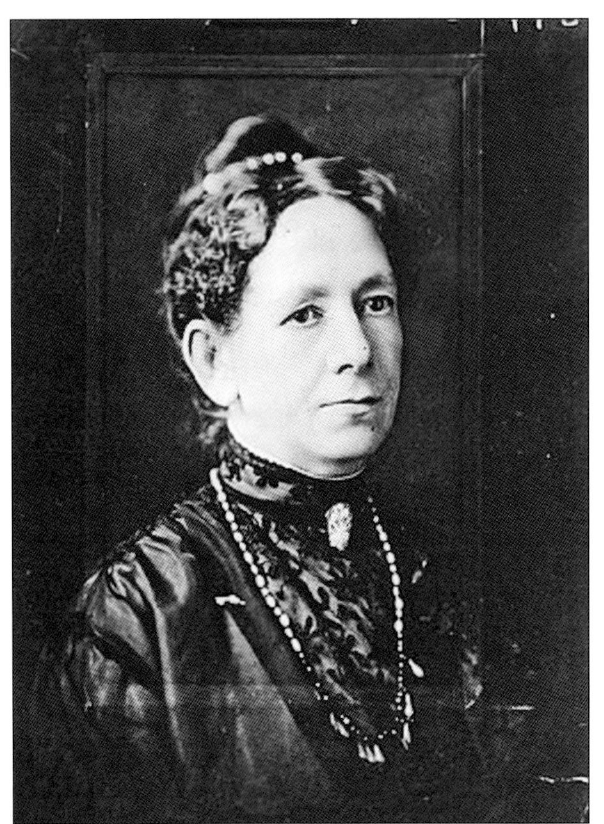

Mattie Cone Sleeth (1852–1934) was a leader of the Oregon Women's Christian Temperance Union and the suffrage movement. She preached in Oregon on prohibition, temperance, and suffrage, was one of the first women jurors in the state, and ran, unsuccessfully, for the state legislature. In 1914, Oregon passed prohibition—five years earlier than national prohibition. Women's groups fought for decades to curb alcohol in the Wild West. Lucy White told of her 1902 arrival to Portland, "The stench of stale beer and whiskey often mixed with the nauseating smell of vomit on the sidewalks, and drunken staggering men blocking my way almost turned my stomach." The 1920s image below shows Portland police with Jane M. Donaldson of the Women's Christian Temperance Union (formed in 1881 in Portland) with 108 confiscated cases of liquor. (OHS 010322.)

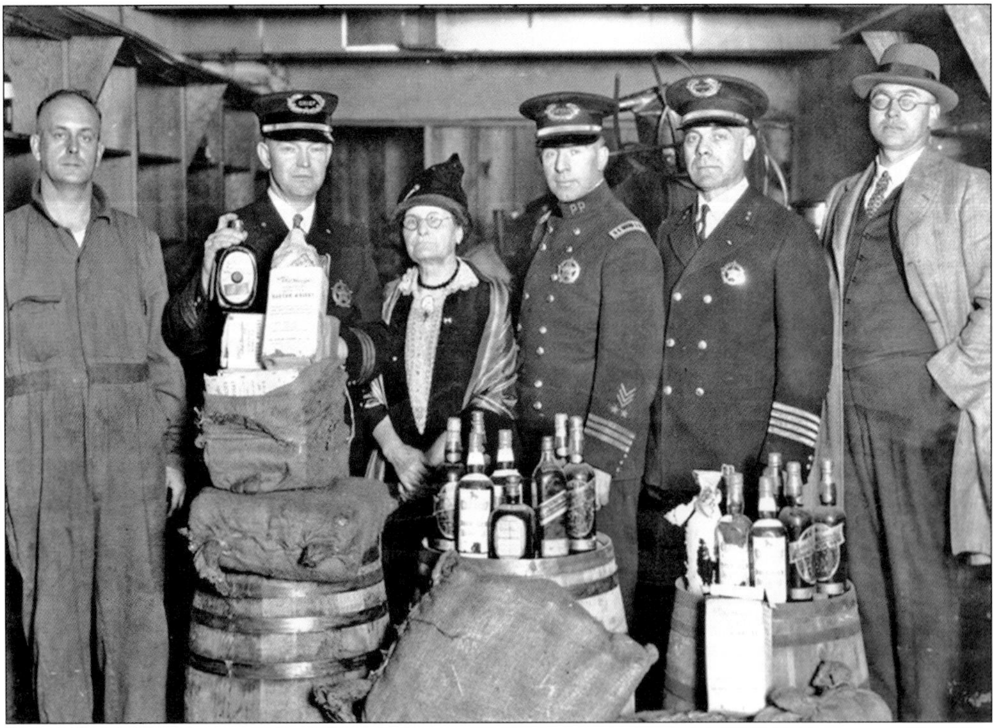

President of the Colored Women's Republican Club Lizzie Weeks (1879–1976), at right, was an African American activist who helped black women register to become voters and invited political candidates to speak at the club. She was the first African American female social worker for Multnomah County, as a matron at the Frazier Detention juvenile home. In 1912, she was a commissioner for the National Emancipation Commemorative Society. (OHS.)

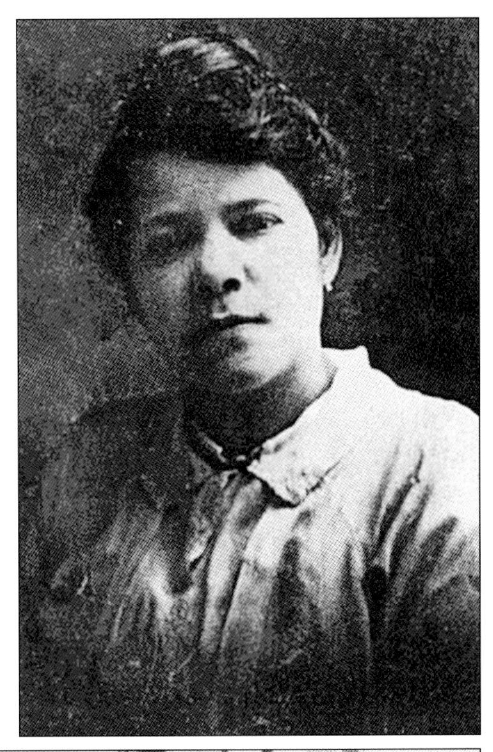

Below, Sarah Bard Field (1882–1974) was a Portland poet and a women's suffrage leader, including making a 5,000-mile automobile journey to carry a petition to Pres. Woodrow Wilson in 1915 (pictured left, with Maria Kindberg, Ingeborg Kindstedt, and the banner greeting them). Field wrote several books, including *Barabbas: A Dramatic Narrative* (1932) and *Darkling Plain* (1936). She is perhaps best known for her controversial relationship with married fellow suffragist C.E.S. Wood. (LOC.)

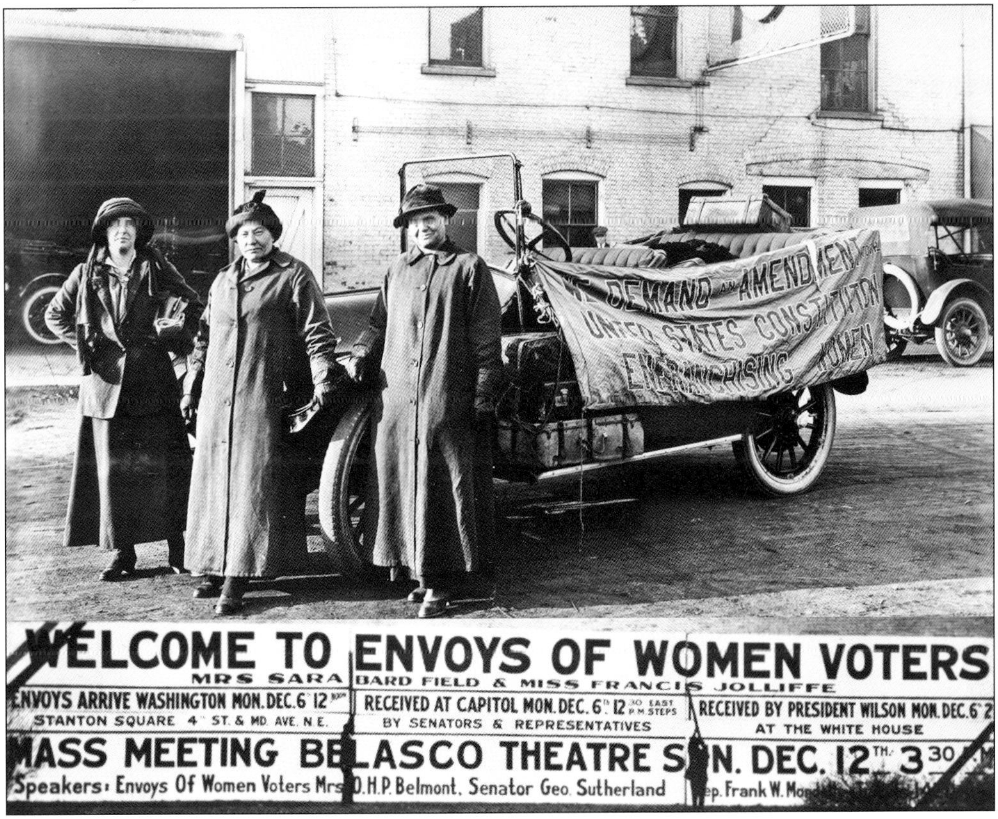

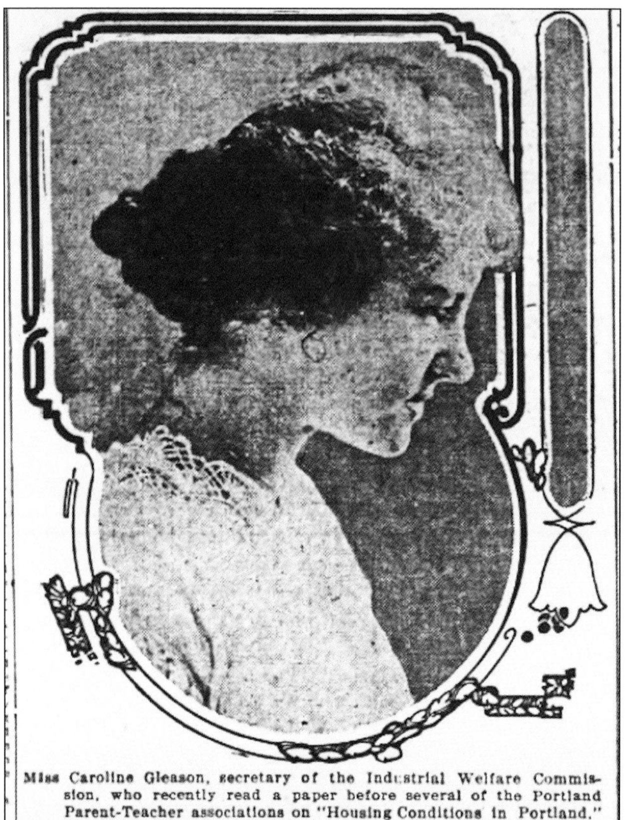
Miss Caroline Gleason, secretary of the Industrial Welfare Commission, who recently read a paper before several of the Portland Parent-Teacher associations on "Housing Conditions in Portland."

The March 8, 1914, *Oregon Daily Journal* depicts Caroline J. Gleason (1886–1962), who later became the nun Sister Miriam Theresa, PhD. She worked for better housing and work conditions, building codes, sanitation, and consumer protections. When working conditions for poorly paid women and children were often dangerous, her tireless labor advocacy and undercover research helped pass Oregon's 1913 wage and hour law, the first minimum wage and maximum hours law in America. She worked for the Portland Health Department, as director of Oregon's Consumer's League, as executive of Oregon's Industrial Welfare Commission, and as head of the Department of Sociology at Marylhurst College. Below, women workers are seen at New System Laundry, at 1001 Northeast Flanders Street, in 1935. (Below, CoPA.)

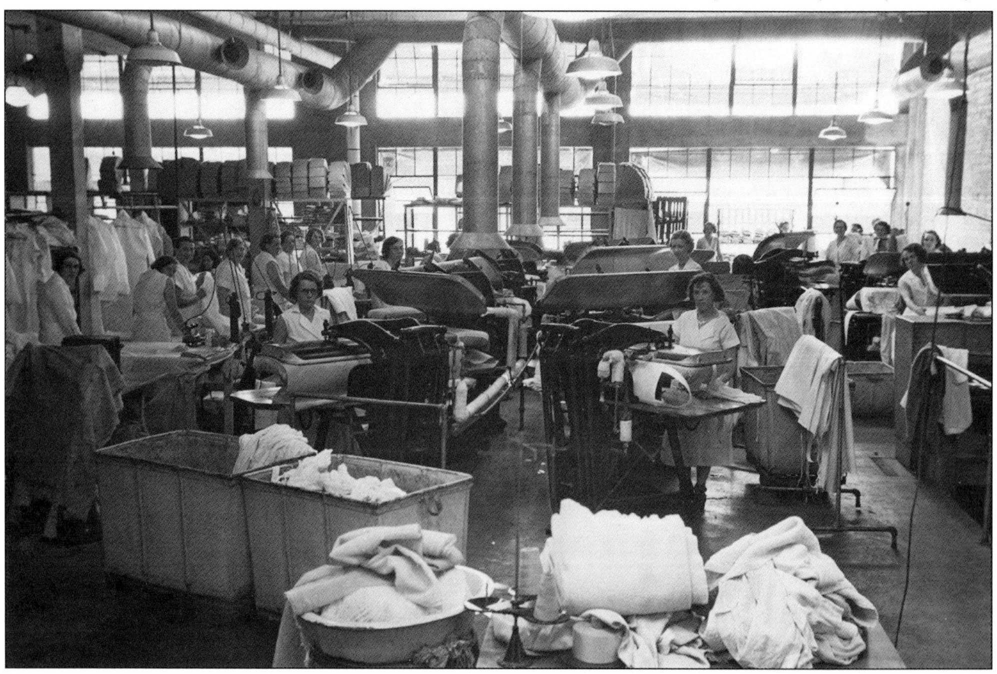

The National Woman Suffrage Association printed this 1917 map to inspire America to follow Canada's lead: "The Canadian provinces of British Columbia, Alberta, Saskatchewan and Manitoba extended full suffrage to their women in 1916. Ontario gave them full suffrage in March, 1917. How long will the Republic of the United States lag behind the Monarchy of Canada?" (W.)

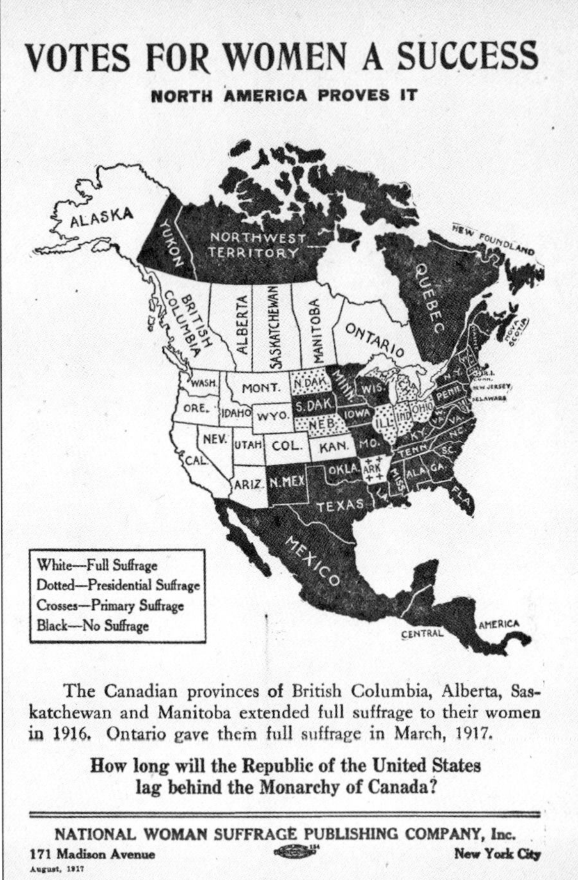

A 1912 suffrage parade in New York City is seen below. Oregon women continued to fight for full suffrage until 1920 when the Nineteenth Amendment to the Constitution was ratified, stating, "The right of citizens of the United States to vote shall not be denied or abridged by the United States or by any State on account of sex." (LOC.)

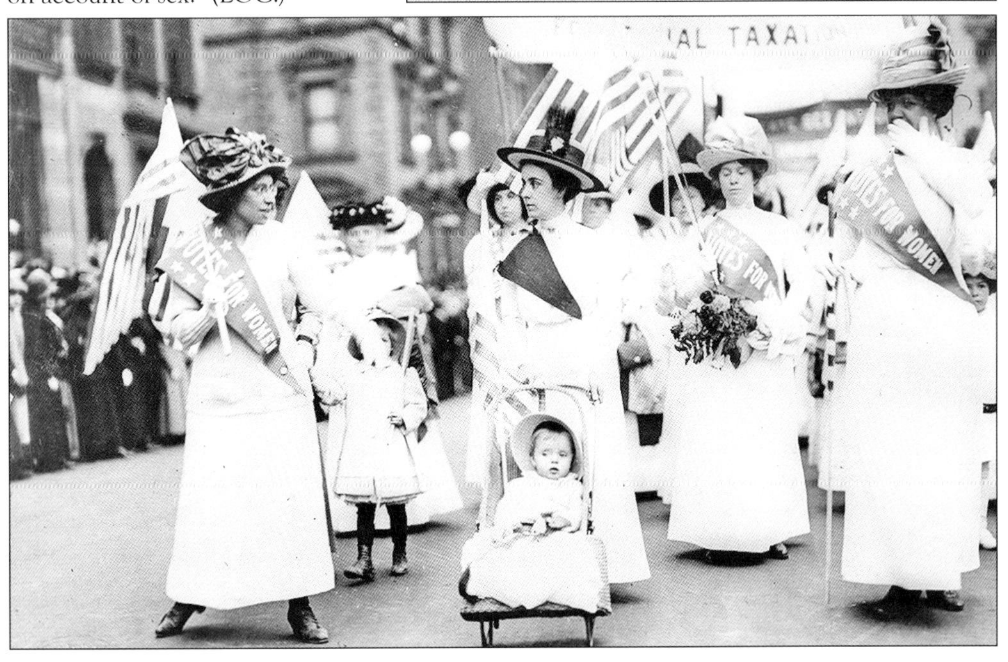

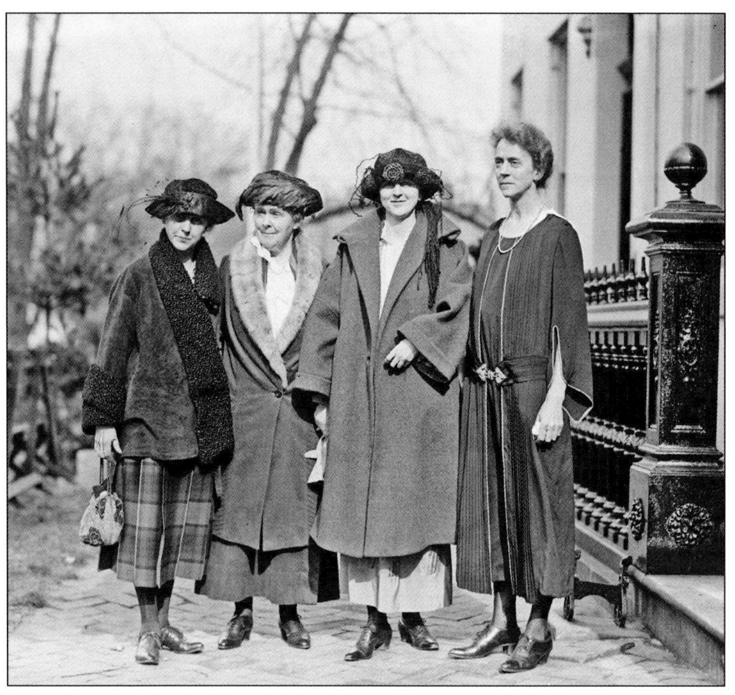

Emma Wold (1871–1950) was an attorney and women's legal rights advocate. She formed the College Equal Suffrage League in Oregon, chaired the Women's Committee for World Disarmament, and was active in the National Women's Party (pictured on the left at the 1922 equal rights conference). In 1930, Pres. Herbert Hoover appointed her as the first woman to represent America at the International Law Codification Conference at The Hague. (LOC.)

Native American Women Win Suffrage in Oregon: 1924

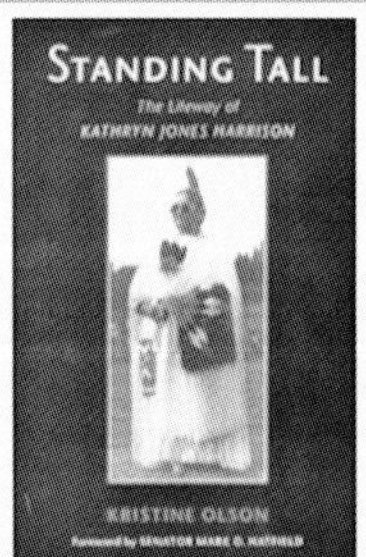

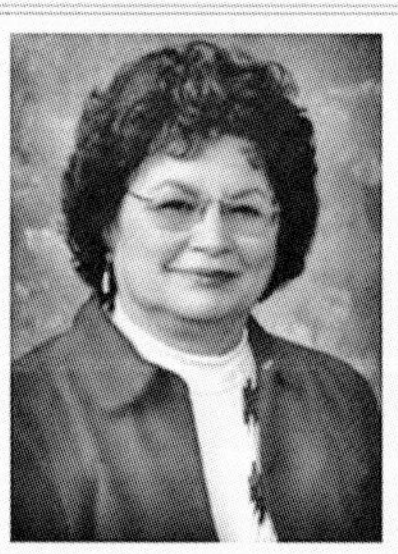

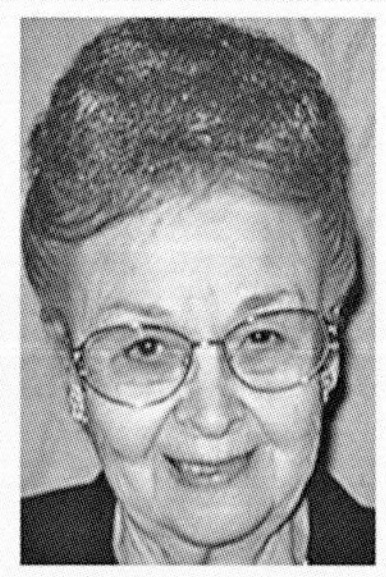

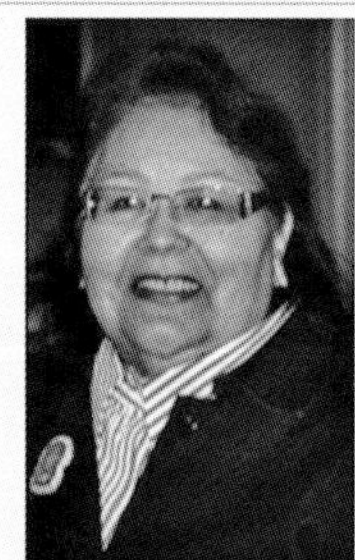

- Kathryn Harrison, Former Chair of Confederated Tribes of the Grande Ronde
- Delores Pigsley, Chair of the Confederated Tribes of the Siletz
- Sue Shaffer, Former Chair of the Umpqua Cow Creek Band
- Cheryle Kennedy, Chair of the Confederated Tribes of the Grand Ronde Community

This is a slide from Portland State University Center for Women's Leadership's excellent grade 6–12 curriculum "Oregon Women Making a Difference." When Oregon women obtained suffrage in 1912, it was not granted to Native American and Asian American women. Native American women did not receive the right to vote until 1924, Chinese American women until 1944, and Japanese American women until 1953. (PSU.)

Three

Women of World War I and World War II 1914 to 1945

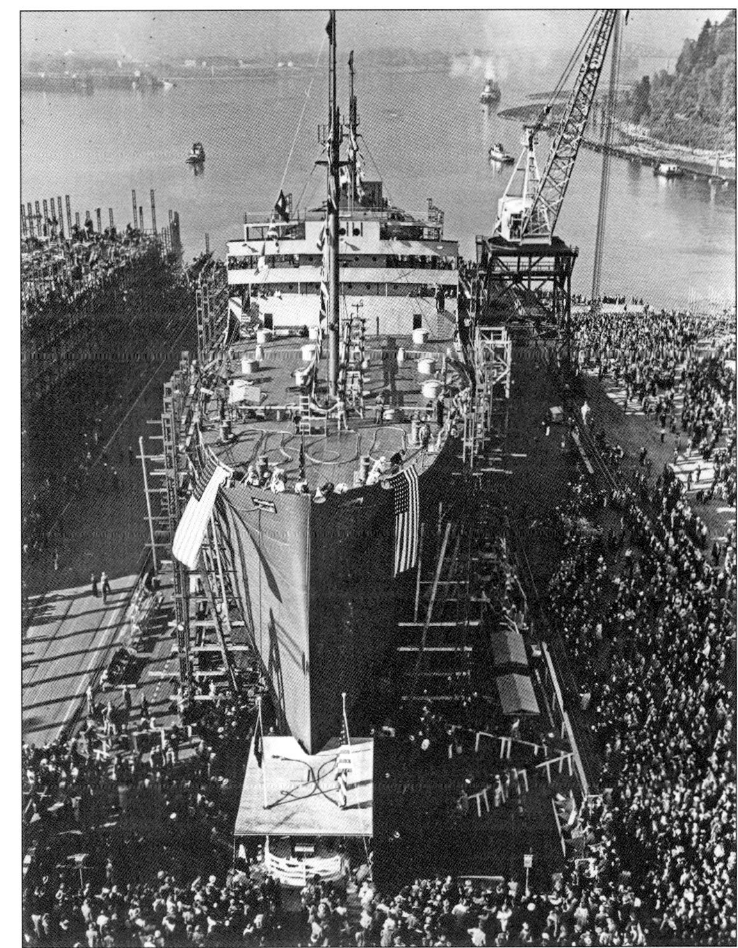

World Wars I and II brought profound changes for Portland women. Women's labor in the traditionally male workforce was encouraged during both wars as a way to free up men to fight overseas. During World War I, women were nurses, volunteers, and Yeomanettes. During World War II, women comprised 35 percent of the workers in Portland's roaring shipyard industries, creating Pres. Franklin D. Roosevelt's "great arsenal of democracy," such as this Liberty ship launching from Kaiser's Swan Island shipyard. Local shipyards built over 1,614 Navy vessels. (Gholston.)

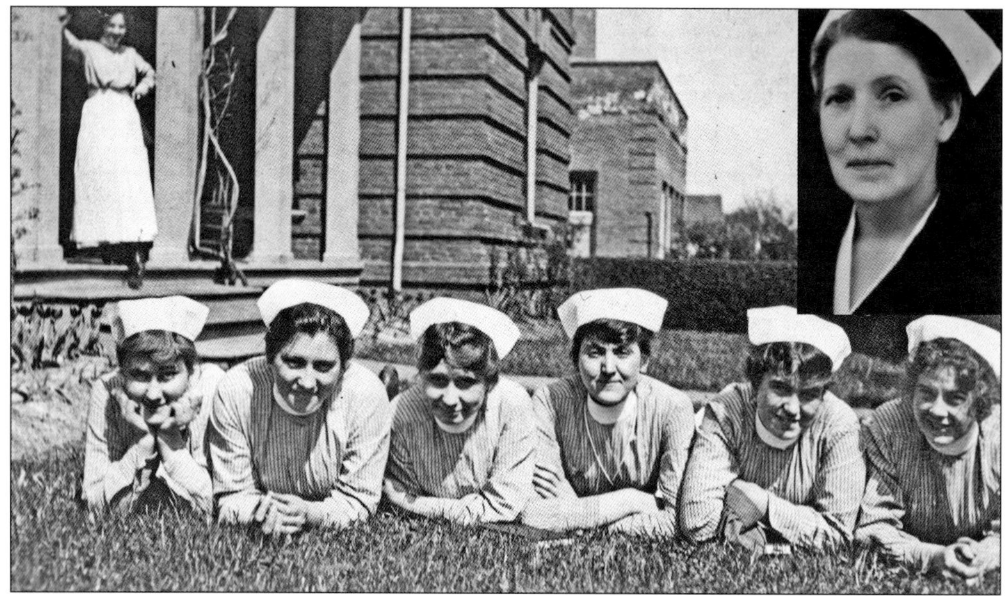

World War I (1914–1918) impacted Portland women as they signed up to join the war effort as nurses, as volunteers and employees with the Red Cross, as Navy Yeomanettes, and as volunteers with the Women's Service League. During the Great War, Grace Phelps (1871–1952) was the chief nurse for the University of Oregon Medical School unit in Bazeilles-sur-Meuse, France. She founded what is now called the Oregon Nurses' Association and organized nursing services for the Portland Red Cross Center. Phelps was superintendent of nurses at Multnomah County Hospital and later superintendent of Doernbecher Memorial Hospital for Children. Above are Portland nurses in 1917. Below, nursing students gather in the cafeteria at Good Sam Hospital. Many Portland nurses served in World War I, stateside and overseas. (Both, Gholston.)

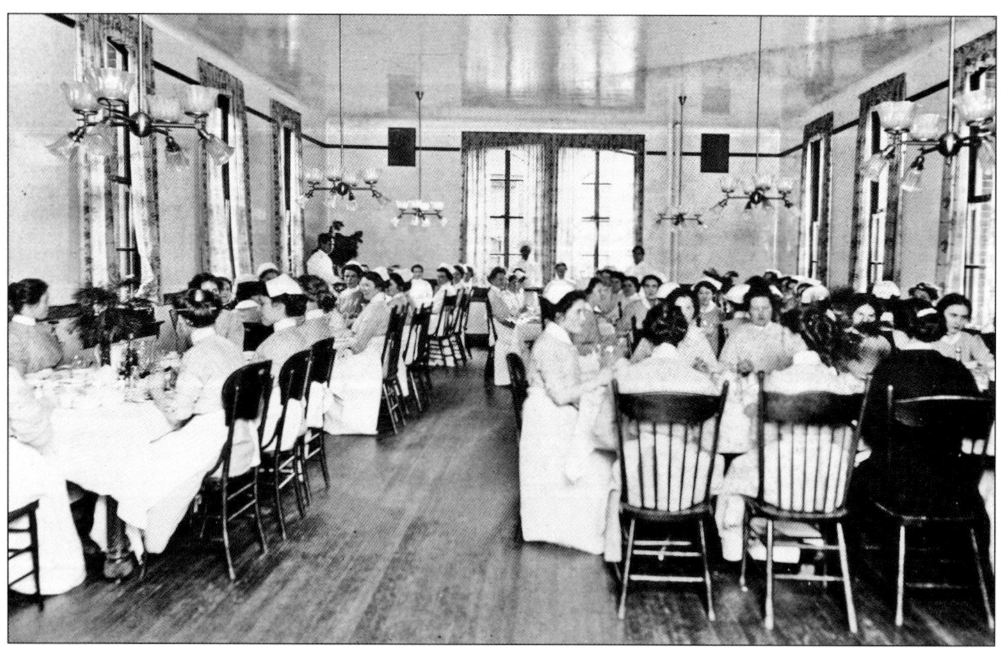

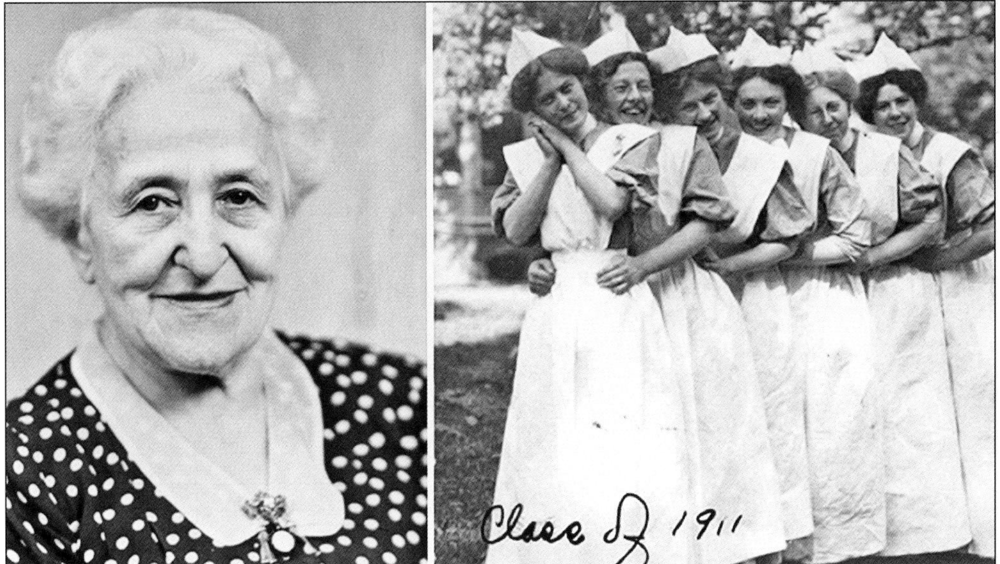

Elnora Thomson (1873–1957) founded the nursing program at what is now Oregon Health and Science University. During World War I, she was director of a Red Cross nursing division. In Italy, she established educational programs for nurses combatting the 1918 influenza epidemic. During World War II, she recruited students for the Cadet Nurse Corps. Thomson was chair of the American Nurses Memorial committee and president of the American Nurses Association. (OHSU.)

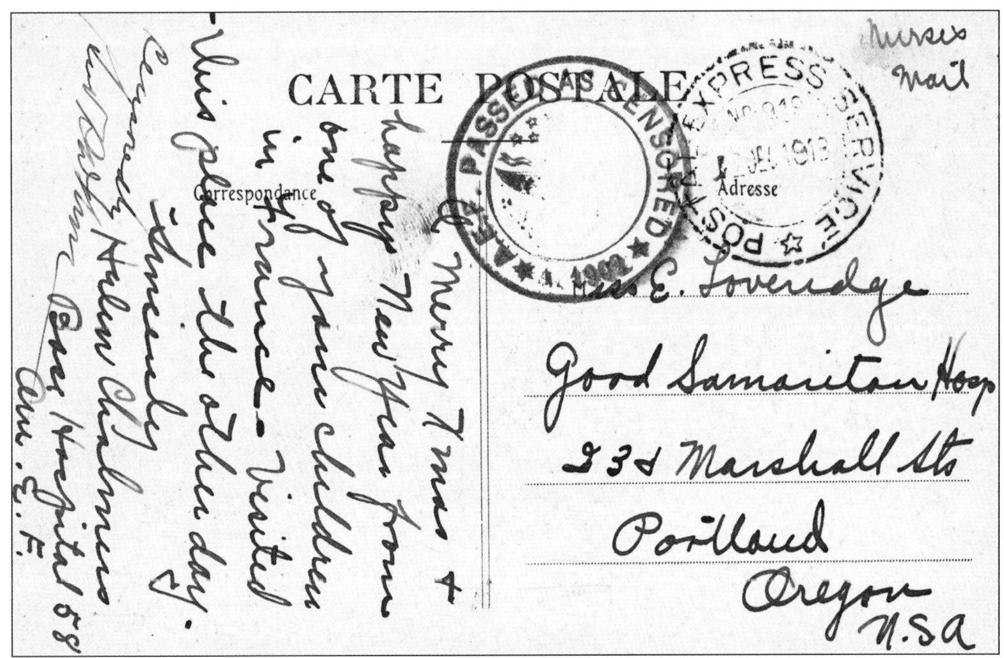
CARTE POSTALE

Correspondance

A merry Xmas + happy New Year from one of your children in France - Visited this place the other day. Sincerely Helen Chalmers Base Hospital 58 Am. E.F.

Adresse

Nurses Mail

A.E.F. PASSED CENSOR

POSTAL EXPRESS SERVICE

Miss E. Loveridge
Good Samaritan Hosp
23d Marshall Sts
Portland
Oregon
U.S.A

This poignant postcard was sent during World War I from Helen Chalmers, a nurse stationed in Europe, to her teacher at Good Samaritan's Nurses School, Emily Loveridge (see page 25). (Gholston.)

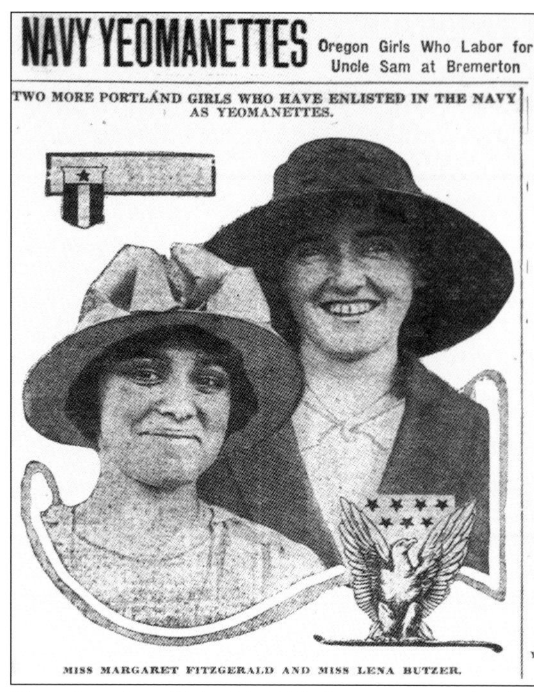
NAVY YEOMANETTES Oregon Girls Who Labor for Uncle Sam at Bremerton

TWO MORE PORTLAND GIRLS WHO HAVE ENLISTED IN THE NAVY AS YEOMANETTES.

MISS MARGARET FITZGERALD AND MISS LENA BUTZER.

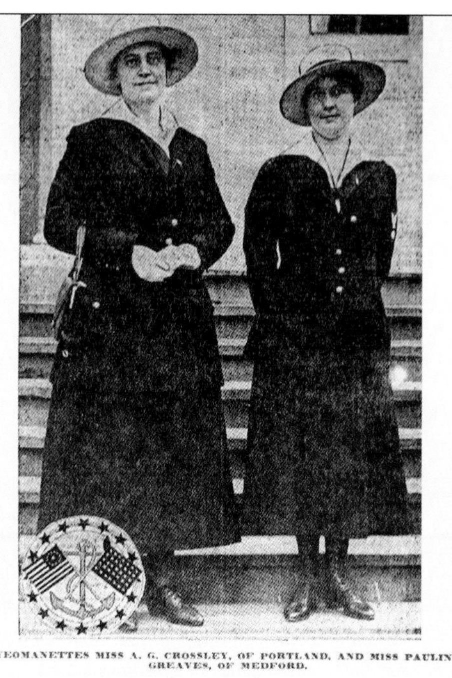
YEOMANETTES MISS A. G. CROSSLEY, OF PORTLAND, AND MISS PAULINE GREAVES, OF MEDFORD.

These June 8 and May 31, 1918, *Oregonian* articles show local women joining the Navy's Yeomanettes going to Puget Sound Navy Yard in Bremerton, Washington. The 1916 Naval Act referred to "persons" rather than men, so the Navy recruited 11,000 women to serve in World War I, with the rank of Yeoman (F)—*F* for female. When pronounced, it sounded like "Yeomanettes," so the nickname stuck. Hired to do home front jobs, freeing up men to be shipped overseas, they were nurses, drivers, messengers, clerks, radio operators, and researchers, receiving the same pay as men. Below are the Yeomanettes marching in Washington, DC, and the University of Oregon faculty listing for the first woman pathologist in Oregon. Dr. Harriet J. Lawrence (1883–1974) called herself a "microbe hunter." During World War I, there was a pandemic of Spanish influenza. The Oregon State Board of Health brought a flu virus culture to Lawrence, who developed an anti-influenza serum. It was sent to doctors across Oregon to treat the infected and immunize others.

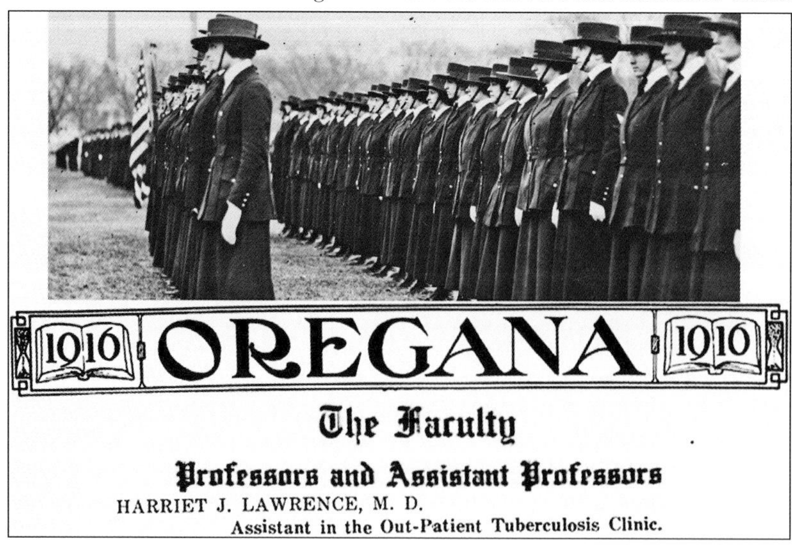
1916 OREGANA 1916

The Faculty

Professors and Assistant Professors

HARRIET J. LAWRENCE, M. D.
Assistant in the Out-Patient Tuberculosis Clinic.

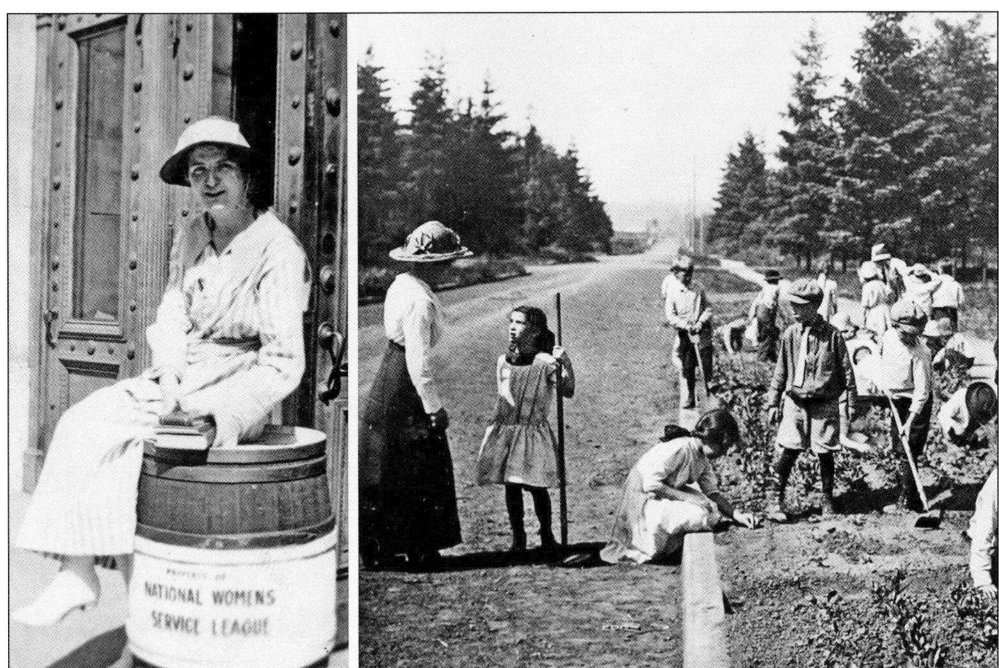

During World War I, the National League for Woman's Service Portland chapter cultivated "war gardens" on vacant land, knitted, sewed, supplied "Flying Squadrons" of women as dance partners for military dances, were wireless operators, and assisted refugees. Above left, a Portland woman is collecting books for the war effort. At right, a woman helps Portland children make a war garden on the strip of land beside the road. The Portland chapter was unique in organizing Uncle Sam's Kanning Kitchen with 25 workers canning daily, as pictured below from the 1920 book *For God, for Country, for Home* (the Women's Service League's motto). Volunteers did farm and urban gleaning to gather all the fruits and vegetables they could get their hands on. Nothing was wasted. In one five-month period, they canned 15,000 quarts of fruit, which was sent to feed soldiers, veterans, and war workers in regional military and hospital facilities. (Above left, Gholston; right, OSU P146:2158.)

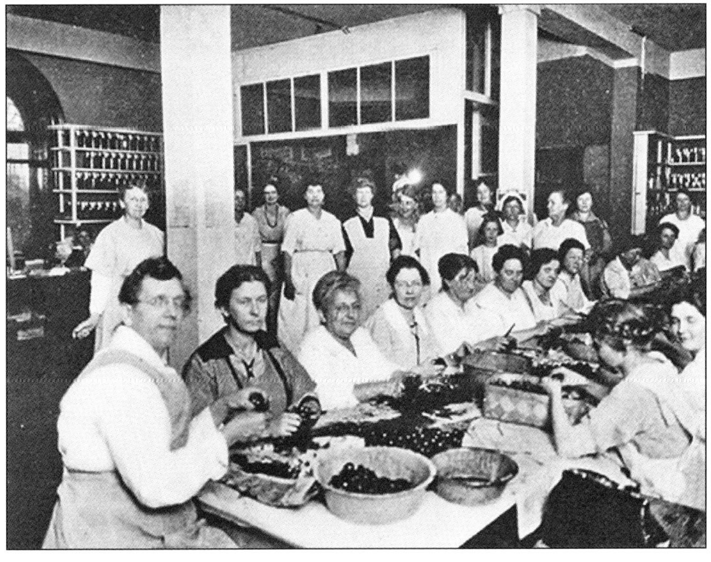

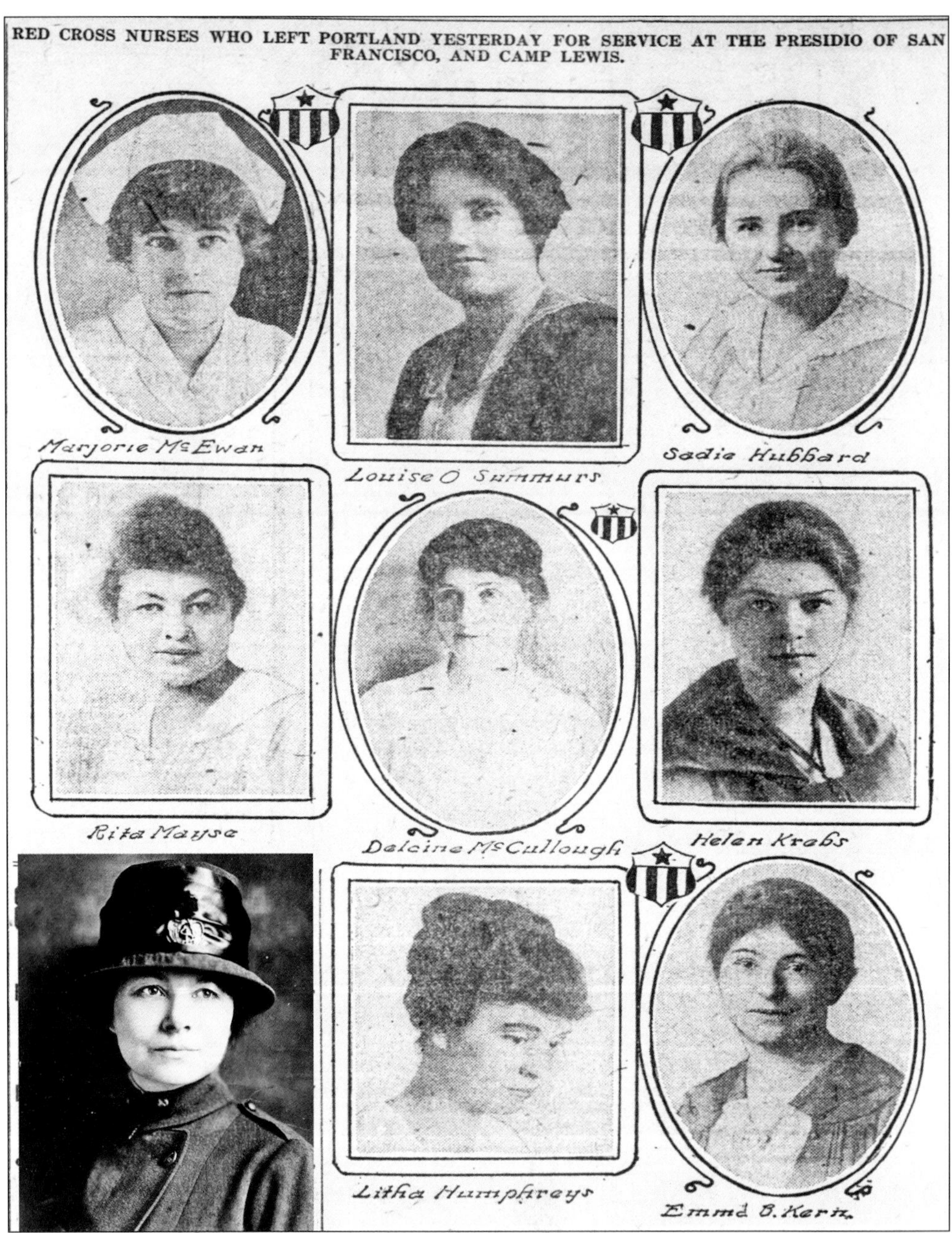

RED CROSS NURSES WHO LEFT PORTLAND YESTERDAY FOR SERVICE AT THE PRESIDIO OF SAN FRANCISCO, AND CAMP LEWIS.

Marjorie McEwan

Louise O Summurs

Sadie Hubbard

Rita Mayse

Delcine McCullough

Helen Krebs

Litha Humphreys

Emma B. Kern

The Red Cross was pivotal to war efforts on the home front during World War I. The November 27, 1917, *Oregonian* proudly featured these Portland women who are heading to Red Cross duty at the Presidio and Camp Lewis. Red Cross women sewed bandages, hospital gowns, and clothing for refugees; knitted sweaters, mittens, and hats; had fundraisers with carnivals, bake sales, plays, and ice-cream socials; fed soldiers who were passing through town on trains; and cared for disabled veterans. Dr. Esther Pohl Lovejoy, inset photograph lower right—shown in her Red Cross uniform—was the first woman to serve on the American Red Cross Commission to France. In 1919, she was the founder and president of the Medical Women's International Association. Another suffragist, Dr. Viola Coe was also active with the Red Cross during World War I.

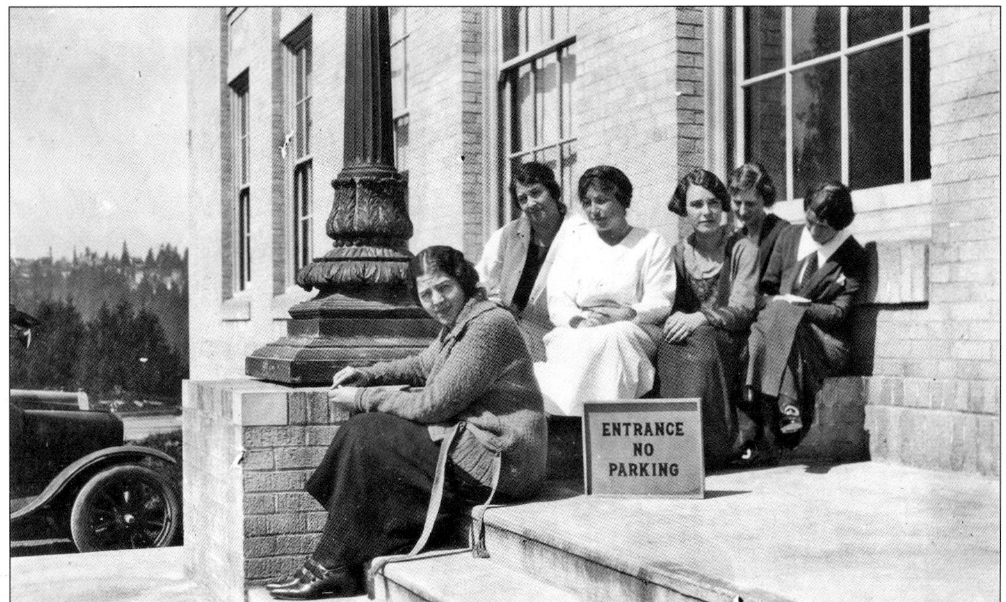

After World War I, life in Portland returned to a normal routine, but the war had demonstrated strong role models to inspire women to be involved in medicine and to attend medical school. This 1920s photograph shows female medical students on the steps of Mackenzie Hall at the University of Oregon Medical School. (OHSU.)

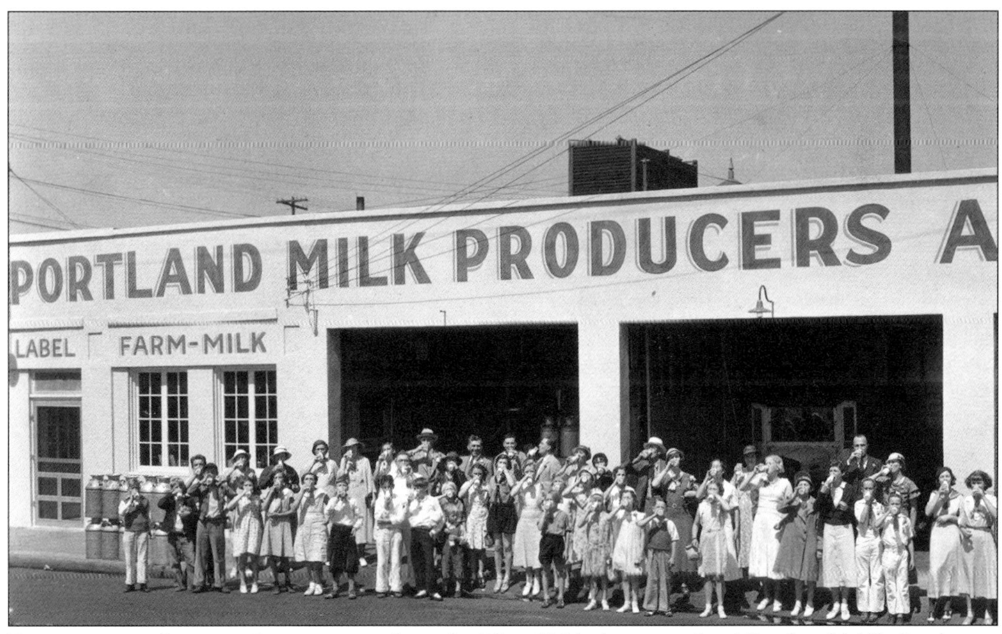

For centuries, dairy work was women's work. This 1934 photograph of Portland Milk Producers Association distribution plant employees and their children shows many women employees. Decades of Portland women worked in this dairy operation at 409 Northeast Roselawn Street, which produced over 10,000 gallons of milk a day. (CoPA.)

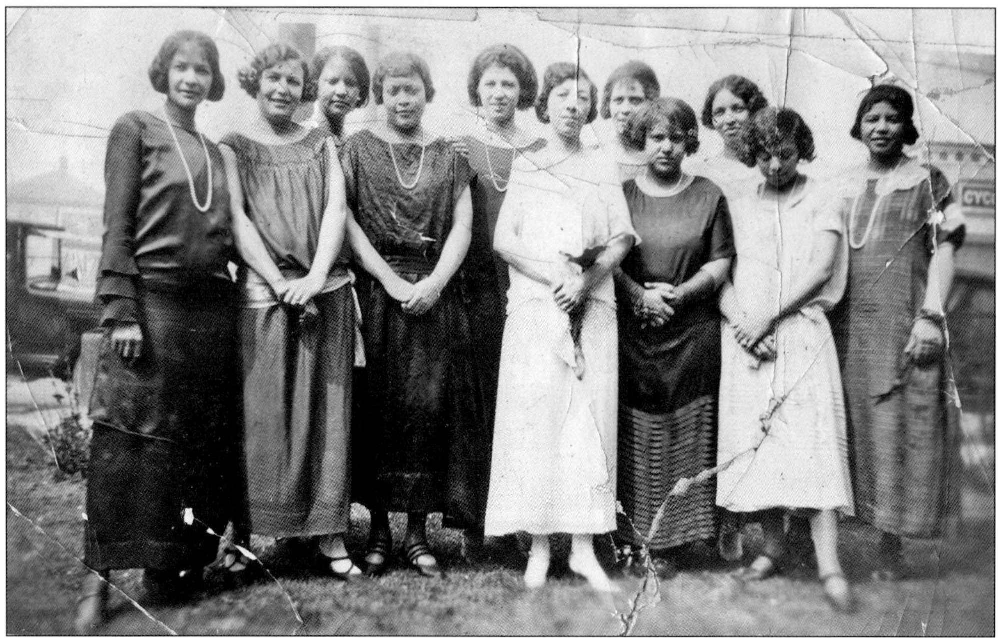

An African American women's social and service group, Portland's Culture Club, founded 1924, was affiliated with the National Association of Colored Women's Clubs, Oregon Association of Colored Women, and the Urban League—teaching history with "Negro History Teas," exhibits, and study clubs, and raising money for scholarships. Its motto, "To Labor is a Pleasure," indicated working to uplift the community with pleasurable activities. Above, charter members are, from left to right, Lula Gragg, Hazel Cage, Estella Gragg, Marion Brown, Thelma Flowers, Clifford Dixon, Maud Booker, Ruth Flowers, ? Flowers, Ina Pierce, and Susan Pierce. Below, with African Americans excluded from the Masons until the 1960s, black men and their families found social and service connections with the Black Masonic Grand Lodge. Members traveled in 16 train cars in 1937 to a Portland State convention. These photographs are in the Verdell Burdine and Otto G. Rutherford Collection at Portland State University; Verdell and Otto were civil rights leaders in the state who were active in both groups (see page 84).

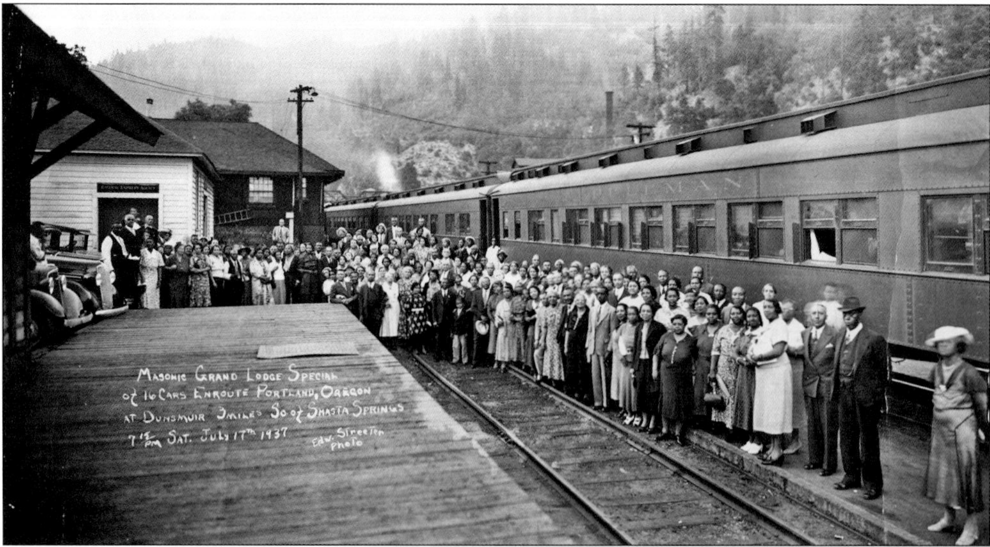

World War II (1939–1945) brought incredible demographic change to women's lives as factories relied on women's labor to replace men who were at war, as at the Kaiser shipyard in St. Johns, pictured. America entered the war December 7, 1941, when the Japanese bombed Pearl Harbor. Government propaganda encouraged women to take such jobs: "Can you use an electric mixer? If so, you can learn to operate a drill!" (Gholston.)

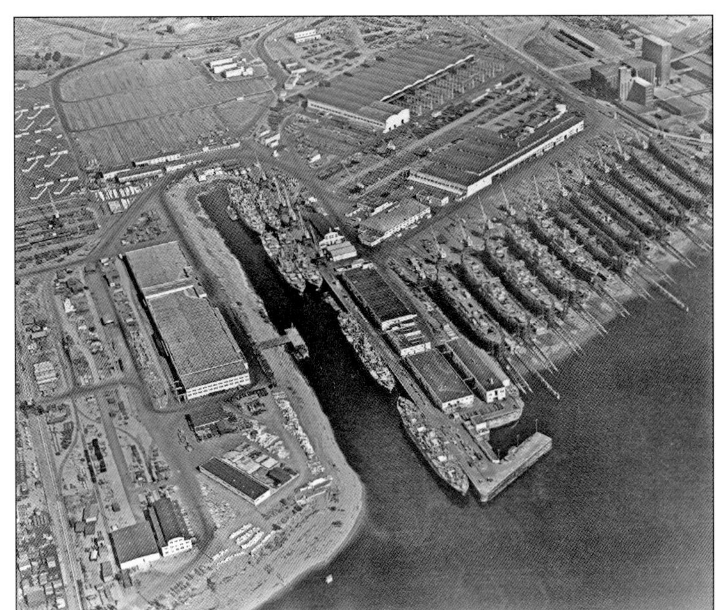

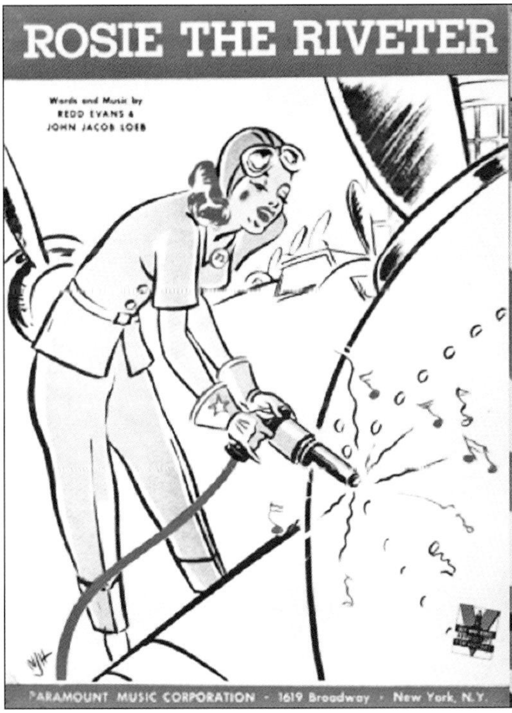

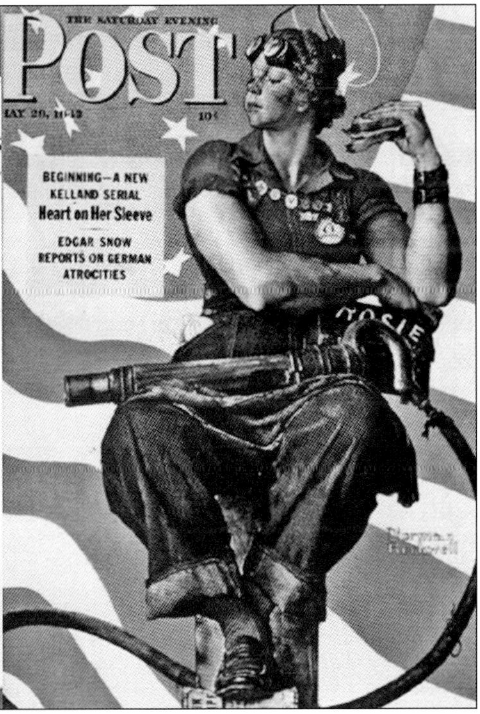

The World War II need for women to take jobs traditionally done by men prompted a patriotic recruitment song (left), "Rosie the Riveter." The lyrics include, "All the day long / Whether rain or shine / She's part of the assembly line / She's making history / Working for victory / Rosie the Riveter." An American icon was born and more firmly cemented in the popular imagination with Norman Rockwell's famous 1943 illustration for the *Saturday Evening Post*. They were also known as Wendy the Welders.

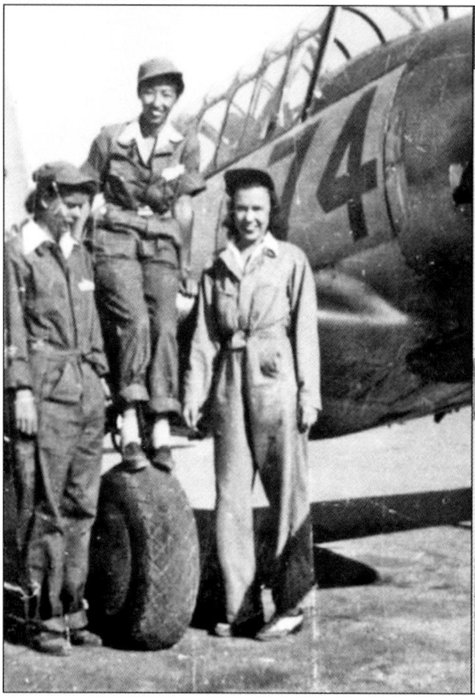

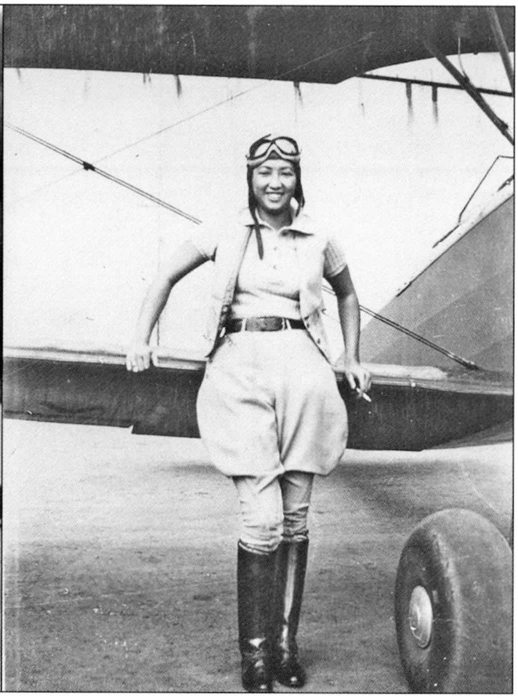

Born in Portland, Hazel Ying Lee (1912–1944) was licensed as a pilot in 1932. During World War II, she joined the Women Airforce Service Pilots (WASP), becoming the first Chinese American women to fly for the American military. She flew aircraft from factories to military destinations. At age 32, she died in a mid-air collision due to low visibility and air traffic control errors. (W.)

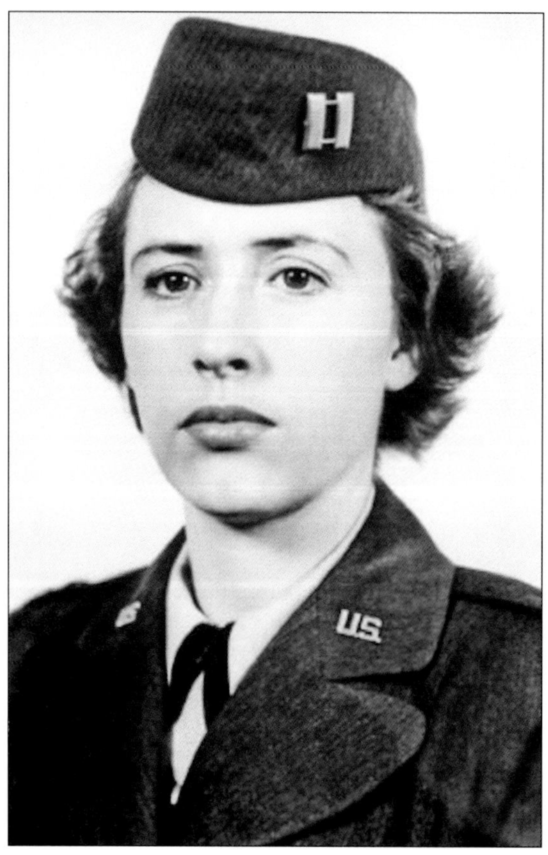

Jeanne M. Holm (1921–2010) enlisted in World War II's Women's Army Auxiliary Corps (WAAC) as a truck driver and was the first woman to attend the Air Command and Staff College in Alabama. Holm was the director of Women in the Air Force from 1965 to 1973 and one of the first women promoted to colonel. In 1971, she was the first woman promoted to brigadier general, and in 1973, she was the first woman to be major general. (National Archives.)

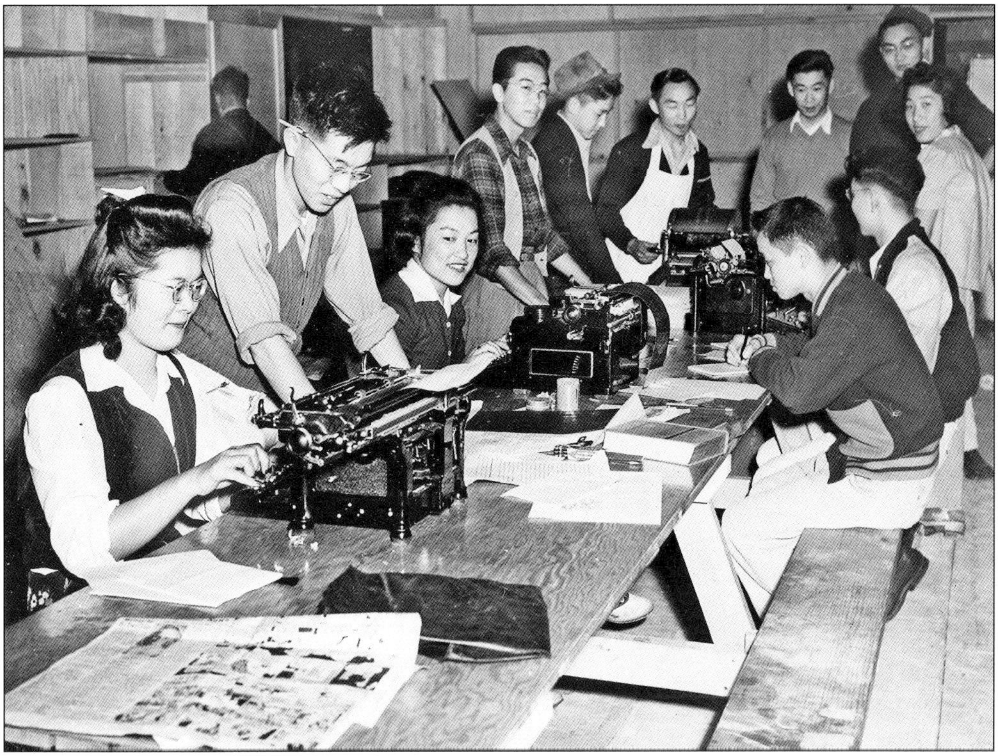

In 1942, Pres. Franklin D. Roosevelt signed Executive Order 9066, which led to the incarceration of many people with Japanese ancestry and some with German, Jewish, and Italian ancestry—people thought to possibly have suspect loyalties since their ancestor countries were at war with America. In May 1942, Japanese American residents of parts of Oregon and Washington were ordered to the International Livestock Exhibition Center, renamed as Portland Assembly Center (now the Expo Center). Internees created *Evacuazette*, a semiweekly newspaper. *Evacuazette* staff (including many women, as pictured here) were prohibited from writing about the war, so they wrote about the 3,676 internees. In September, these internees were sent on trains to Idaho, California, and Wyoming internment camps. This World War II history is memorialized at the Expo Center MAX Station, where artist Valerie Otani created five torii—Japanese gates marking a sacred place. Metal strips hanging between the timbers represent identity tags worn by internees. (Above, OHS.)

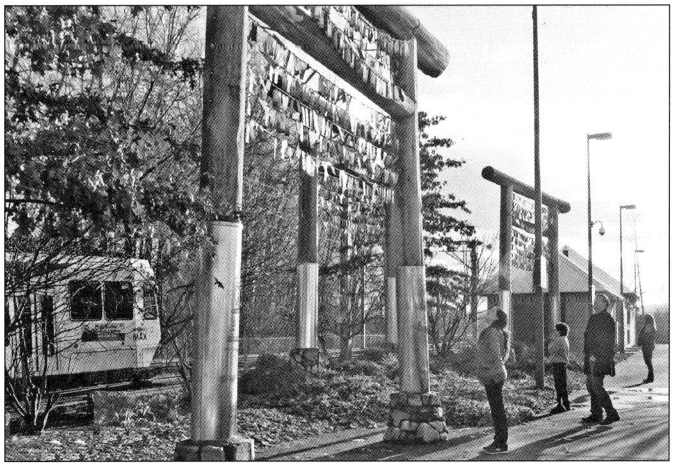

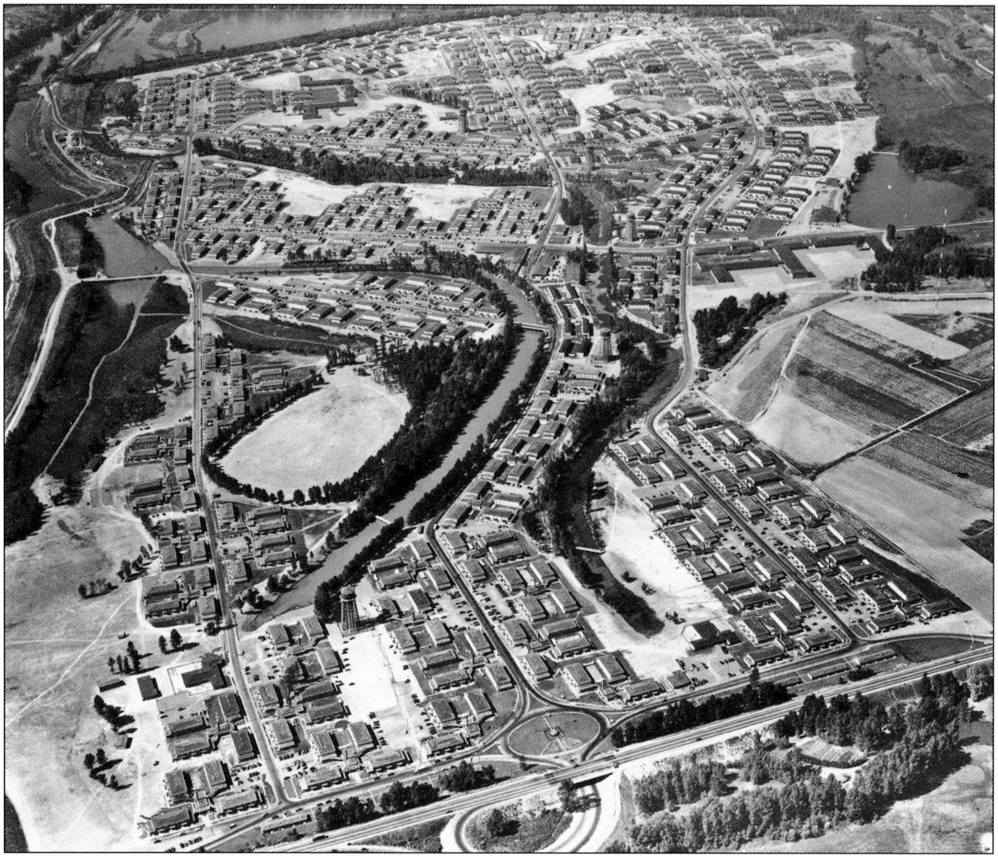

With 140,000 people employed in Portland-area defense industries and people streaming in from across the country, worker housing was woefully insufficient. Also, African Americans recruited to come to work in Portland's defense industry could not find housing, since banks would not lend to blacks and the Portland Realty Board required members to refuse to sell to Asians or blacks. So, Kaiser shipyards secured federal funding to build 9,568 units of temporary defense industry housing on a Columbia River floodplain in North Portland. Vanport, a city from 1942 to 1948, had 42,000 residents, including 6,000 African Americans. Housing and medical facilities were racially segregated, while schools were integrated. Residents were employed at Kaiser shipyards on the Willamette River in St. Johns and Swan Island and on the Columbia River in Vancouver. Vanport was a self-contained city, with schools, grocery stores (pictured below), a movie theater, recreation centers, a hospital, and 24-hour childcare. (Both, Gholston.)

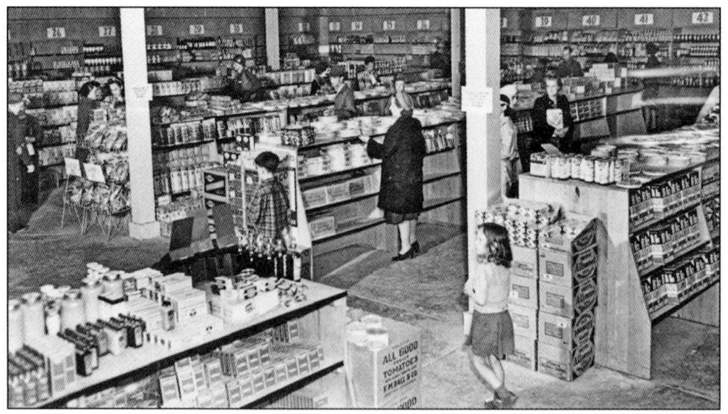

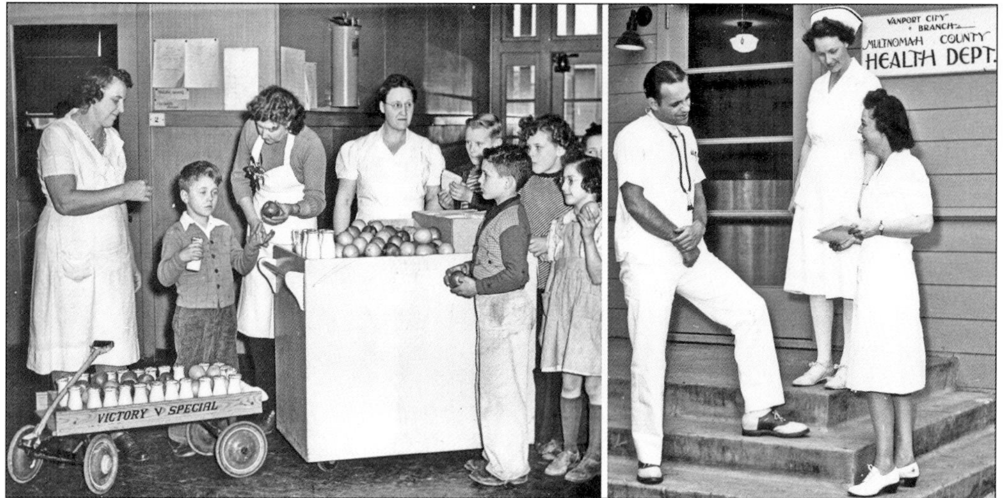

America's largest wartime housing development, Vanport had stores stocked with processed prepackaged foods, and women could pick up prepared meals for their families. Though these food conveniences are common now, they were not then. Since women shipyard workers had reduced time to prepare meals, this Kaiser perk allowed women to be able to work more, with fewer encumbrances. Such benefits as prepared foods, on-site childcare, schools (left), and a hospital (right) were groundbreaking corporate benefits that Kaiser was rightfully proud of, but these benefits also assured that women shipyard workers maintained maximum productivity and had reduced absenteeism. This allowed Kaiser shipyards to have unrivaled productivity. Below, women work at Vanport with a Red Cross sewing unit of volunteers. (Above, Gholston; below, CoPA.)

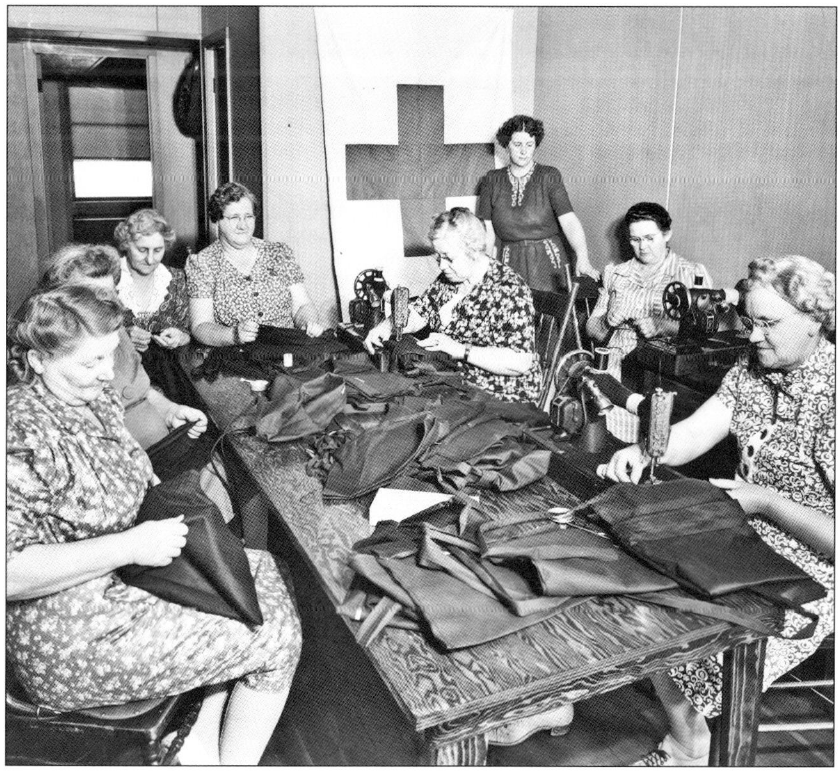

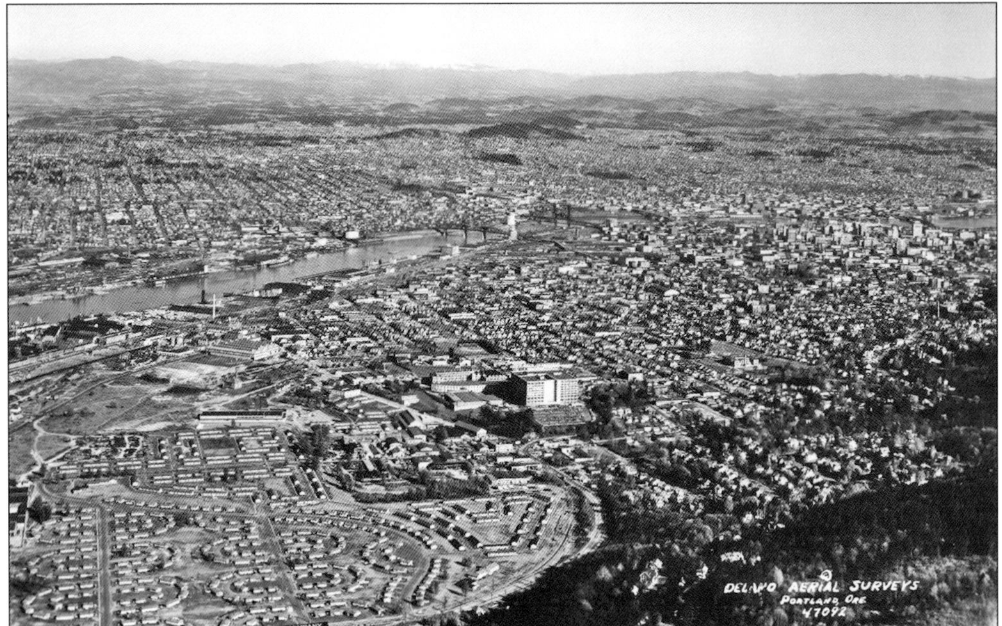

In Northwest Portland's Slabtown neighborhood, Guild's Lake war housing, built on an infilled lake, held 10,000 defense industry workers and their families—many working at Gunderson and Willamette Iron and Steel Company (WISCO). Half of the residents were African Americans who lived in segregated housing on the north end. Though schools were integrated, societal prejudices toward people pejoratively called "the swamp kids" prevented true integration. (Gholston.)

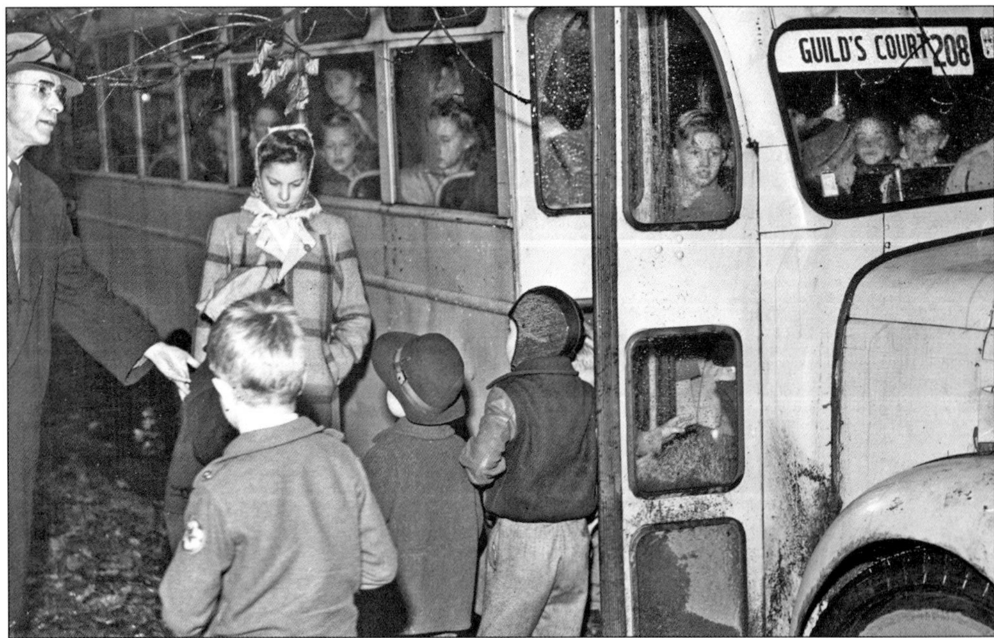

Portland schools such as Portsmouth and Chapman Grade Schools held classes in shifts to accommodate the children of women who worked swing shifts. With 2,000 children at Guild's Lake, nearby Chapman Grade School was bursting at the seams. This bus is taking children home from Chapman's night shift. Eventually, another school was built at Guild's Lake. (Gholston.)

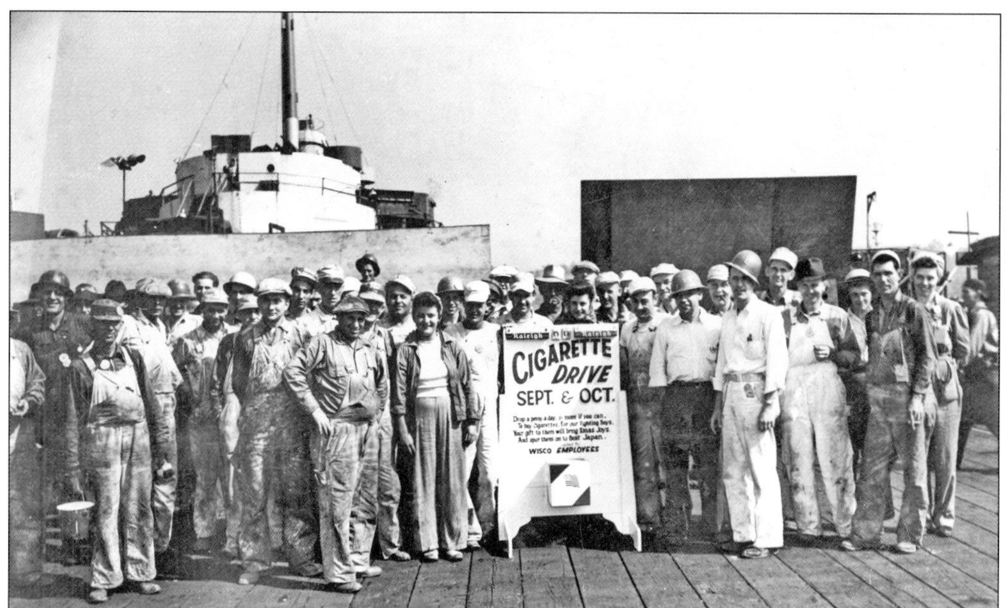

Northwest Portland's Willamette Iron and Steel Company workers, including four women, show support for the troops by raising money to send them cigarettes. "Drop a penny a day & more if you can." WISCO made 70 Navy minesweepers, subchasers, landing craft, and auxiliary aircraft carriers, and many locomotives. (Gholston.)

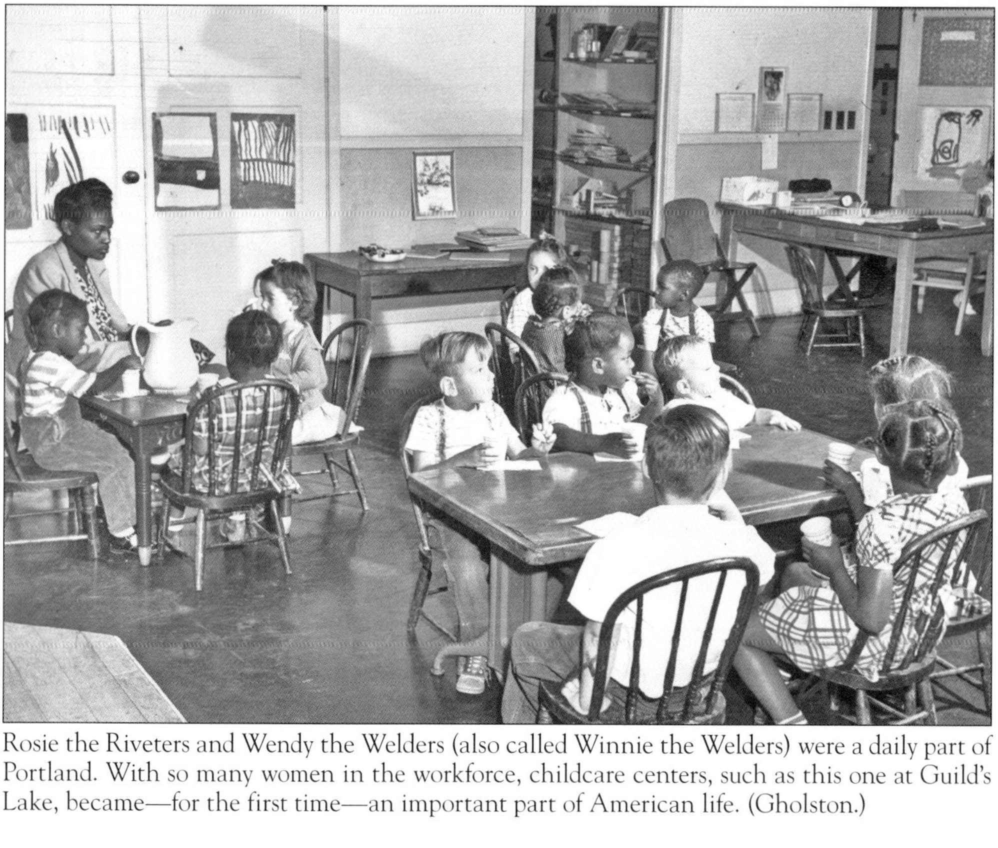

Rosie the Riveters and Wendy the Welders (also called Winnie the Welders) were a daily part of Portland. With so many women in the workforce, childcare centers, such as this one at Guild's Lake, became—for the first time—an important part of American life. (Gholston.)

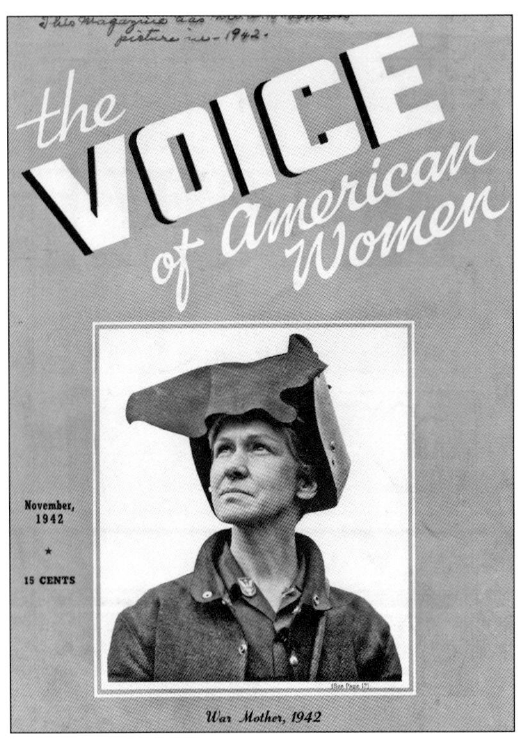

A 1942 Portland shipyard newspaper, the *Voice of American Women*, shows "War Mother" Mary Carroll in her welding gear. Mary is striking and powerful—a war hero. She decided to work in the war effort when her 27-year-old son was reported missing in the Philippines. Below, women are eagerly scanning the shipyard newspaper to see "who is the champion woman shipyard welder?" It was suddenly socially acceptable for women to do jobs that would have been considered men's work before the war. Portland recruiters went door to door, convincing women that a woman's place was in the shipyard. Women had opportunities never before experienced. After the war, the pressure was intense for women to drop out of those jobs for men returning home. For a brief time in American history, women were encouraged and celebrated for their ability to do hard, skilled, gritty manual labor. (Both, Gholston.)

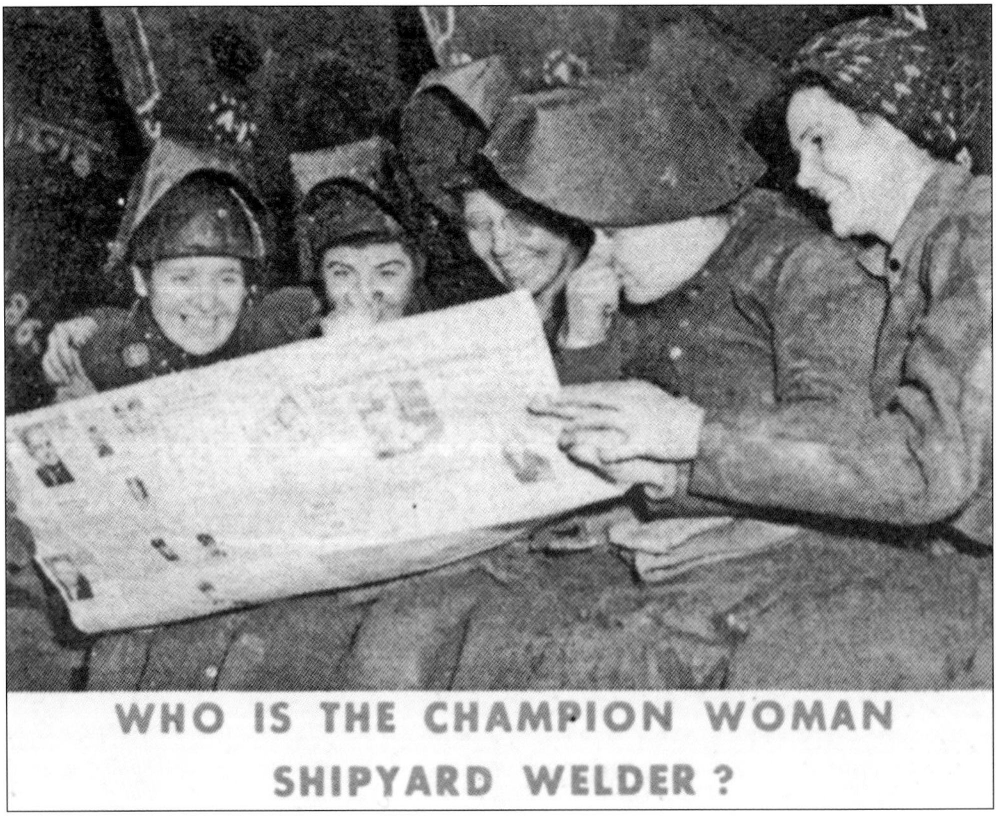

WHO IS THE CHAMPION WOMAN
SHIPYARD WELDER ?

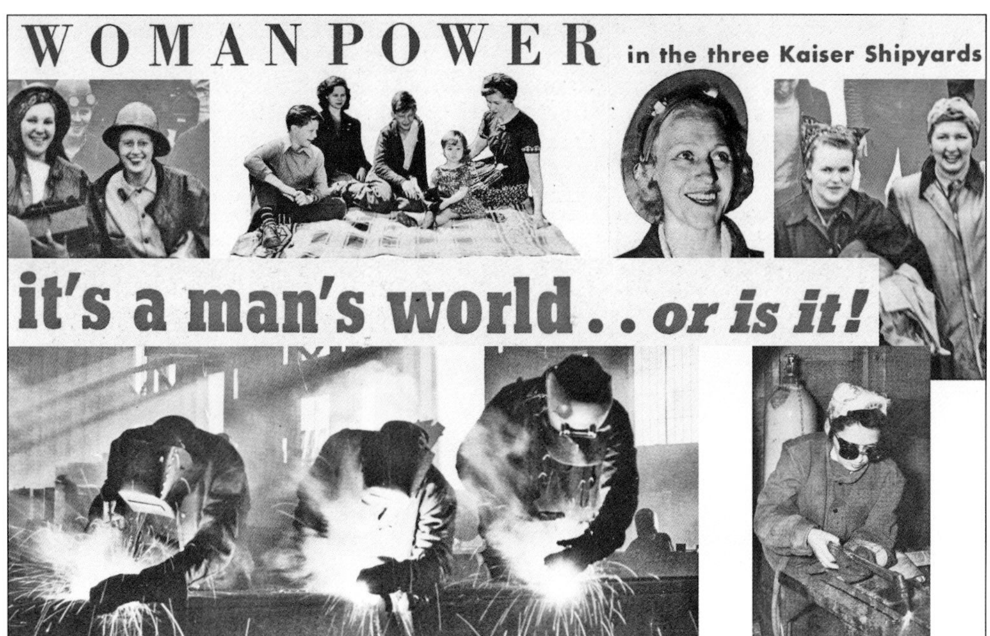

"Woman power, it's a man world . . . or is it?" Kaiser Shipyards *Bos'n's Whistle* newsletters depicted women in many facets of work—smiling and eager to be involved in what were once considered men's jobs—helped women feel proud of their jobs, and educated them about technical aspects of the work. Many women were single parents (because of the war or other circumstances) and were happy to find jobs to support their families that provided skills training, housing, and childcare. (Gholston.)

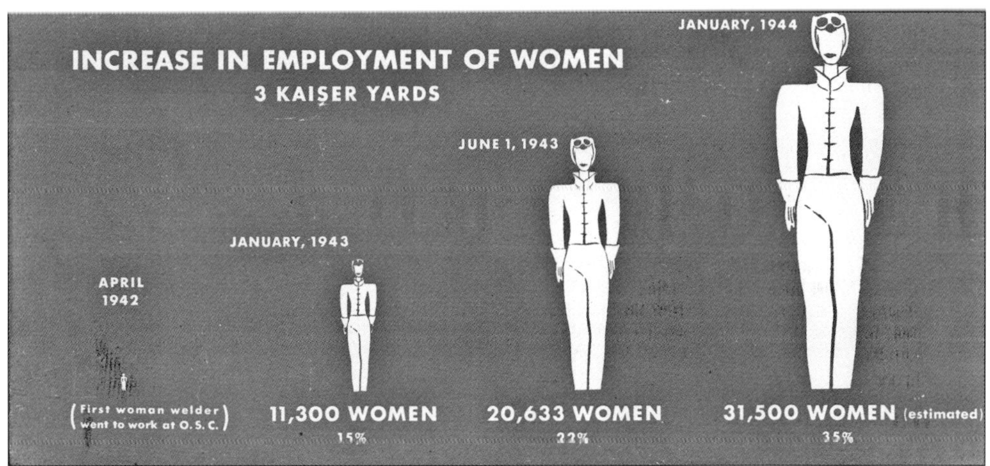

In 1944, women made up 35 percent of Kaiser's Portland/Vancouver shipyards workforce. OSC stands for Oregon Shipbuilding Corp., the name of Kaiser's St. Johns location. OSC produced 453 ships, including Liberty ships, Victory ships, and attack transporters. Kaiser's Swan Island shipyard made 140 tankers, and Kaiser's Vancouver shipyards made 118 ships, according to the website USMM.org. (Gholston.)

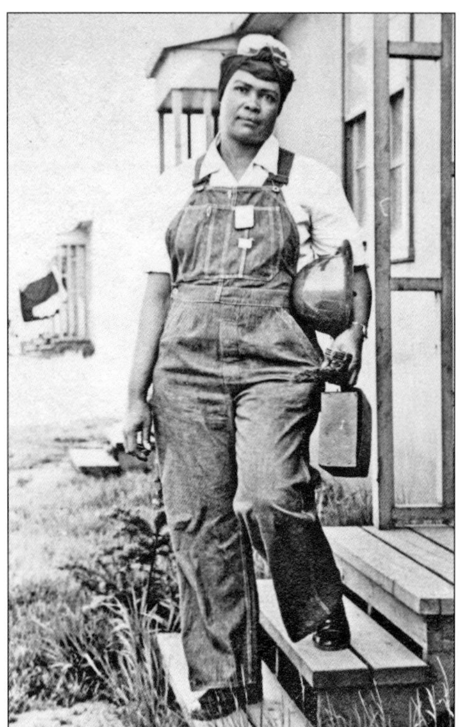

At Guild's Lake wartime housing, Ninie Mae Locke leaves for work in 1943. In 1941, President Roosevelt signed Executive Order 8802, forbidding discrimination based upon "race, creed, color, or national origin" in defense industries. This meant improved employment access for people of color. However, in comparison to other Wendy the Welders, African American women were often paid less than white women, relegated to lower-level positions, and faced discrimination at work and in the city. Pictured below are, from left to right, shipyard workers Phyllis Branch, Elsie Foster, and Mary Fowler. Kaiser's Portland and Vancouver shipyards produced at least 711 ships. According to the book *Her Finest Hour,* other area shipyards made another 903 steel ships (181 subchasers at Albina Engine and Machine Works, 442 landing craft and 2 tugs at Gunderson, 70 minesweepers, patrol, attack, troop, and landing vessels at WISCO, and 208 tugs, minesweepers, patrol, escort, ammunition, and landing vessels at Commercial Iron Works. (Left, CoPA; below, Gholston.)

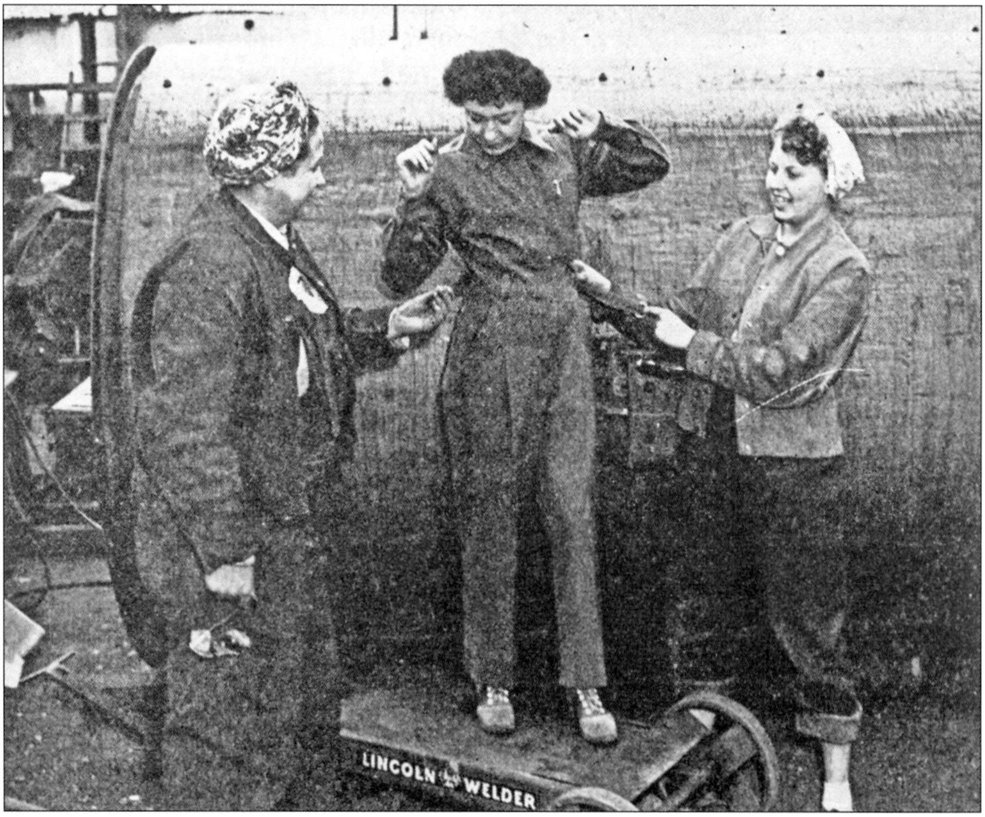

Kaiser shipyard women workers are talking to Muriel King, women's industrial clothing designer, about their ideas on proposed new uniforms. From left to right are Mary May, V. Kingsley, Mary Fowler, Ethel Dodson, Elaine Baker, Mabel Siegfried (seated), and Lillian Scott. (Gholston.)

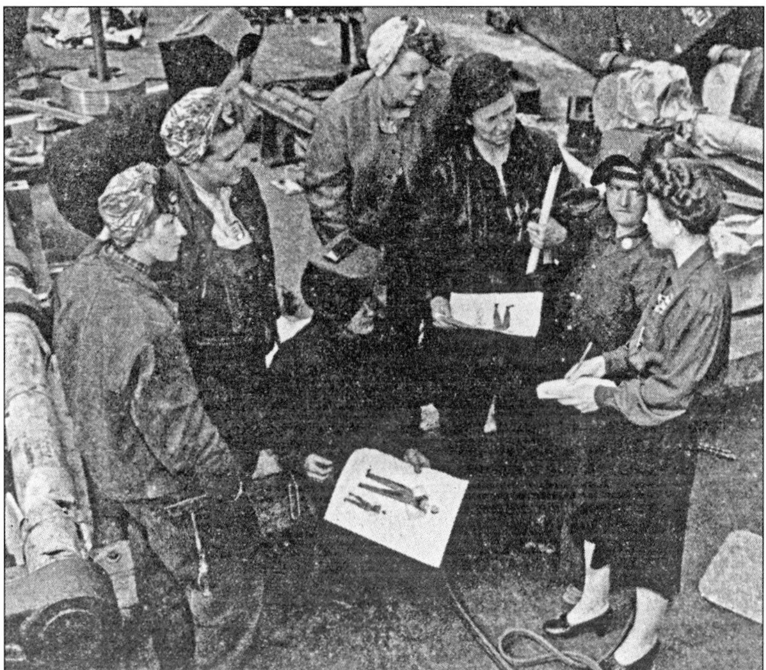

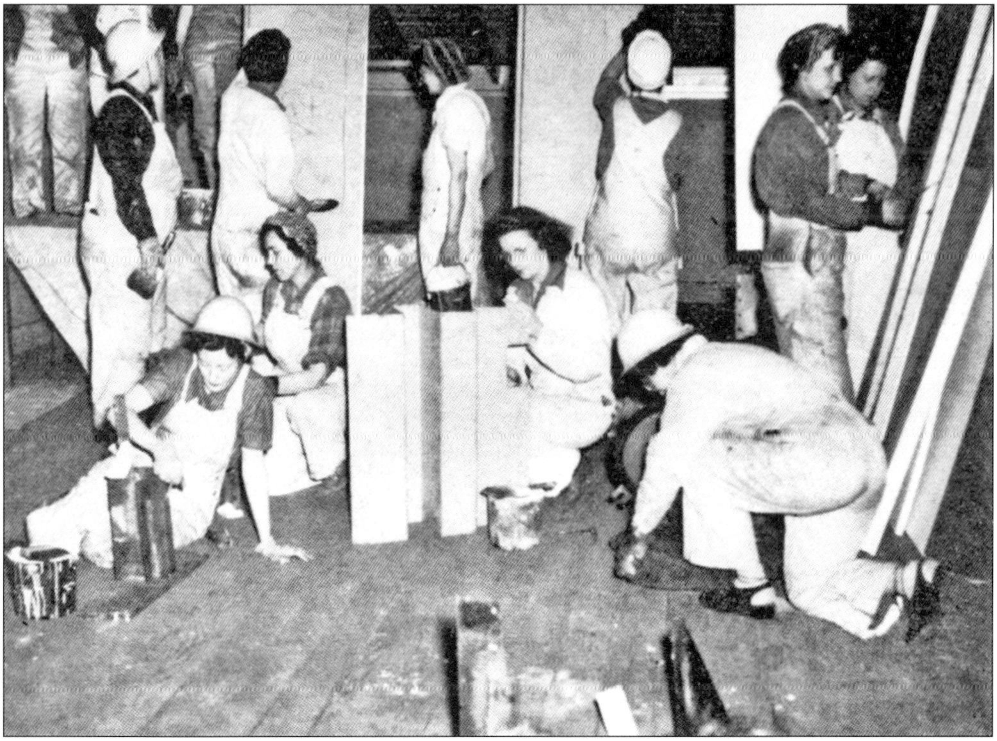

Women are pictured painting at WISCO. Other jobs held by women in Portland's defense industry included machinists, scalers, time checkers, crane operators, sheet metal workers, draftsmen, messengers, loftsman's helpers, tool checkers, burners, rigger's helpers, material clerks, electrical journeymen, warehousemen, and shipwright helpers, among others. (Gholston.)

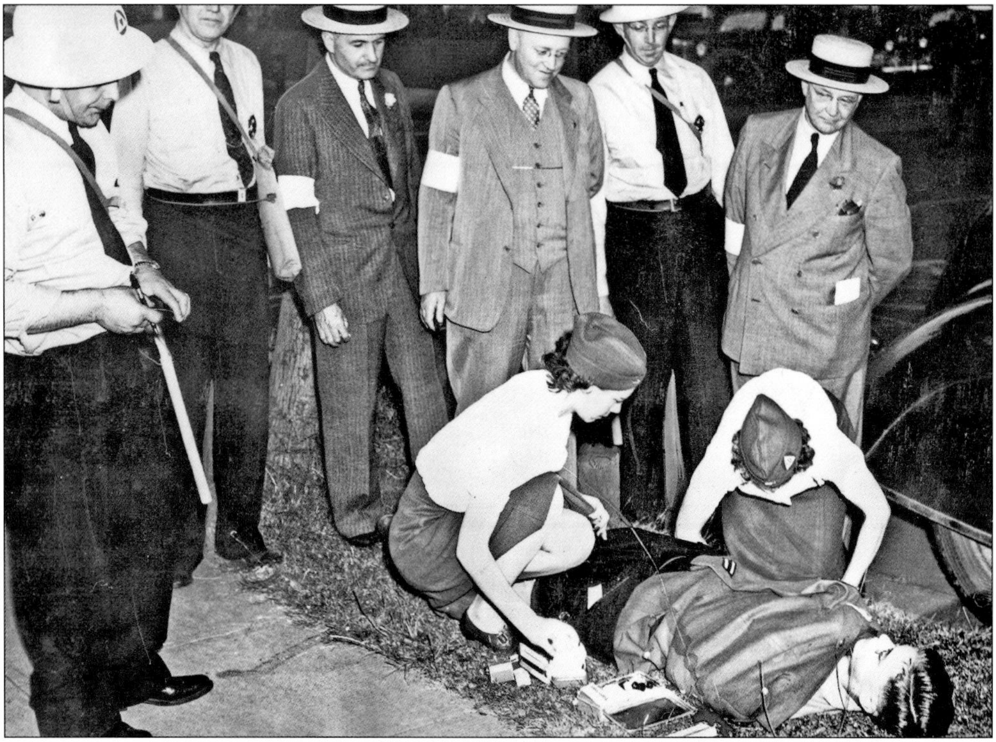

The Women's Emergency Corps conducts a World War II Civil Defense drill in 1943 at Chapman School to train citizens for emergencies. Pvt. Evelyn Bendickson (kneeling) and Sgt. Olive Edwards demonstrate emergency treatments. City commissioner William Bowes (third from right) and Mayor Earl Riley (far right) observe. Below, Portland-area shipyards were a marvel of productivity—often America's most productive. Women contributed greatly as workers in local shipyards, helping build over 1,614 World War II vessels. But Portland has mostly forgotten this history. Richmond, California's shipyards now house Rosie the Riveter Memorial Park. Vancouver's shipyards are remembered with this 2005 Waterfront Renaissance Trail statue by the Women Who Weld collective, with iconography of a Rosie the Riveter–style kerchief and Wendy the Welder's gear. After the war, the shipyards mostly closed. Women were encouraged to, once again, think of a woman's place as in the home. (Above, Gholston.)

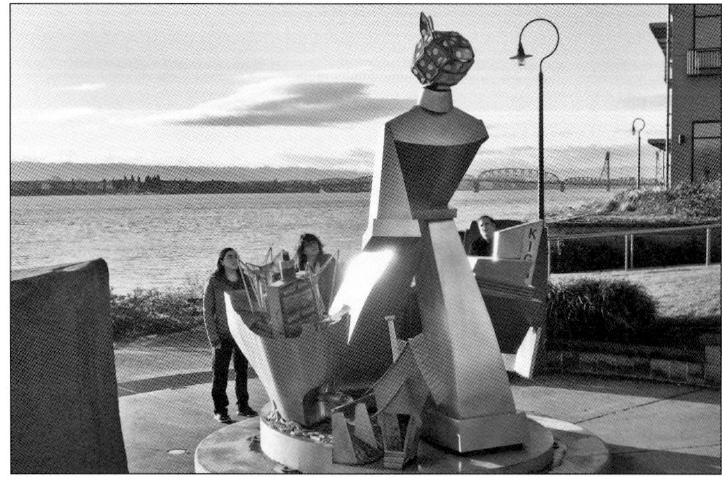

Four

Postwar to Contemporary Women 1945 to Present

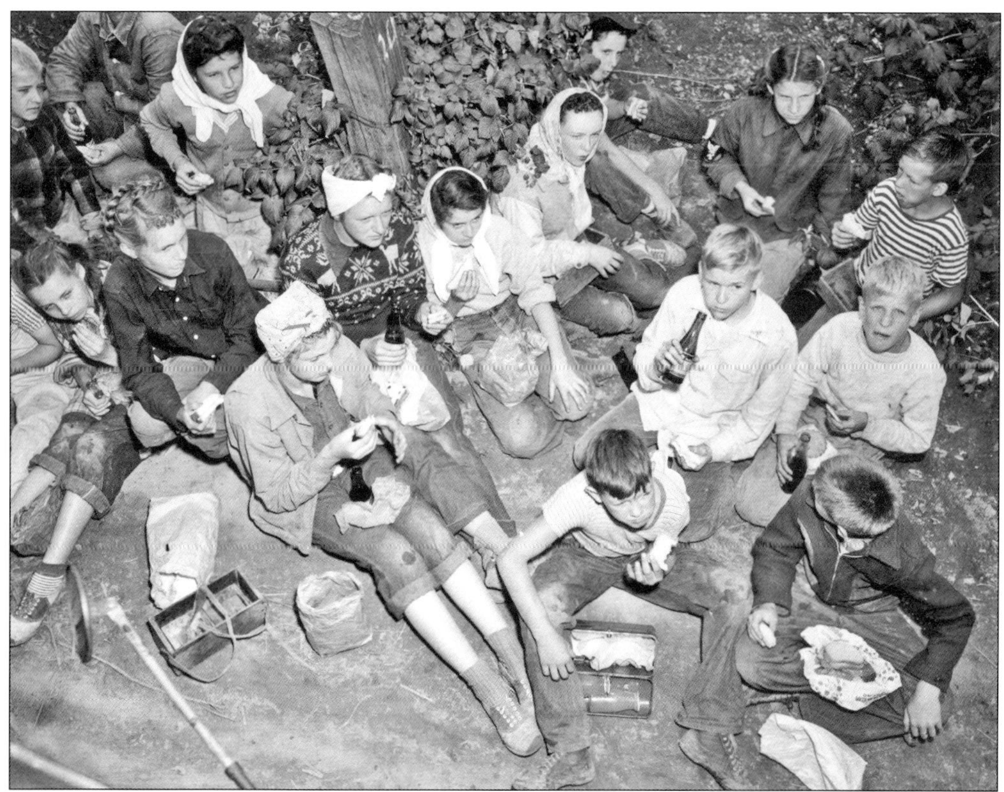

During World War II, the Women's Land Army recruited women for desperately needed farm labor. Victory Farm Volunteers recruited teens for farmwork, continuing for two years after the war. In 1946, youth are taking a break from raspberry picking at Portland Victory Farm near Troutdale. A tradition of city kids, especially girls, helping on farms continued for decades. Many Portlanders reminisce about summer days joining a bus full of kids and picking crops to make some spending money. (OSU.)

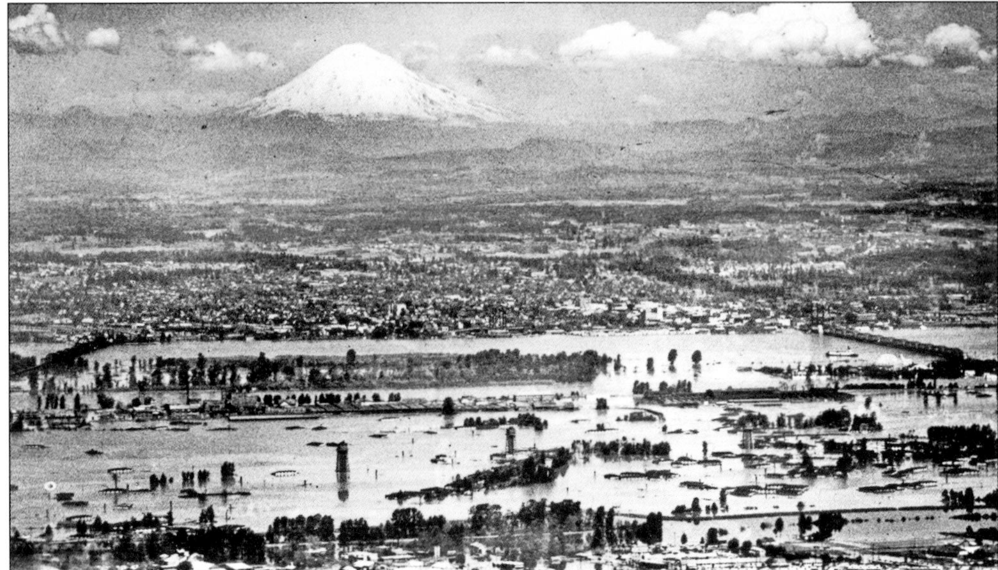

Vanport was completely destroyed by floodwaters on Memorial Day, May 30, 1948. Weeks of rains caused water to rise on the Columbia River, breaching the dikes in the afternoon. That morning, the Housing Authority of Portland had assured residents that there was no flooding threat, stating, "Remember: dikes are safe at present. You will be warned if necessary. You will have time to leave. Don't get excited." When the dikes broke, residents had 35 minutes to escape. Poorly constructed houses quickly swirled in the currents, and 15 people died. Above, this view of flooded Vanport looks north, with Mount. St. Helens looming 50 miles away (before it blew its top in 1980). Below, the view in this image of flooded Vanport looks toward the Tualatin Mountains (locally called the West Hills, though this is completely inaccurate when looking at them from the Tualatin Valley side). (Above, Gholston; below, CoPA.)

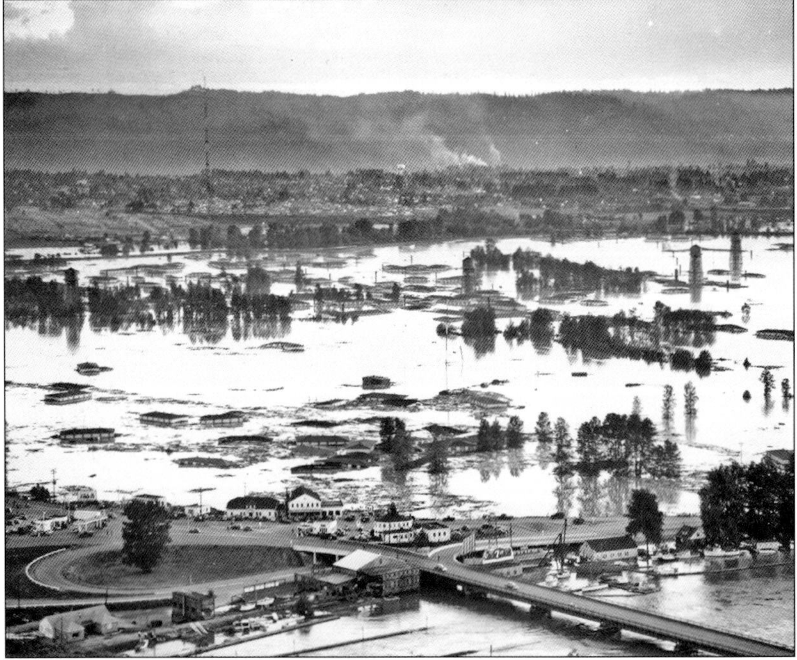

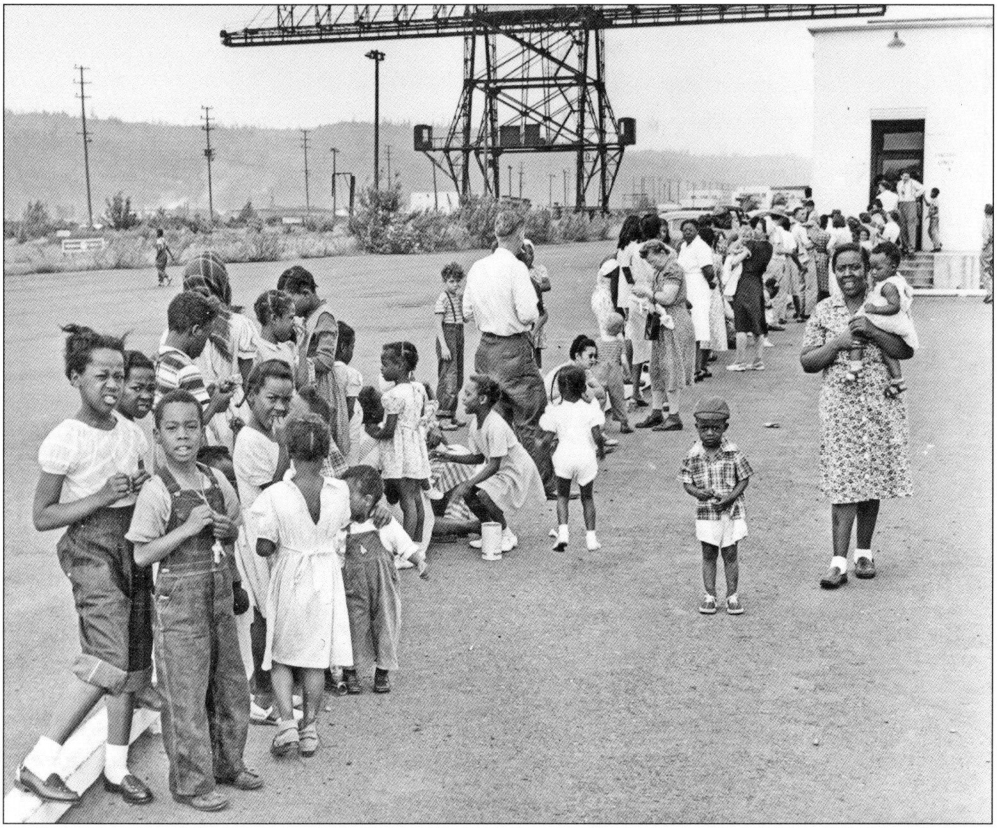

Refugees from the flooding of Vanport—Oregon's second-largest city and the largest public housing project in America—are waiting for emergency services on Swan Island. Approximately 18,500 people were displaced by the flood. Many Vanport refugees were eventually moved to Guild's Lake Courts, formerly war industry housing that later became public housing. Trailers were brought in to accommodate more families. At right, a Vanport flood refugee family waits in temporary housing. (Both, Gholston.)

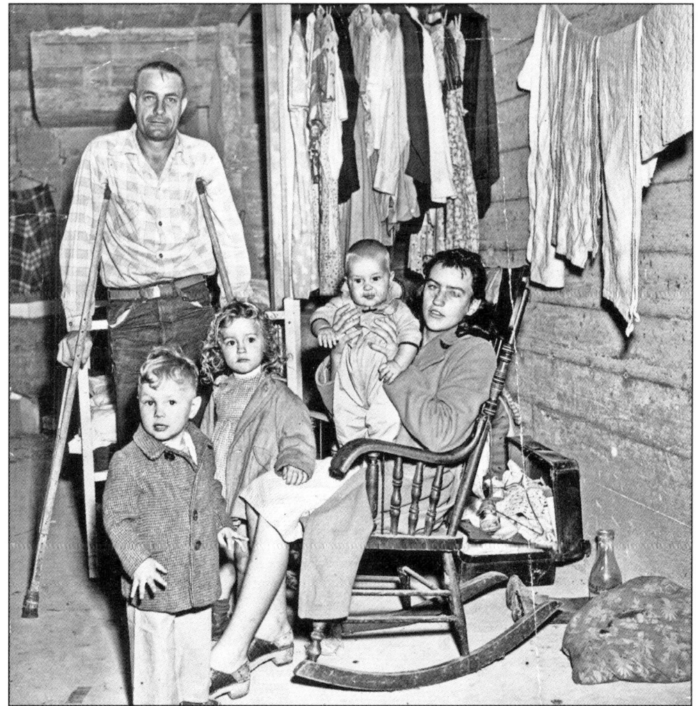

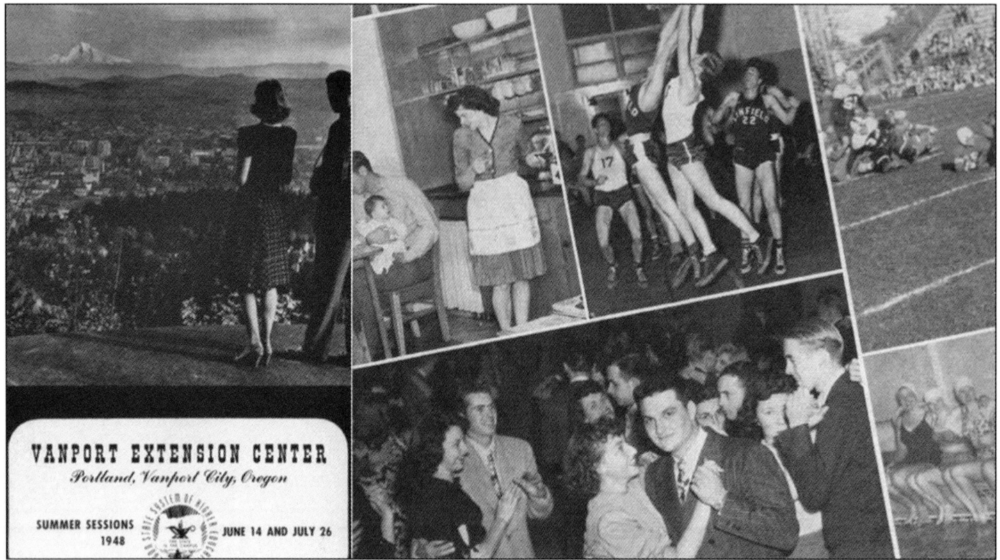

In 1946, 1,924 students enrolled in Vanport Extension Center—the "U by the Slough." Women students were aggressively recruited, with marketing touting childcare, married student housing, part-time degree options, and night classes. This brochure includes a housewife with her husband and baby. After the flood, Vanport College (dubbed "the college that wouldn't die") moved to the former St. Johns shipyards (see page 61) and later to the former Lincoln High School building on Portland's South Park Blocks (now Lincoln Hall), eventually becoming Portland State University (see page 91).

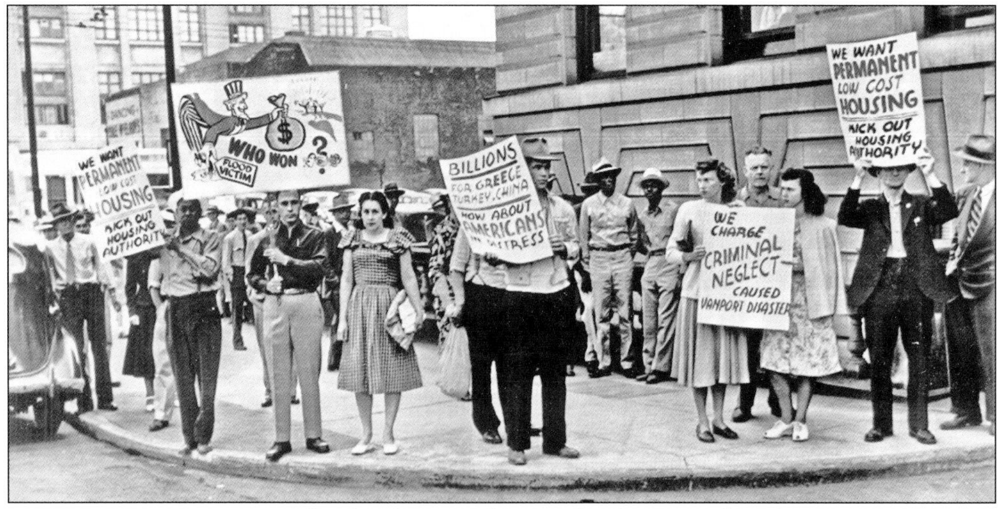

On June 30, 1948, Vanport flood refugees picket Portland City Hall with signs reading, "We charge criminal neglect caused Vanport disaster," and "Billions for Greece, Turkey, China: How about Americans in distress?" They demanded better housing and relief grants. At this time, refugees were being housed in former Navy barracks and in trailers rushed to Portland by the federal housing authority. (Gholston.)

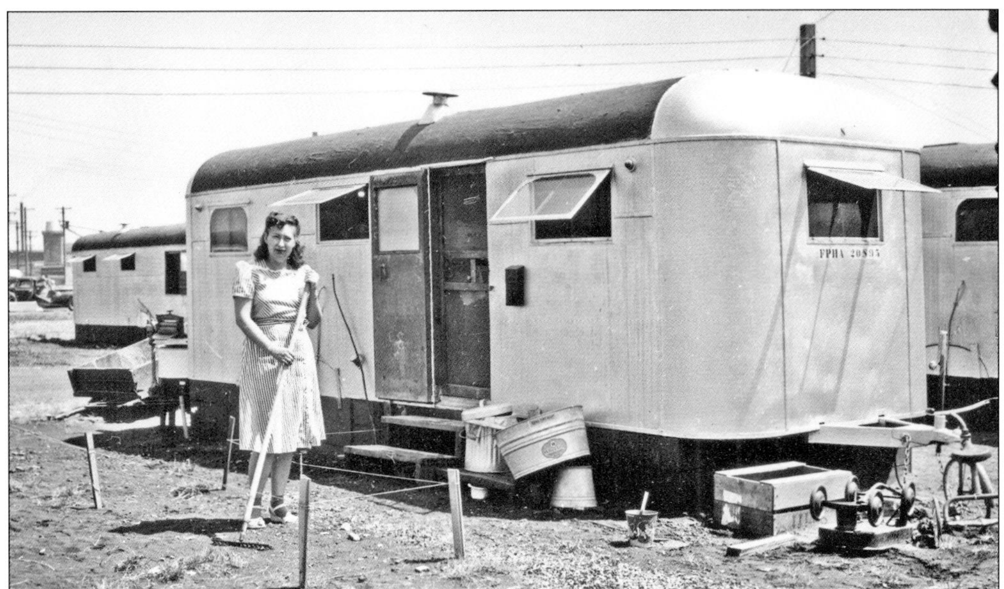

A woman is planting her very modest garden at Guild's Lake after having been displaced by the 1948 Vanport flood. Many flooded-out residents of Vanport were moved to temporary housing in trailers on the former site of Guild's Lake wartime housing. (Gholston.)

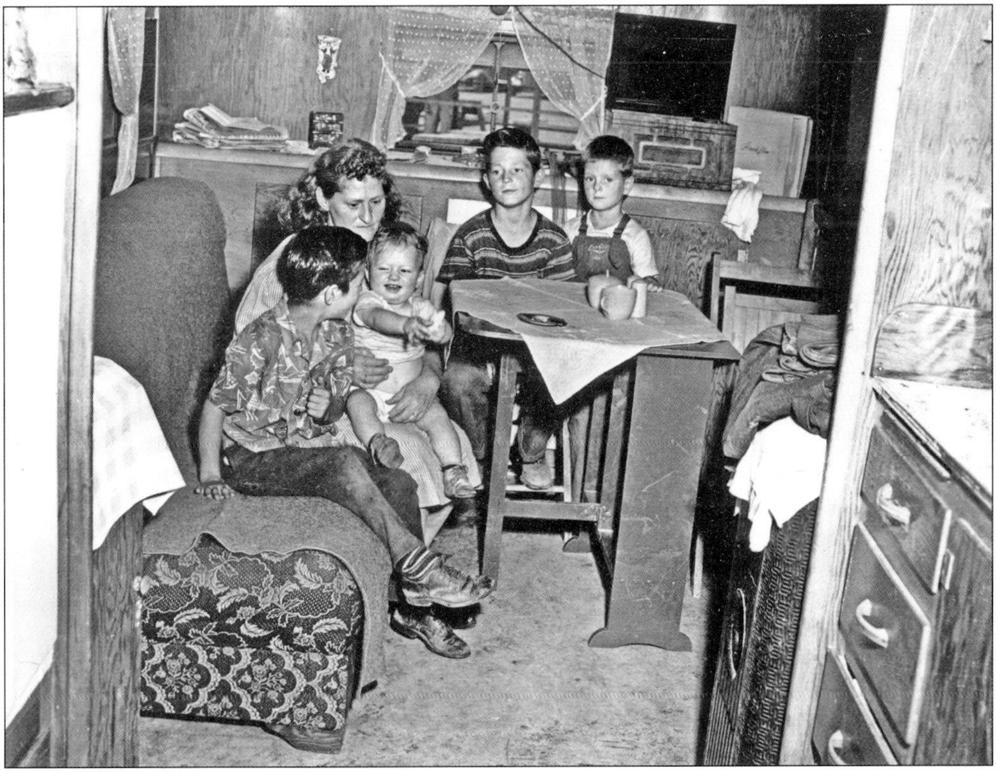

The temporary trailers of Guild's Lake Courts often housed more than the official four-person limit. Seen here are a mother and her four children in a Guild's Lake trailer. Rent was $35 per month. (Gholston.)

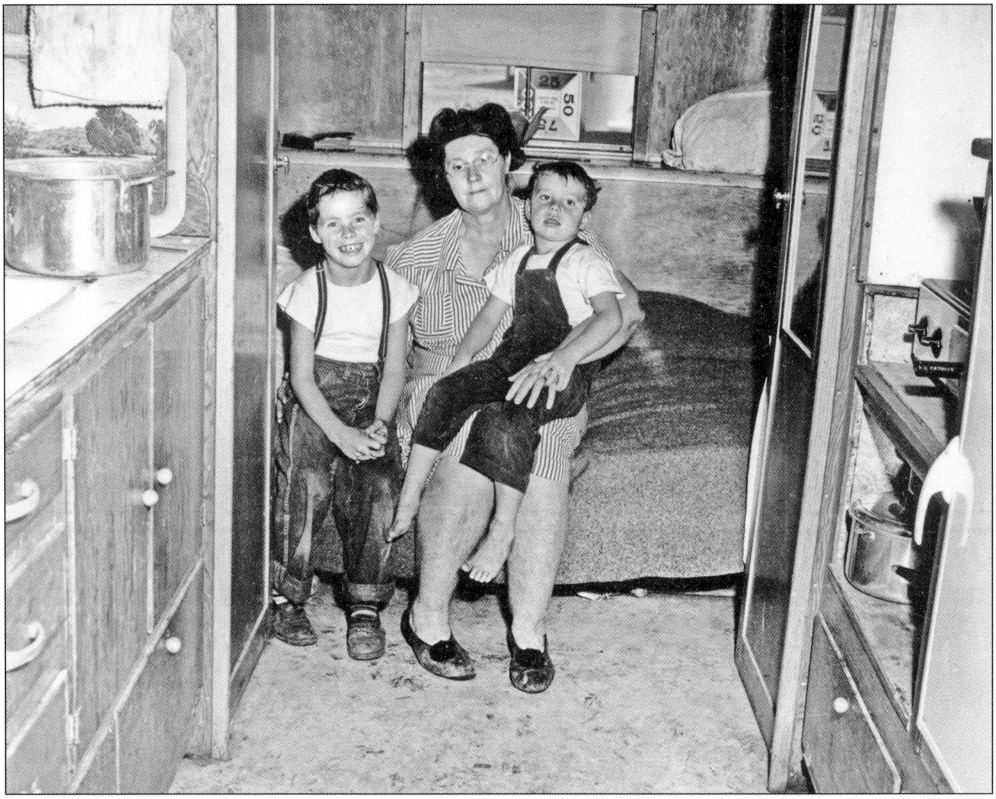

Pictured here are a grandmother and her grandchildren inside their Guild's Lake trailer. (Gholston.)

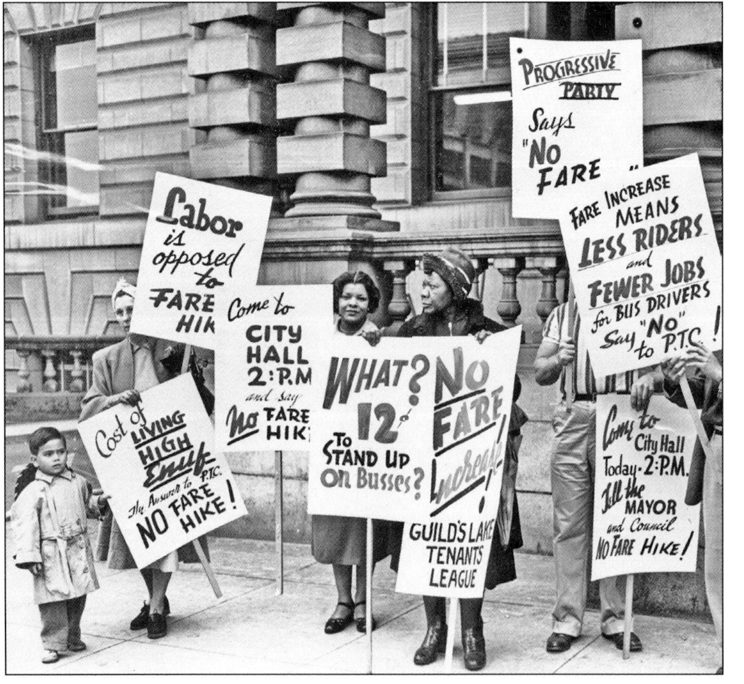

Women of the Guild's Lake Tenants League protest at city hall. Their picketing signs read, "Labor is opposed to fare hike," "Cost of living high enuf," "What? 12 cents to stand up on busses?," and "No fare increase! Guild's Lake Tenant's League." Many households in Guild's Lake housing desperately needed low fares and low rents to survive. (Gholston.)

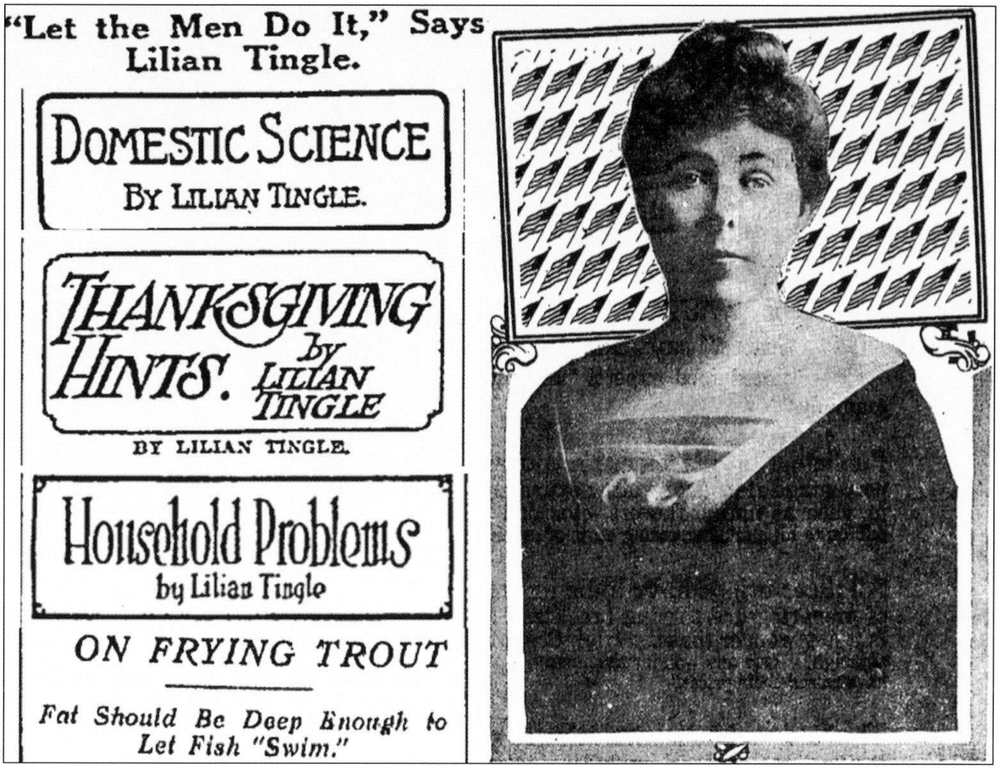

"Let the Men Do It," Says Lilian Tingle.

DOMESTIC SCIENCE
By Lilian Tingle.

THANKSGIVING HINTS. by Lilian Tingle

BY LILIAN TINGLE.

Household Problems
by Lilian Tingle

ON FRYING TROUT

Fat Should Be Deep Enough to Let Fish "Swim."

Lilian Ella Tingle (1872–1951) taught domestic science homemaking skills of cooking, cleaning, sewing, cleanliness, and nutrition as the director of the Portland School of Domestic Science at the YWCA. She was the author of *Oregonian* columns (excerpted), and later, faculty head of the Department of Household Arts at the University of Oregon. She also led a consumer advocacy crusade to improve sanitary conditions at grocery markets. Below is a domestic science class at a Portland school. (Below, Gholston.)

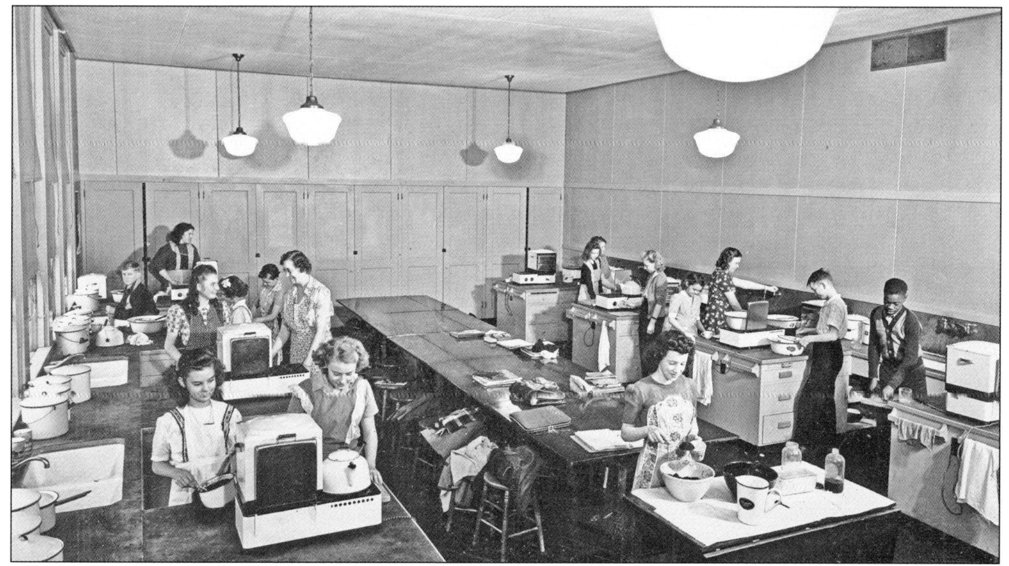

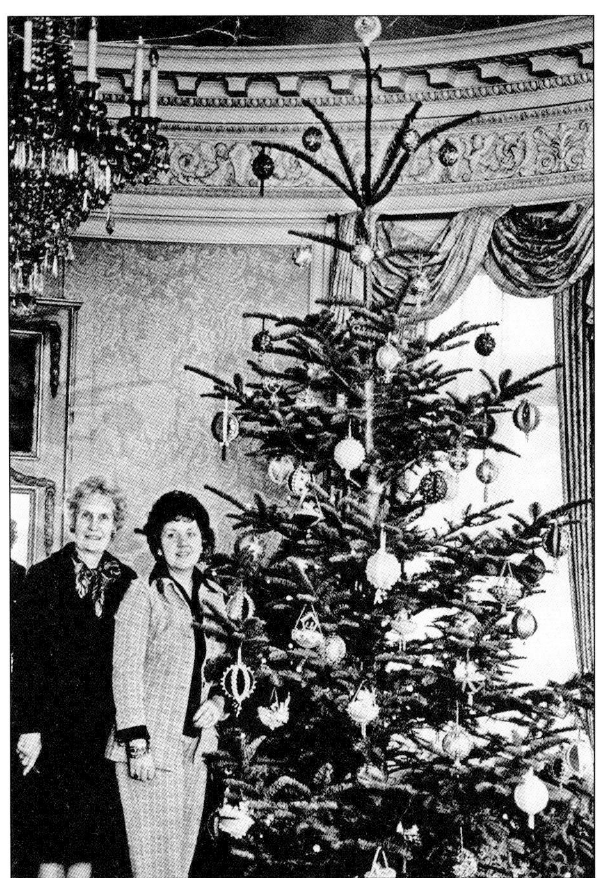

Dorothea Lensch (1907–2000) was Portland's first recreation director from 1937 to 1972. She developed recreation programs and facilities like music, theater, arts, ball fields, gymnasiums, and sports teams and pushed for public activities in spaces such as Washington Park. She was one of the first people in Oregon to promote sports activities for girls. Lensch founded the Children's Museum and was a founder of the Portland Opera Guild, Chamber Music Northwest, and the Japanese Garden. As president of the Opera Guild, she poses left at the Pittock Mansion's Christmas tree, decorated by Guild member Mrs. Berenson (right). Under Lensch's leadership, Portland women had much better access to sports activities through Portland Parks and Recreation, as seen below in a 1949 women's softball game with Betty Turner at bat, a 1956 women's exercise class titled "Reaching for glamour," and children at a wading pool in the 1950s. (Below, CoPA.)

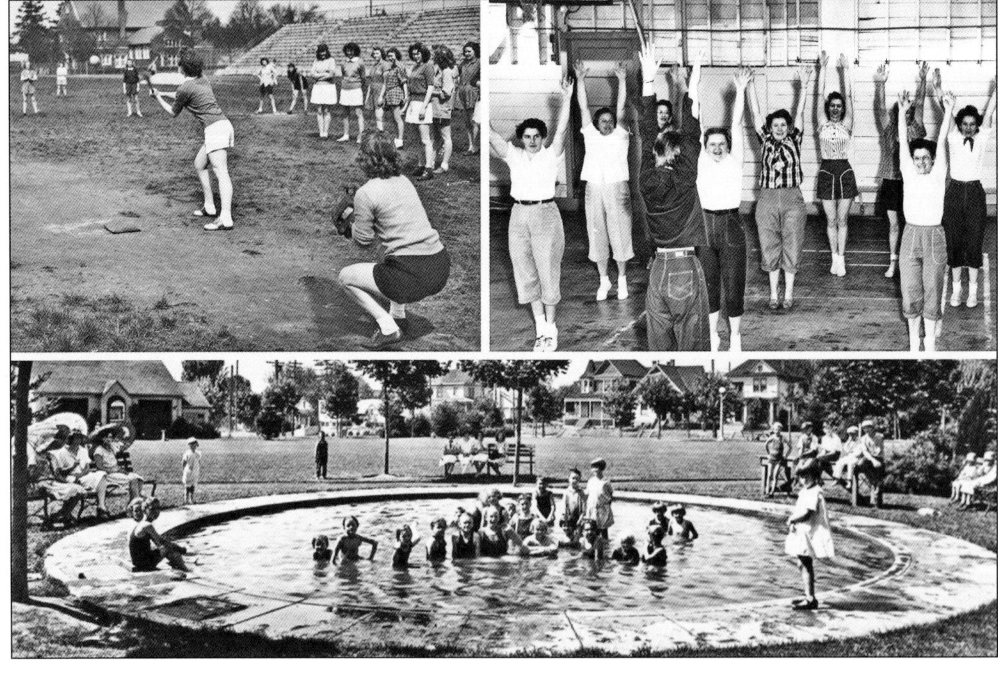

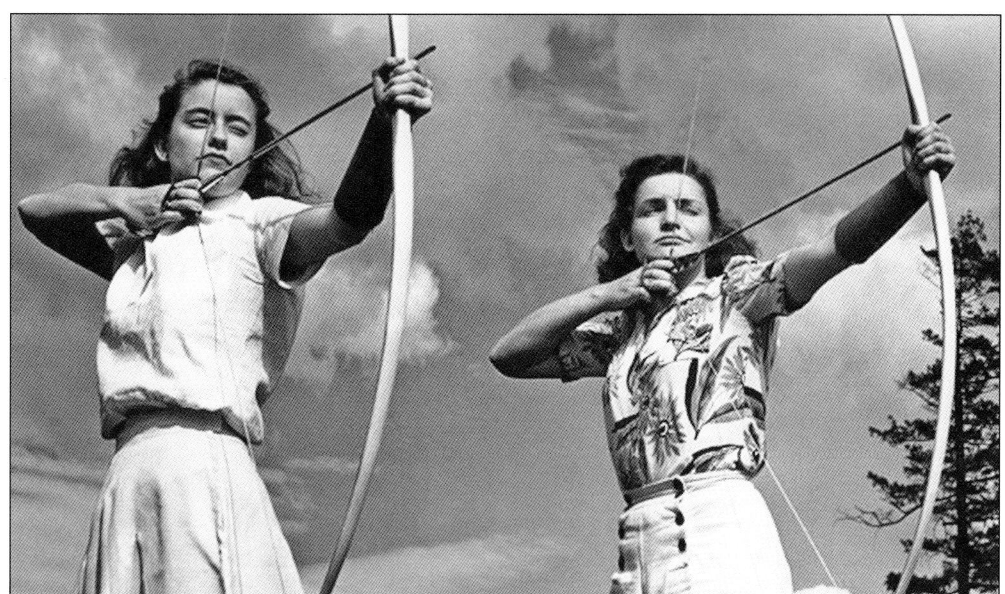

In the post-war era, women had much greater access to a variety of sports than they had before. In the image above, women students at Reed College are practicing archery in 1948. Below, a 1950s women's gymnastics class is held at the Multnomah Athletic Club (MAC) in Goose Hollow. Many Portland women were Olympic athletes (often with connections to the MAC), including Rayma Wilson, 800 meters (1928 Olympics); Nancy Lees, swimming (1948); Suzanne Zimmerman, swimming (1948); Julia Cornell, swimming (1952); Carolyn Wood, swimming (1960); Cathy Jamison, swimming (1968); Deanne Wilson, high jump (1972); Cindy Brown, basketball (1988); Debra Sinclair, shooting (1992); Tonya Harding, figure skating (1992 and 1994); Katy Steding, basketball (1996); Tiffany Milbrett, soccer (1996 and 2000); Jennifer Devine, rowing (1996 and 2004); Ellen Estes, water polo (2000 and 2004); Kate Johnson, rowing (2004); Whitney Ping, table tennis (2004); M'fon Udoka, basketball (2004); Mariel Zagunis, fencing (2004, 2008, and 2012); Elsie Windes, water polo (2008 and 2012); Ana Montoya, soccer (2012); and Jacqueline Wiles, alpine skiing (2014). (Above, Reed; below, Gholston.)

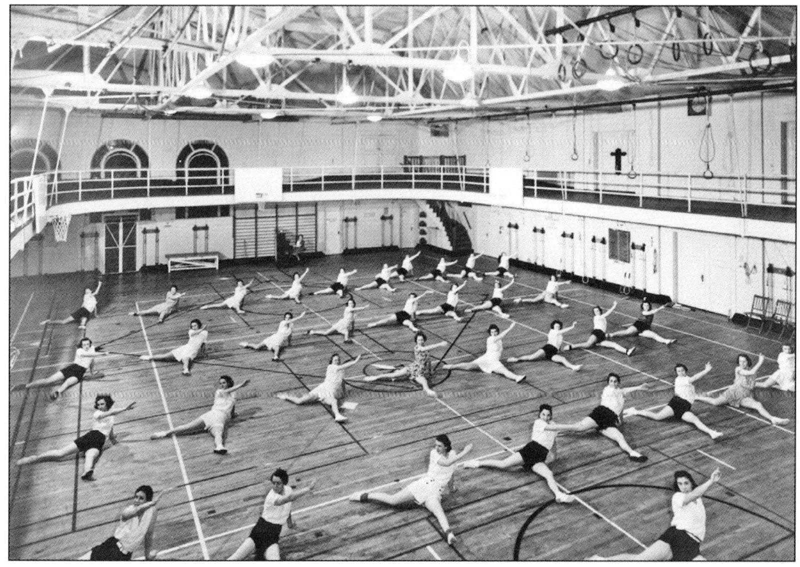

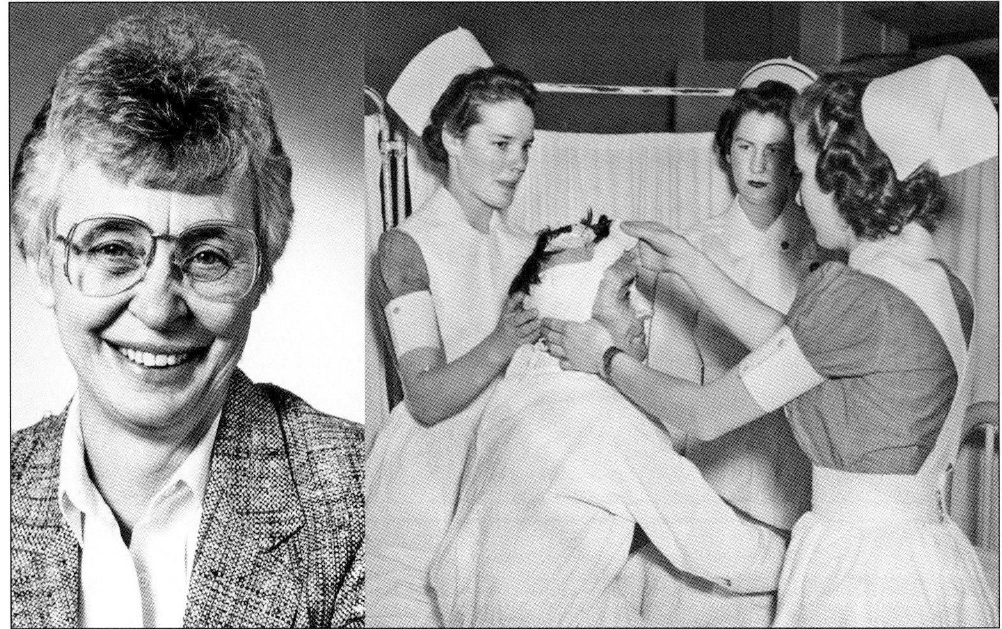

In 1976, Carol. A. Lindeman (born 1935), PhD, RN, FAAN (Fellow of the American Academy of Nursing), became dean of the University of Oregon Health Sciences Center, School of Nursing (now Oregon Health and Sciences University). She helped create a statewide system of nursing programs to address nursing shortages, started a PhD program in nursing, served on American Nurses' Association and American Nurses' Foundation committees, and received four honorary doctorates for her work promoting nursing education. (OHSU.)

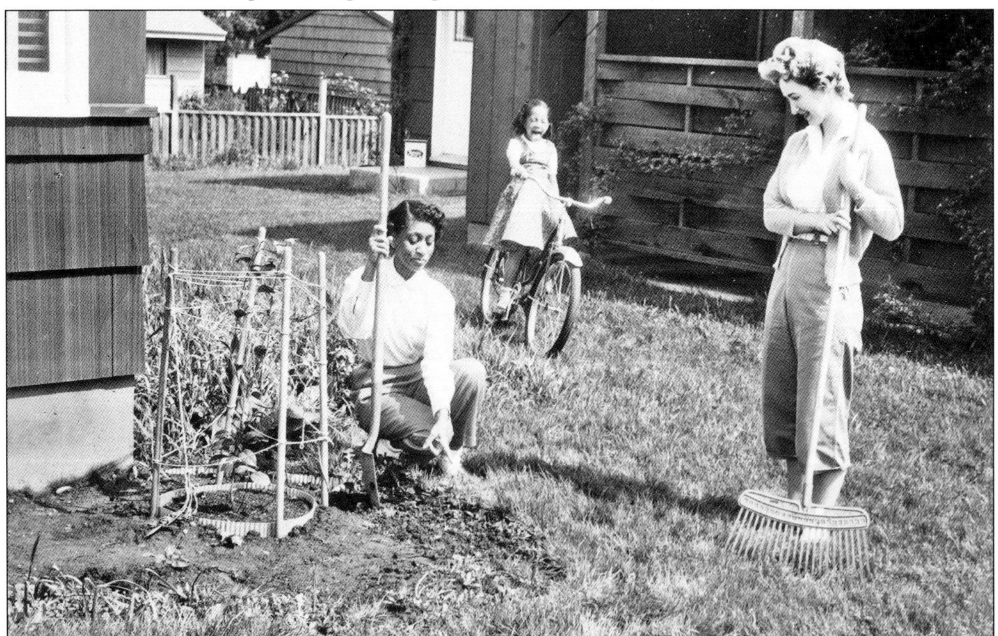

In this 1958 image, titled *Neighbors sharing gardening hints in North Portland*, Mrs. Samuel Brown (left), her daughter Cheryl, and Mrs. Marvin Dewald chat while tending their yards. (OSU Archives–Urban League Collection.)

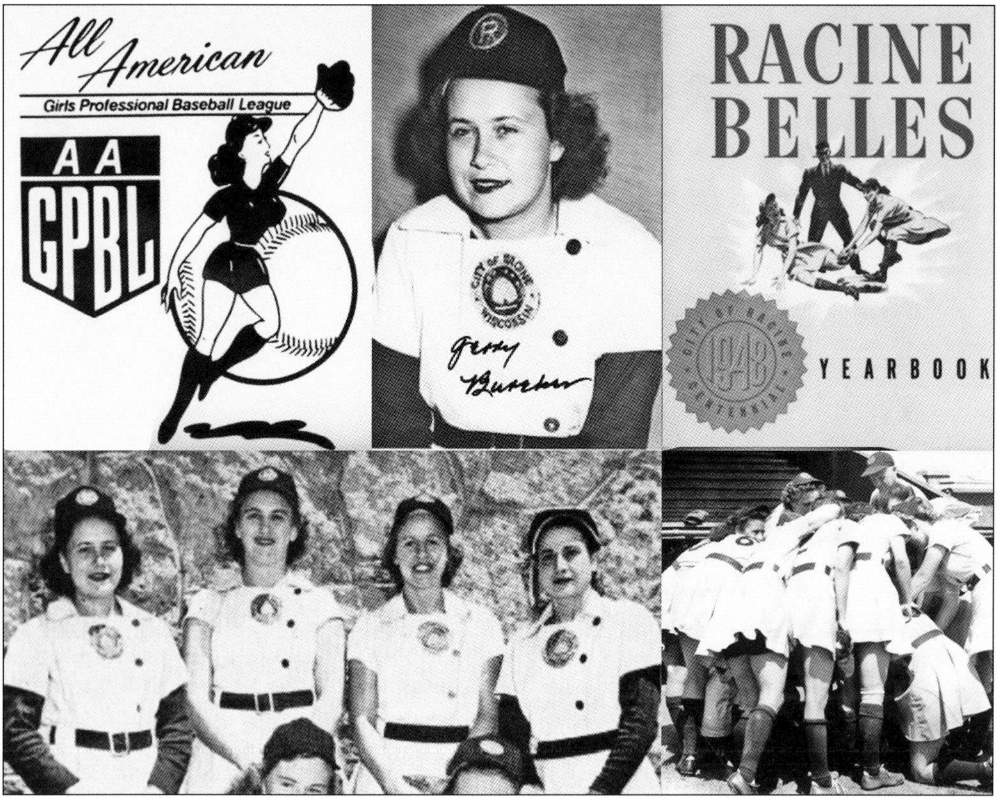

Geraldine Bureker (1924–2009) played in the All-American Girls Professional Baseball League (AAGPBL). Her team, the Tonseth Flowers, won the Oregon State Championship in 1945. She played Chicago softball circuits before joining the AAGPBL. In 1948, she was an outfielder with the Racine Belles, who were memorialized in the 1992 movie *A League of Their Own*. AAGPBL has a permanent exhibit at the Baseball Hall of Fame.

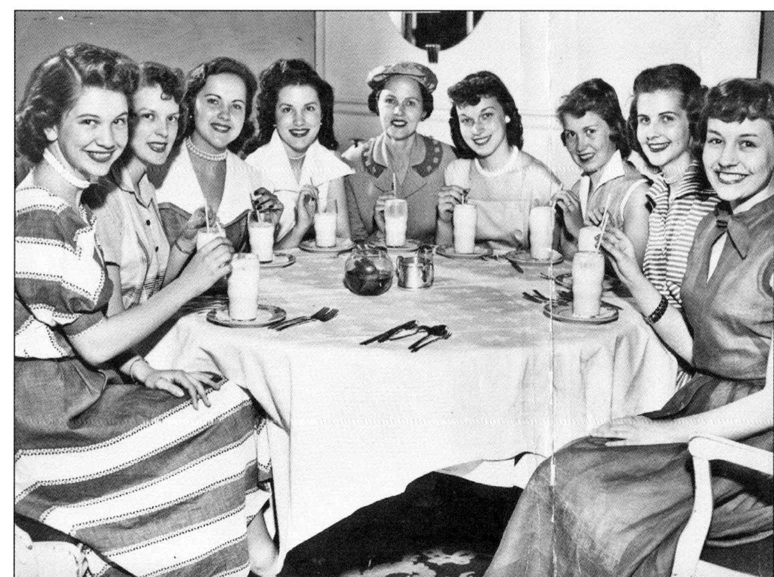

The 1952 Rose Festival Court and chaperone are having milkshakes at the Multnomah Hotel; pictured are, from left to right, Barbara Richmans, Jeanne Wallace, Cecily Ley, Patti Throp, Mrs. James Bryson, Naomi Mooney, Patricia Morud, Zola Wyly, and Valerie Cowls. (Gholston.)

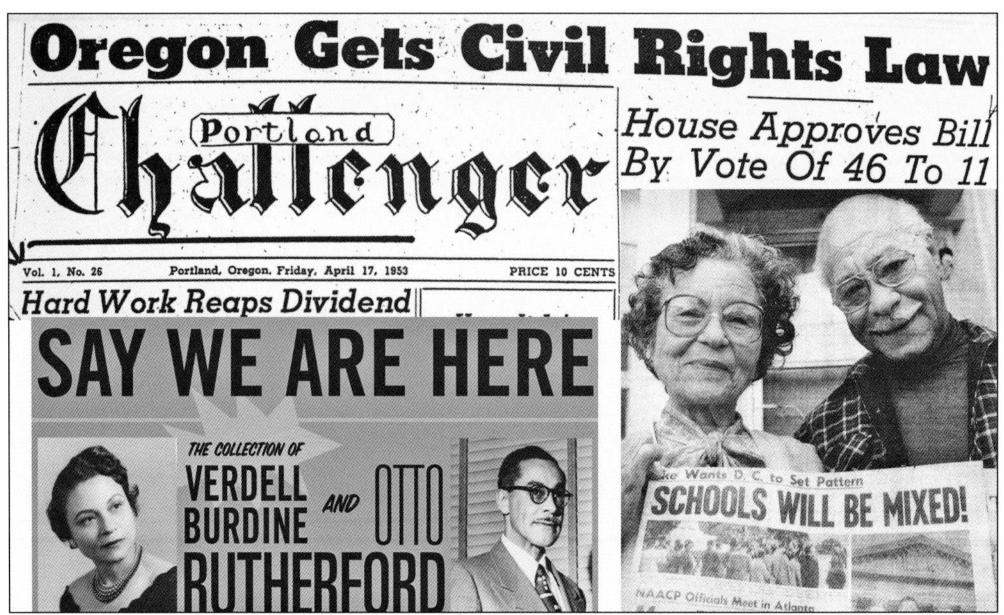

Verdell Burdine Rutherford (1913–2001), an Oregon civil rights leader, was the secretary of Portland's NAACP chapter from the 1940s to 1962. Her husband, Otto, was president of the Portland NAACP chapter in the 1950s. Their work was pivotal to help pass the 1953 civil rights public accommodations law that failed 17 times before it was passed. Discrimination was outlawed in hotels, motels, restaurants, and recreational facilities. This work put Oregon a decade ahead of the nation in passing civil rights laws. (Photographs are excerpted from the PSU exhibit on their legacy.)

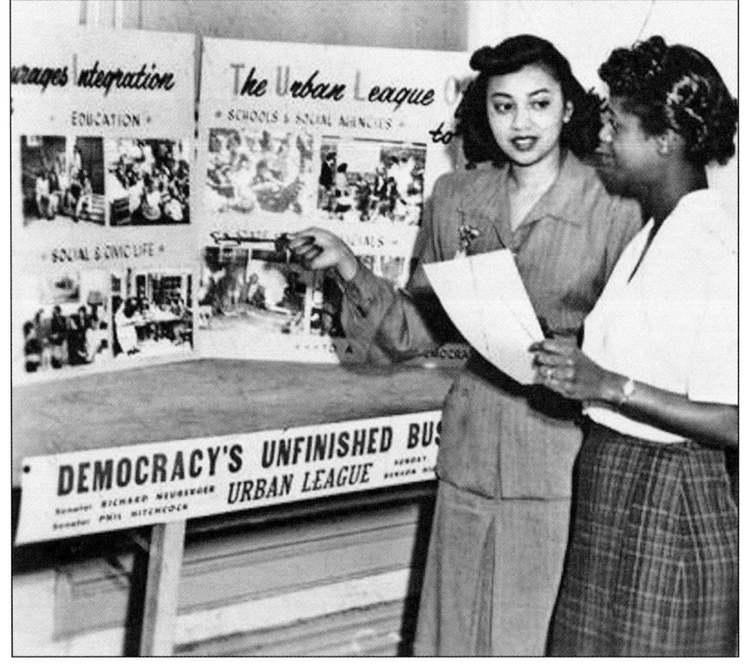

Gertrude Williams Rae and Myrtle White Carr (right) staff an Urban League presentation on "Democracy's Unfinished Business," which encouraged the passage of the accommodation law: "The Urban League encourages integration in education, social and civic life, schools and social agencies, and state and local officials." (Urban League Archives at OSU.)

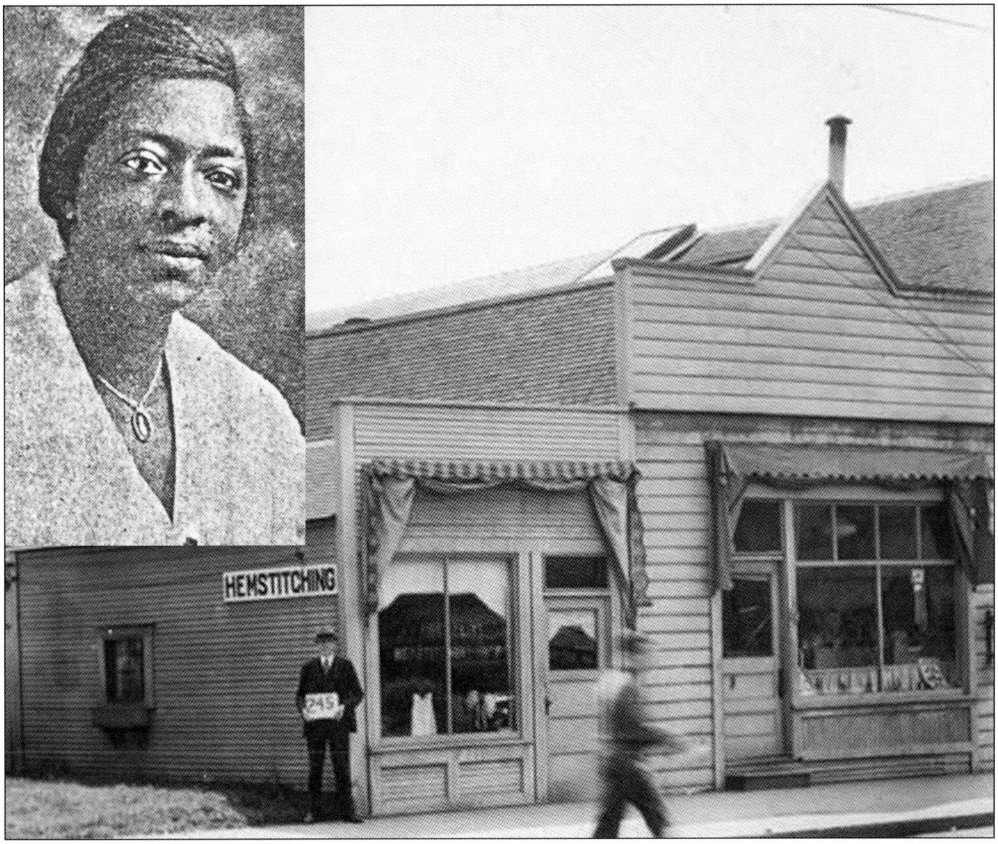

Katherine Gray (1870–1956) was a founder of the Harriet Tubman Club, co-founder of the Colored Women's Equal Suffrage League, a leader in the protests of *The Birth of a Nation*, president of the Oregon Federation of Colored Women's Clubs, and president of the Colored Women's Council with her daughter Edith as secretary. Her family lived at the house (above) at what is now 3962 Northeast Martin Luther King Boulevard. Historic preservationists are protecting what was later known as the Burger Barn to commemorate the house's Gray history, its role in the 1960s as a hub for civil rights protests, and the 1981 racially charged Opossum Incident, when police officers left dead animals there and were later fired. Below, June Roe Runnels Key was director of education for the Urban League, an educator in Portland Public Schools, and a member of the Portland Alumnae Chapter of Delta Sigma Theta. In 2012, the first African American–owned commercial Living Building in the United States was dedicated as the June Key Delta Community Center in her honor. (Above, CoPA; below, OSU.)

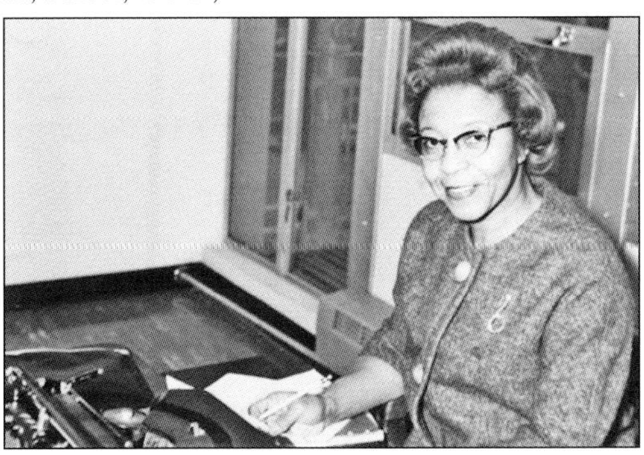

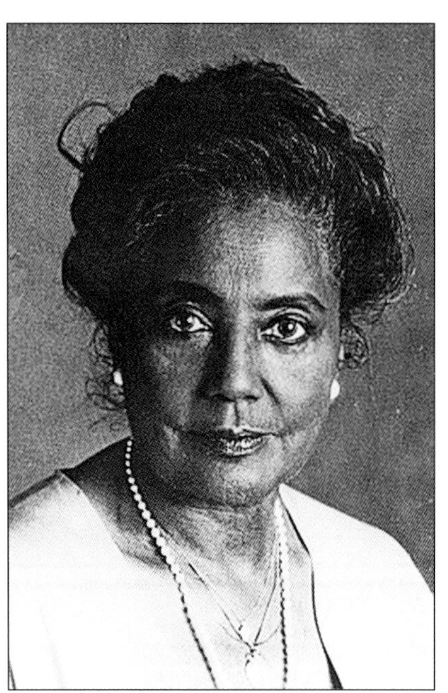

Kathryn Hall Bogle (1906–2003), a journalist, social worker, and civil rights activist, was known for her 1937 *Oregonian* article "An American Negro Speaks of Color," describing the harsh realities of black life in Portland. It was the first time the *Oregonian* paid an African American journalist to write an article. Bogle helped found the Friends of Golden West to secure historical status for the Golden West Hotel, the first local hotel to allow African American patrons and a social hub for the African American community. A member of Portland's NAACP and founder of Portland's Links, Inc., she promoted equality through educational and civic activities. (OHS ba018784.)

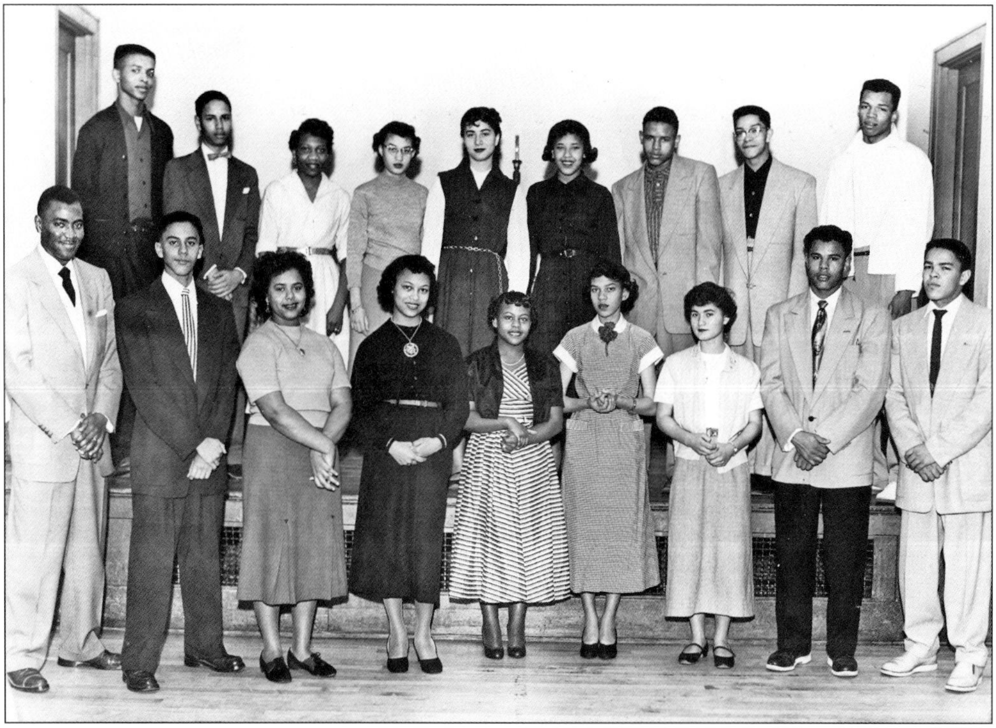

In Portland, women played a strong role in the National Association for the Advancement of Colored People (NAACP), where half of the members were women and many leadership positions were held by women. This 1950s photograph of the NAACP youth group, from the Verdell A. Burdine and Otto G. Rutherford Family Collection, shows the strong participation of women in the organization, including Rutherford's daughter Charlotte (in the first row, wearing the dark dress). (PSU.)

A labor and political activist and journalist, Julia "Kathleen" Godman Ruuttila (1907–1991) founded and headed the ladies' auxiliary and recruited mill workers for the International Woodworkers of America. The auxiliary supported workers and families to maintain solidarity. She wrote about her work in the *Timberworker*, of which she later became editor. She also wrote for the *Dispatcher* newspaper of the International Longshoreman's and Warehouseman's Union (ILWU), where she was a labor leader and peace activist for decades. In this photograph, she is protesting labor issues in 1966 at the Red Lion. (OHS 85712.)

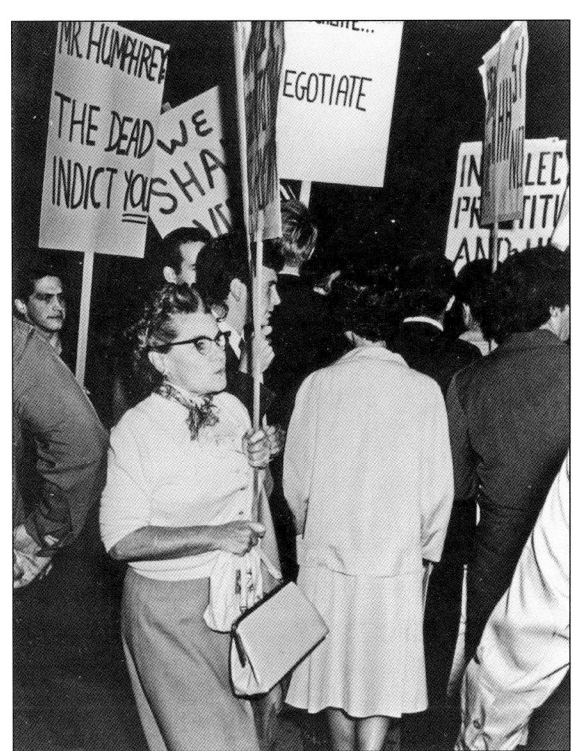

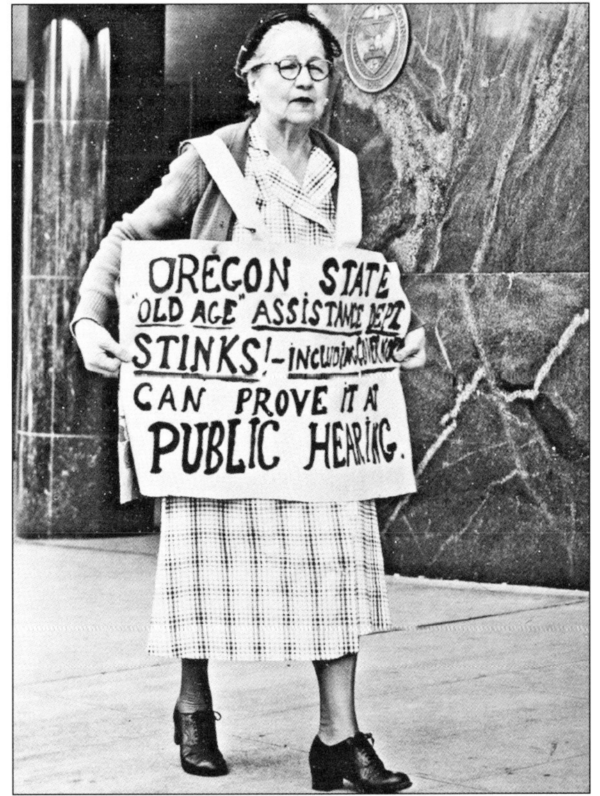

An actress on the East Coast, Grace Wick (1888–1958) moved to Portland in 1927, working as an actress and radio producer. The Depression affected her work prospects, so for three decades, she was a protest fixture around Portland. She was often spotted marching down Broadway or at city hall in a barrel with slogans and her political opinions taped to the side. She ran for many political offices but was never elected. (OHS ba019192.)

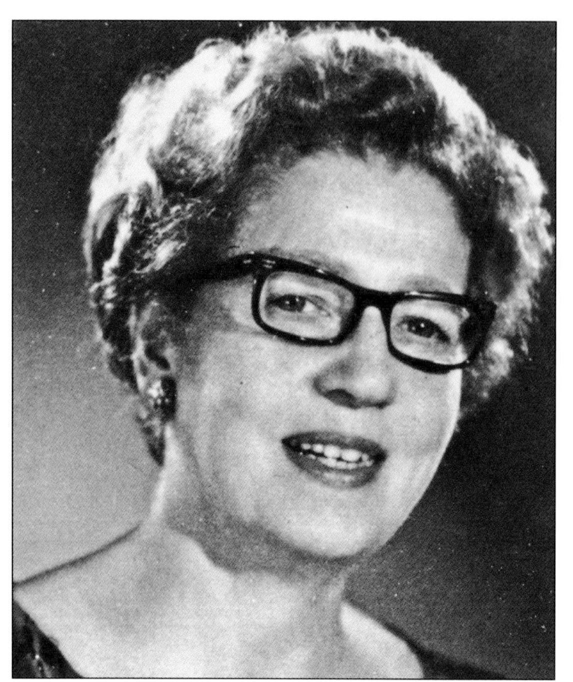

Dr. Lena Nemerovsky Kenin (1897–1968) graduated from the University of Oregon Medical School in 1929 and practiced obstetrics and gynecology. In 1961, after a psychiatric program at the University of Pennsylvania and residency at the Philadelphia Hospital for Mental and Nerve Disorders, she established a psychiatry practice. In 1962, she published the first major article on postpartum depression in women. Dr. Kenin was an associate professor of psychiatry and chief consultant for the University of Oregon Medical School's health services. Her work helped Oregon practitioners understand postpartum depression before it was widely studied. (Gholston.)

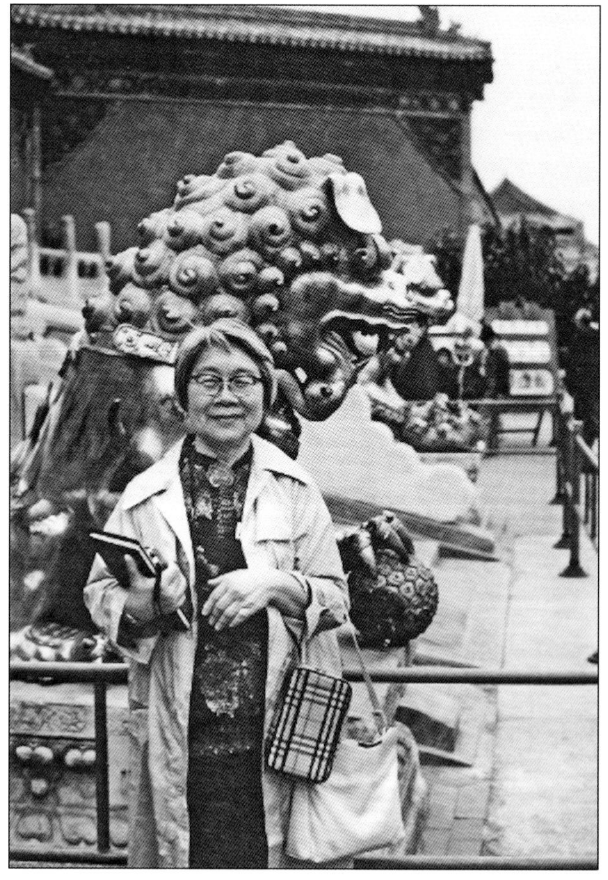

Kwan Hsu, PhD (1913–1995), was born in Guangxi province in China but lived in Shanghai from early childhood until moving to America in 1947 to pursue graduate studies. She graduated from the University of California, Berkeley, in 1960 and arrived in Portland in 1964 to teach biophysics at Portland State University, where she focused artificial lipid membranes. Hsu created a new biophysics program in the Physics Department. She was active in encouraging trade relations with China and bringing international students to Portland State University. (PSU.)

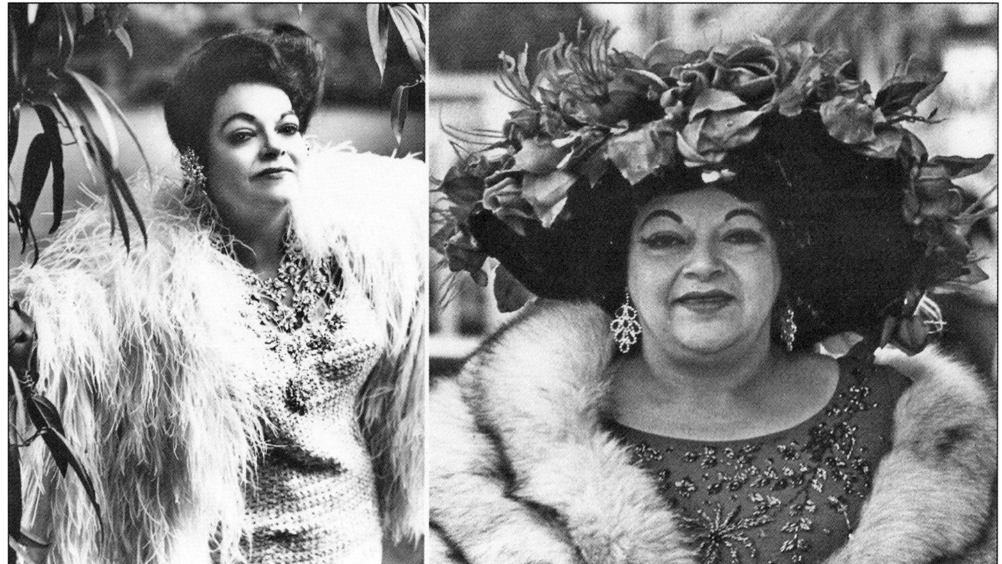

Gracie Hansen (1922–1985) was known for her cabaret shows at Seattle's 1962 World's Fair and later at Portland's Hoyt Hotel. The so-called last of the red-hot mamas declared, "I believe people should raise a little more hell and a little less eyebrow." Her inspirational speech included, "I was fat and 40 and I came out of the hills and I made it. My message is this: if I could, who the hell can't?" Portlanders loved her, and she inspired Darcelle's cabaret shows, which continue today. (trianglepro.org.)

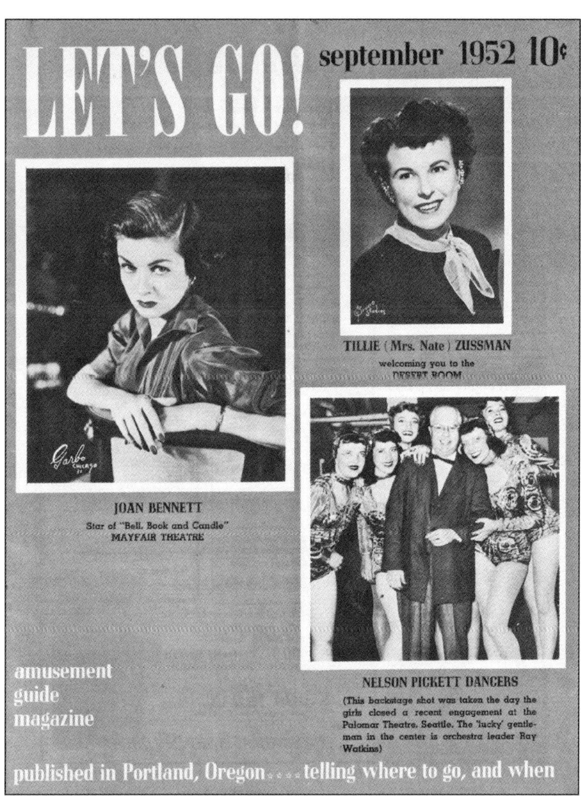

Otillie "Tillie" C.K. Hilderman Zusman (1913–1998) was co-owner with her husband, Nate, of the notorious Desert Room nightclub; it is currently McMenamin's Crystal Hotel with Zeus Café, honoring her nickname Zus (pronounced "Zoose") and with her image as the logo. The Desert Room was headquarters for Portland's criminal, political, and business elite—known for gambling and dancers. The shows were so scandalous that they had to be previewed by the Portland Police Vice Squad. The saying was "you can get anything you want at the Desert Room." Tillie reigned as queen of Portland's nightlife until the nightclub closed in 1970. (Richard Horswell.)

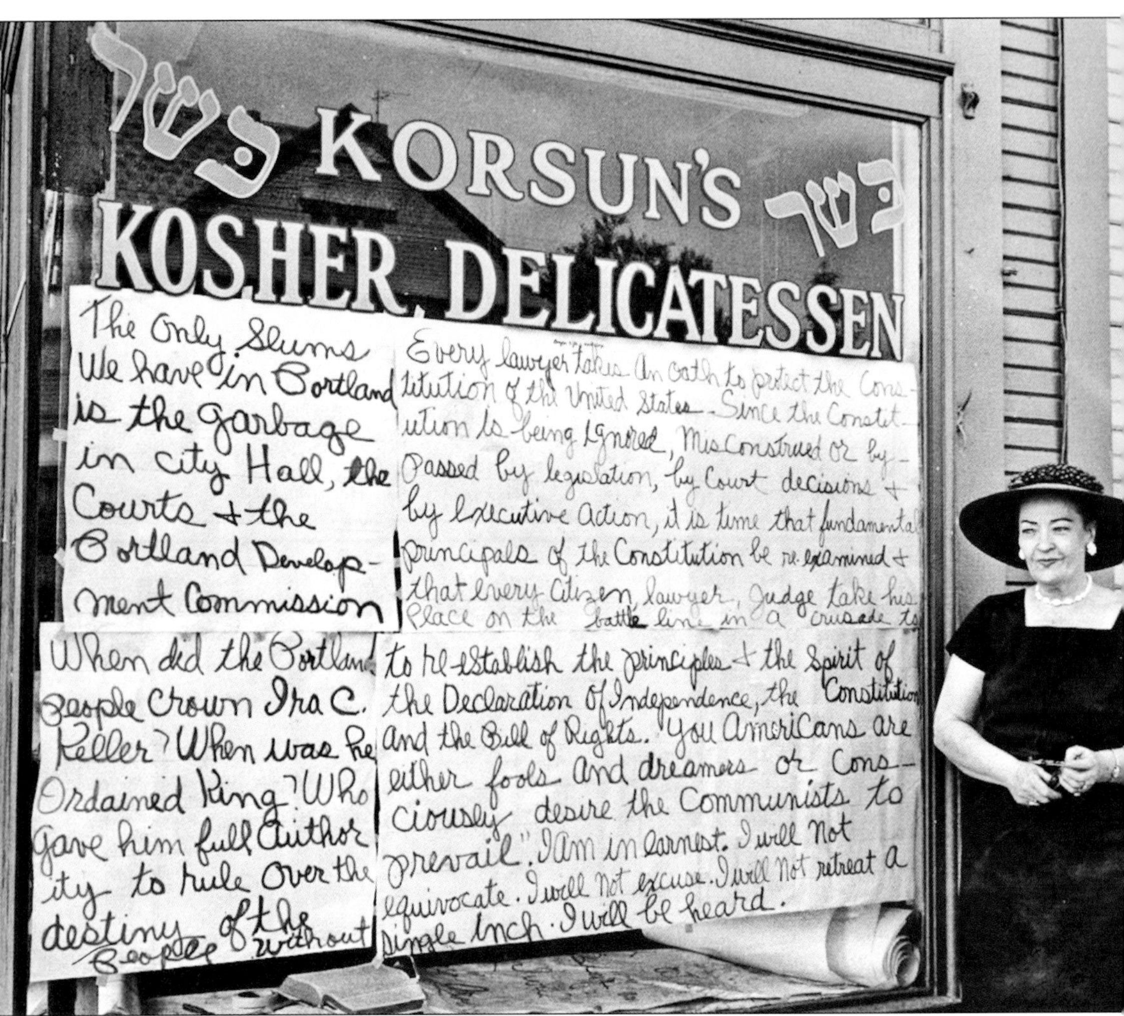

In the 1950s and 1960s, so-called urban renewal was the buzzword used by Portland city planners as an excuse to bulldoze the largely Jewish and Italian immigrant neighborhoods in old South Portland, known today as the southwest part of downtown and a small section of Goose Hollow and Lair Hill. This woman's creative protest uses every square inch of window space to name the people and the policies causing the destruction of her home, her community, and her family business—a Jewish deli. (CoPA.)

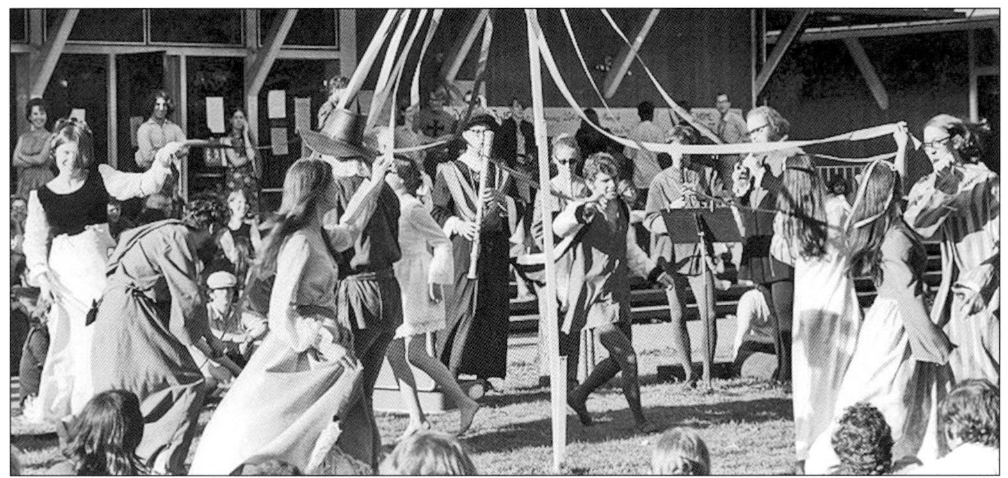

Reed College students enjoy a maypole dance in a photograph capturing the feeling of the late 1960s. Portland women protested with anti-war marches, civil rights picket lines, Freedom Rallies, and sit-ins and were concerned with war, racism, labor issues, capitalism, women's roles, birth control access, pacifism, and the earth movement. Thirteenth Avenue Gallery at 7987 Southeast Thirteenth Avenue was a counterculture Sellwood neighborhood spot popular with Reed College students, who had a reputation for radical political activism. The book *Portland in the 1960s: Stories from the Counterculture* shows that women's roles were complicated. One woman said, "I have mixed feelings about that era. It was after the sexual revolution but before the women's movement. Guys smoked dope while women washed clothes." (Reed.)

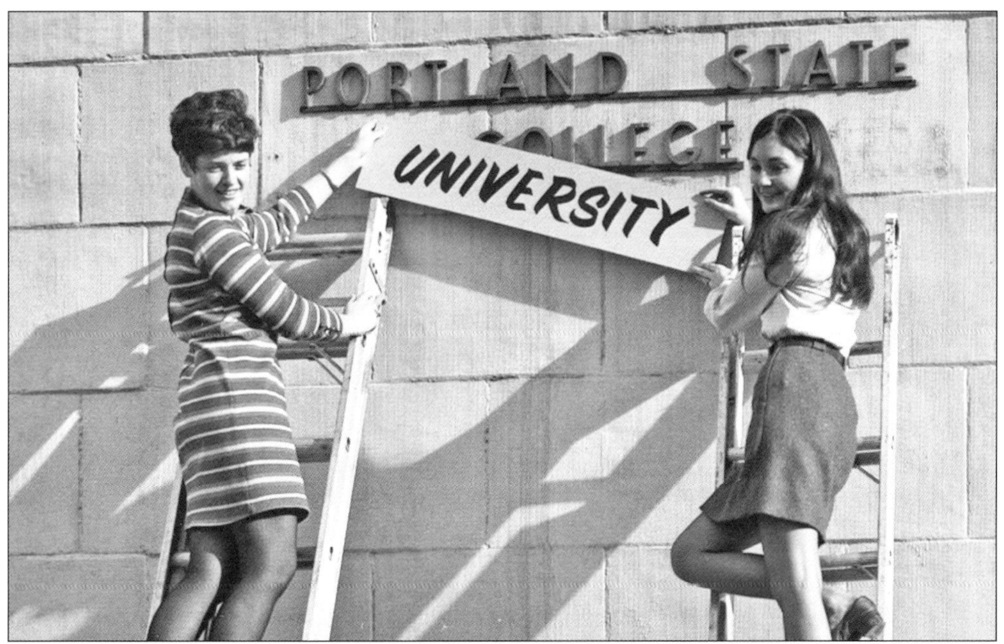

In 1968, women students at Portland State College hang a new sign after the Oregon State Board of Higher Education granted university status to Portland State University. It started in 1946 as Vanport Extension Center in a recreational center at Vanport. It became Portland State Extension Center in 1952 and then Portland State College in 1955. (PSU.)

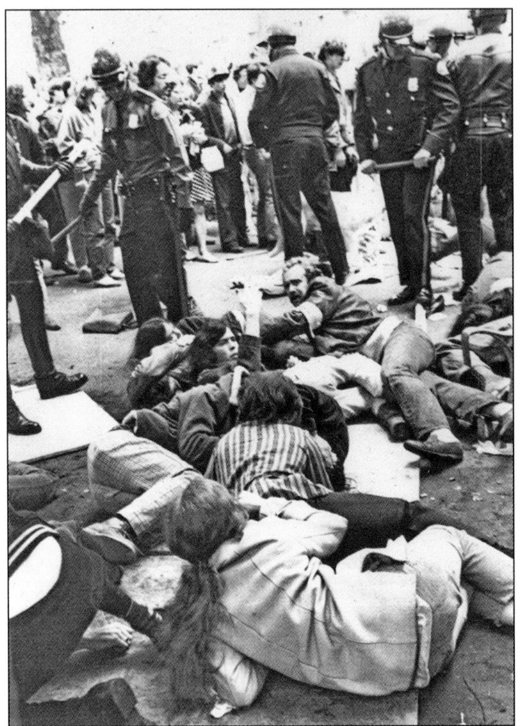

During the Vietnam War, many Portland women joined protests against the war, the draft, and the Kent State students shot by the Ohio National Guard on May 4, 1970. Portland had many antiwar marches, but Kent State galvanized students. Portland State University students went "on strike" as a way to protest along with many nationwide campuses. As pictured in the South Park Blocks, students set up barricades and made demands. Classes were canceled. Because campus walkways were open as roads back then, it halted traffic for several days. Portland police showed up at a first-aid tent the students set up. The students refused to take it down, saying they had a permit, and linked arms near the tent. Officers clubbed students with riot sticks. A total of 31 protesters and 4 policemen were injured, and some had to be taken to the hospital. No officers were charged. (Both, Gholston.)

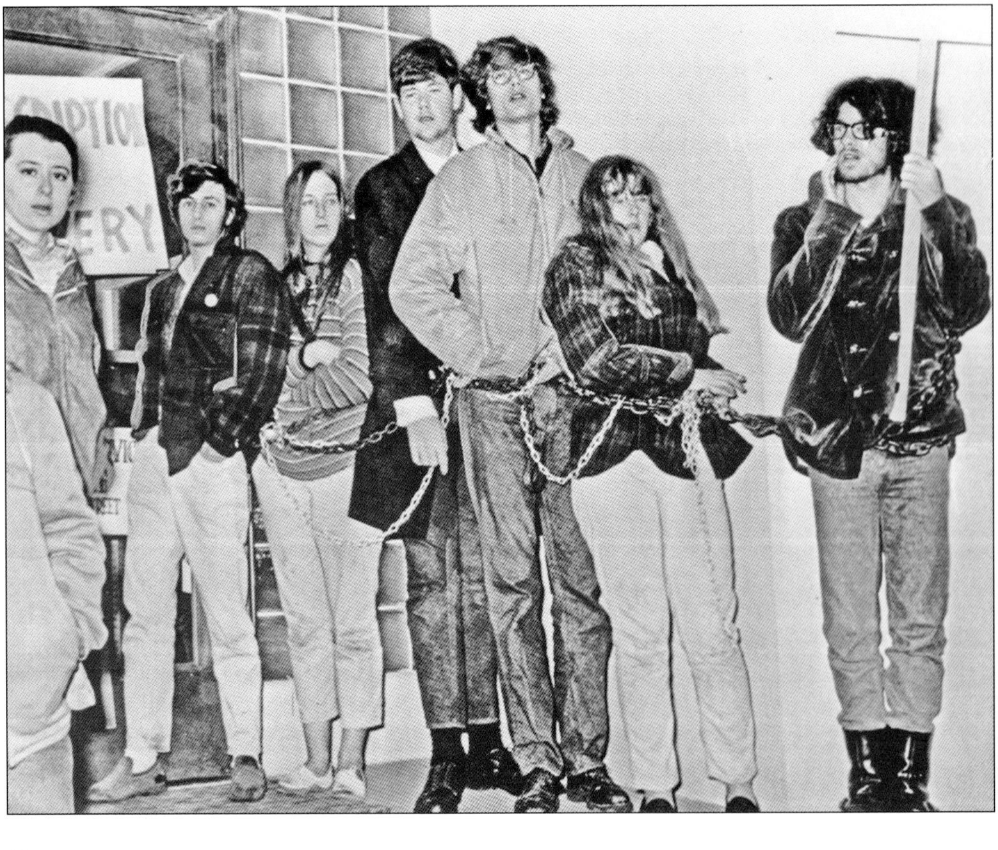

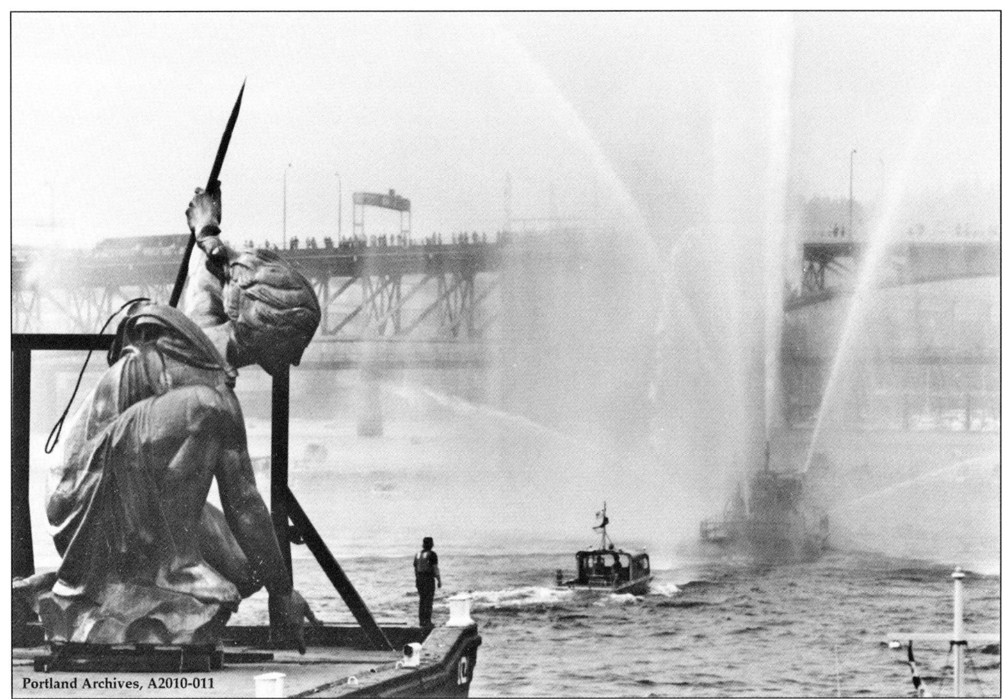

Portland Archives, A2010-011

Part of the Portland Public Art Project Program, the iconic *Portlandia* statue was designed to reflect ideas in the city seal. It was the suggestion of Michael Graves, designer of the Portland Building, to use the seal, Lady Commerce—a woman in classical robes holding a trident— as inspiration. Made by Raymond Kaskey in 1985, it is the second-largest copper repoussé statue in the United States: the largest is the Statue of Liberty. The *Portlandia* statue was floated down the Willamette River on a barge to put it in place at the Portland Building, 1120 Southwest Fifth Avenue. These photographs were taken in October 1985, when it was dedicated. The *Portlandia* statue has become a symbol of Portland. Mayor Vera Katz suggested moving it to the waterfront, since trees and the building's height make viewing it difficult. Both Kaskey and Graves objected, and the cost was deemed prohibitive, so it was not moved. (Both, CoPA.)

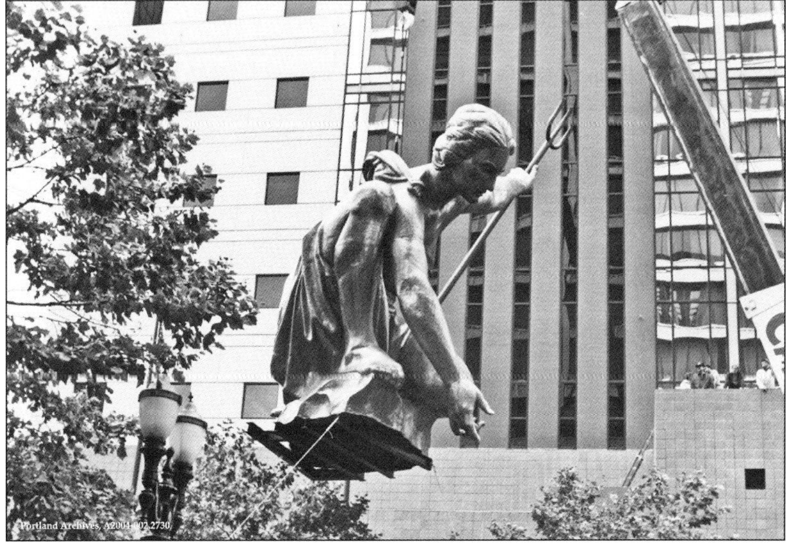

Portland Archives, A2004-002.2730

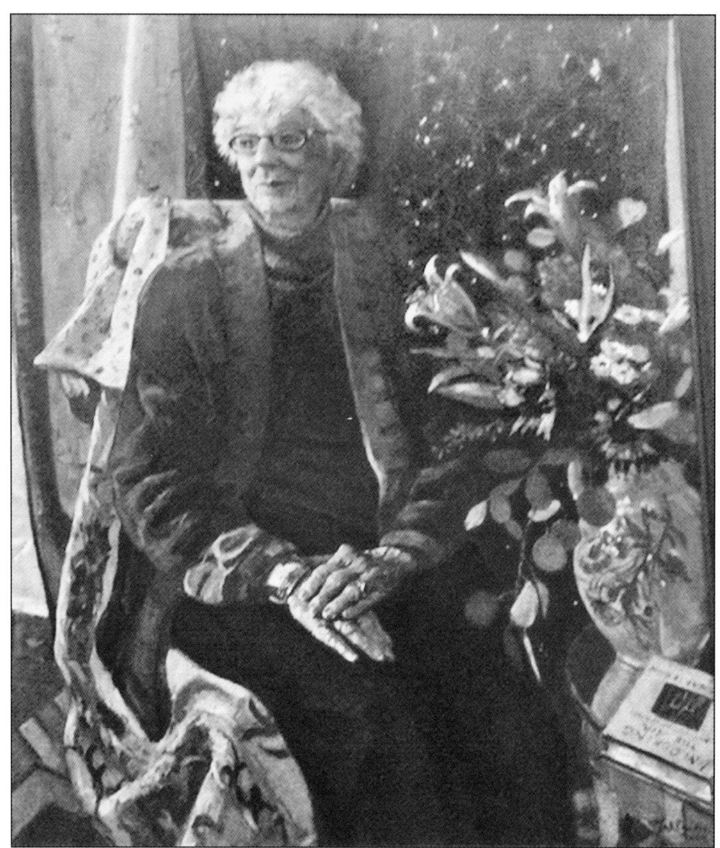

Dorothy Davenhill Hirsch (1916–2007) moved to Portland in the 1940s and served in the Women's Army Corps during World War II. In 2004, she became the oldest person to reach the North Pole, at age 89. She was on the boards of a Northwest Portland community center—Friendly House, the Library Foundation, and the Oregon Holocaust Research Center, was on the Reed College Alumni Board, and was director and treasurer of Friends of the Multnomah County Library. Hirsch was honored with this painting on the second floor of Central Library, which she helped raise money to refurbish.

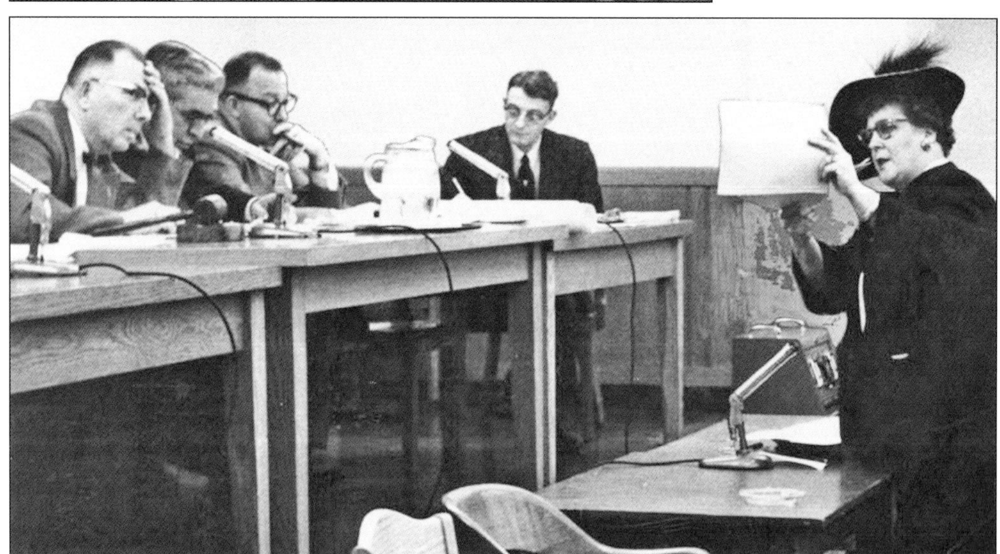

A civic leader and state and national lobbyist, Gertrude (Glutsch) Jensen (1903–1986) worked to make sure that the Columbia Gorge was protected. A board member of Portland's Women's Forum, Jensen also chaired the Columbia River Gorge Commission for 16 years. She oversaw the protection of more than 3,000 acres of land and also created the Save the Columbia Gorge committee. (OHS ba86990.)

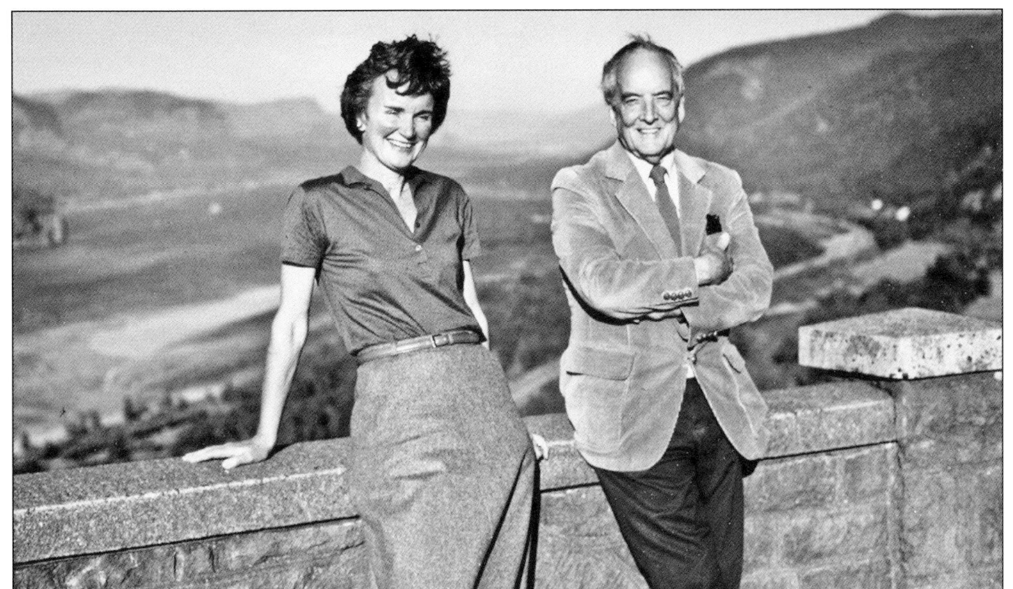

A proposed 1980 subdivision across from Multnomah Falls threatened Columbia Gorge's scenic nature. Nancy Ann Neighbor Russell (1932–2008) was a driving force, with Friends of the Columbia Gorge, fighting for a designated National Scenic Area. This group also included Portland Garden Club members and architect John Yeon (pictured with Nancy), son of the Historic Columbia River Highway's "Roadmaster." After years of lobbying, the Columbia River Gorge National Scenic Area Act was signed by Pres. Ronald Reagan on November 17, 1986. (Friends of the Columbia Gorge.)

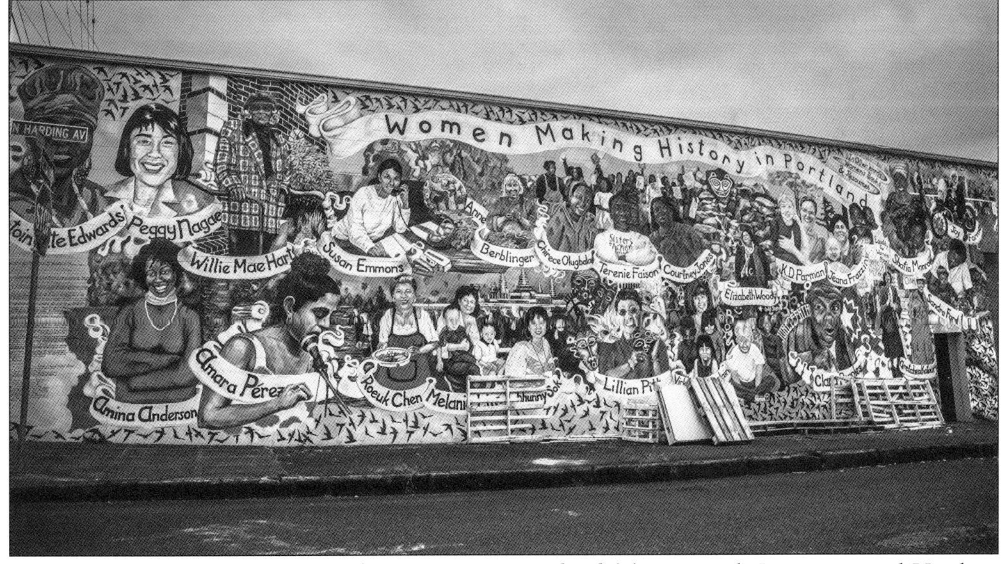

Robin Corbo's mural *Women Making History in Portland* (along North Interstate and Harding Avenues) features Antoinette Edwards, Peggy Nagae, Willie Mae Hart, Susan Emmons, Anne Berblinger, Chirece Olugbala, Terenie Faison, Courtney Jones, Elizabeth Woody, K.D. Parman, Jeana Frazzini, Shafia Monroe, Sandra Ford, Joy Farmer, Vanessa, Vatea, and Valeicia, Amina Anderson, Amara Pérez, Roeuk Chen, Melanie Lim and Chhunny Sok, Lillian Pitt, Vickie Chamberlain, Clara Peoples, and Gretchen Kafoury. (Tony Webster.)

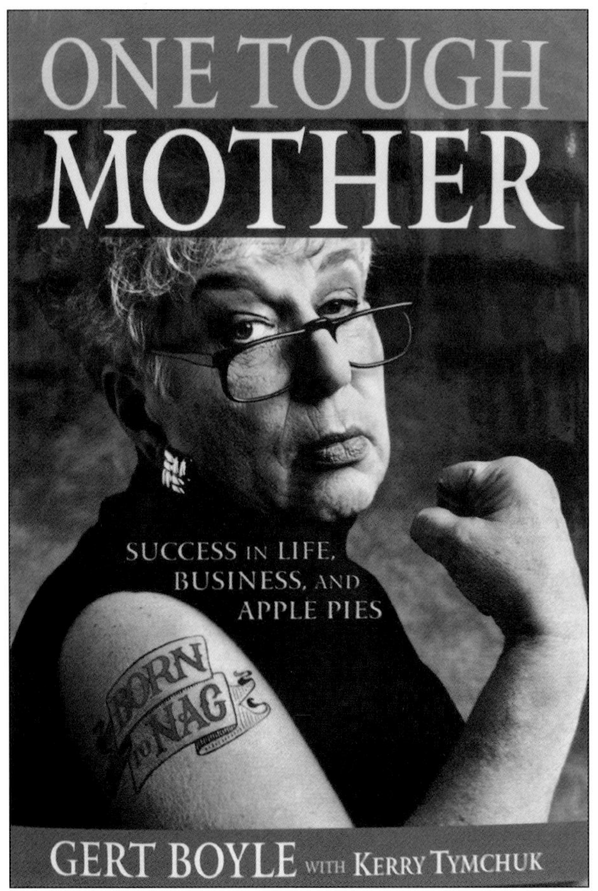

President of Columbia Sportswear, Gertrude "Gert" Lamfrom Boyle (born 1924) was an immigrant to America who fled the Holocaust. Boyle's husband, Neal, diversified her family's hat business into outerwear. When her husband died in 1970, she became president and steered the company to great success. In 1984, Boyle started starring in advertisements as Ma Boyle, "One Tough Mother," who used her son as a test dummy for new products. Royalties from her autobiography benefit Special Olympics and Court Appointed Special Advocates for Children.

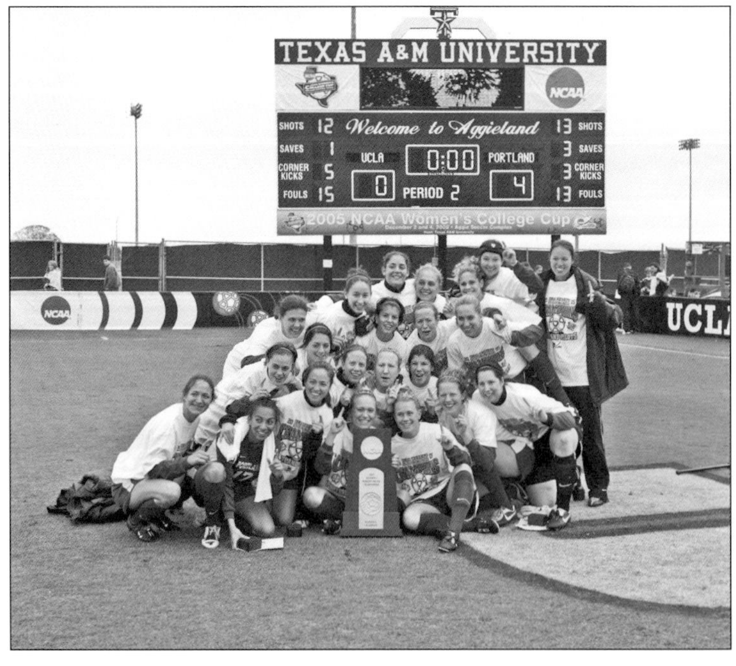

It was a big deal around town when the Portland Pilots (of the University of Portland) women's soccer team won the 2002 and 2005 National Collegiate Athletic Association Division I Women's Soccer National Championships. They are pictured here after the 2005 championship game. (University of Portland Athletics.)

Five

Women in the Arts
1890s to Present

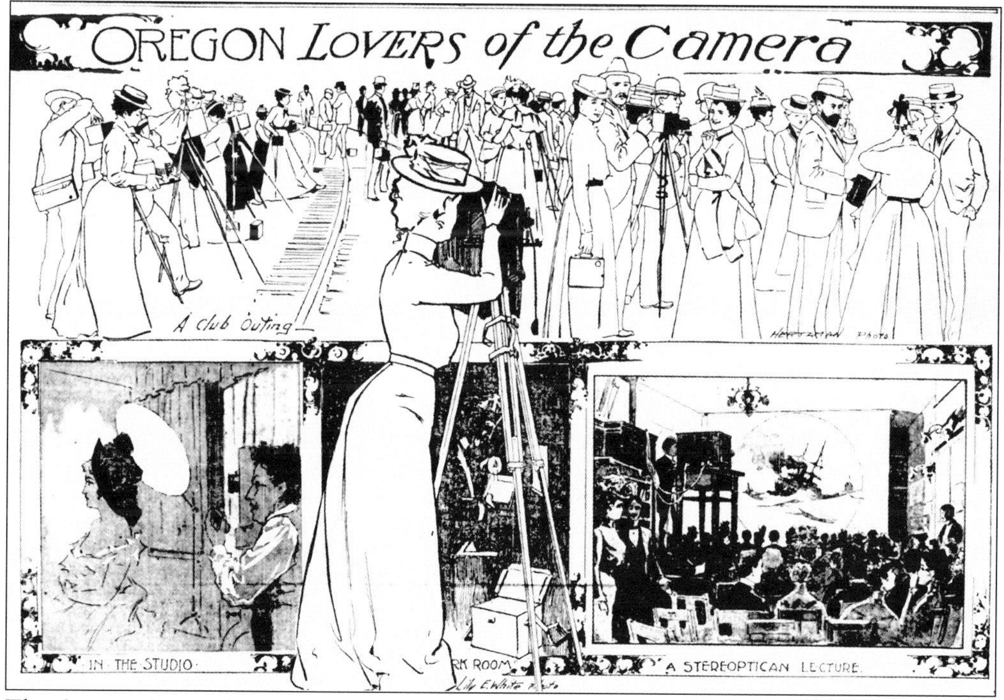

The Oregon Cameral Club formed in 1895 and voted to include many women members. This June 3, 1900, *Oregonian* illustration includes a Lily White photograph (lower center) and shows many women participating. With monthly meetings at the Oregonian Building, the Camera Club provided education, equipment, and outings and promoted the photographs of members in publications and exhibits. Photographers Lily E. White and Sarah Ladd were members who rose to great acclaim.

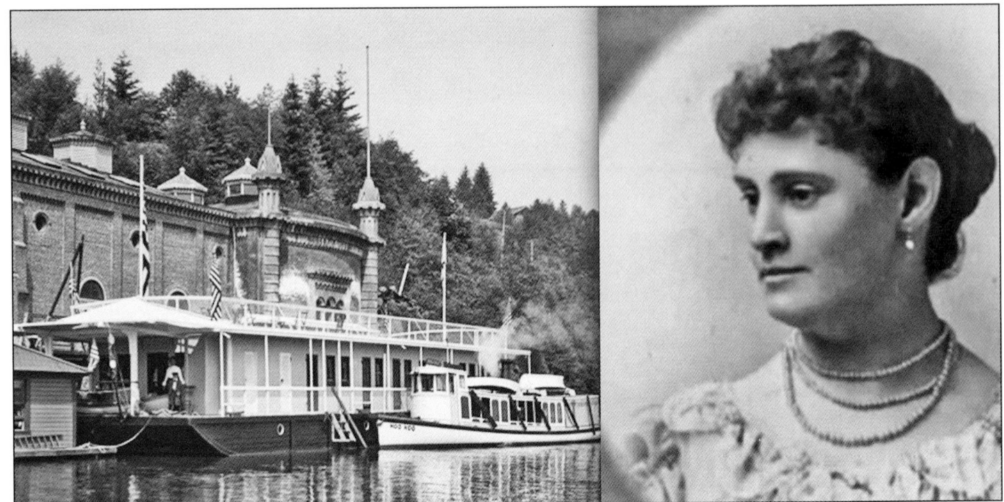

Photographer Lily Edith White (1866–1944), below with a White photograph of a local Native woman, was known for her photographs along the Columbia River and of Native Americans near Portland. White and her friend and photography colleague Sarah Hall Ladd (1860–1927), seen above, took many photographs while traveling on the Raysark houseboat, also above, which was outfitted with a darkroom. White and Ladd photographs were frequently published in travel brochures promoting the region and in the *Pacific Monthly*, owned by Ladd's husband, Charles E. Ladd. White studied art in Chicago and San Francisco. She and Ladd were active in the Oregon Camera Club and the Camera Club of New York, and their works were exhibited in Portland, San Francisco, and New York. White and Ladd were members of the Photo-Secession, an exclusive group of avant-garde photographers led by Alfred Stieglitz in New York. (Below, Doug Magedanz.)

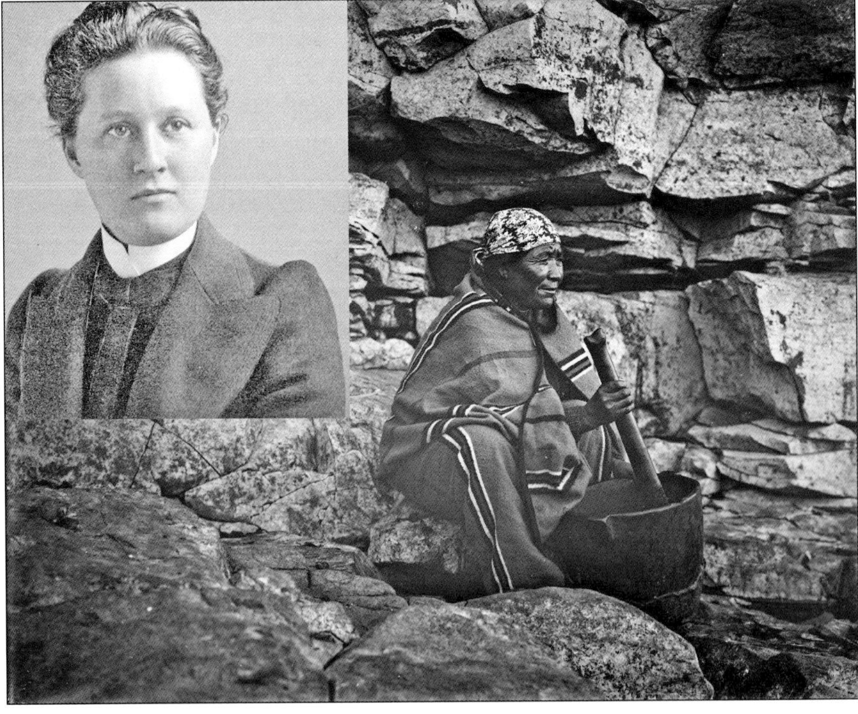

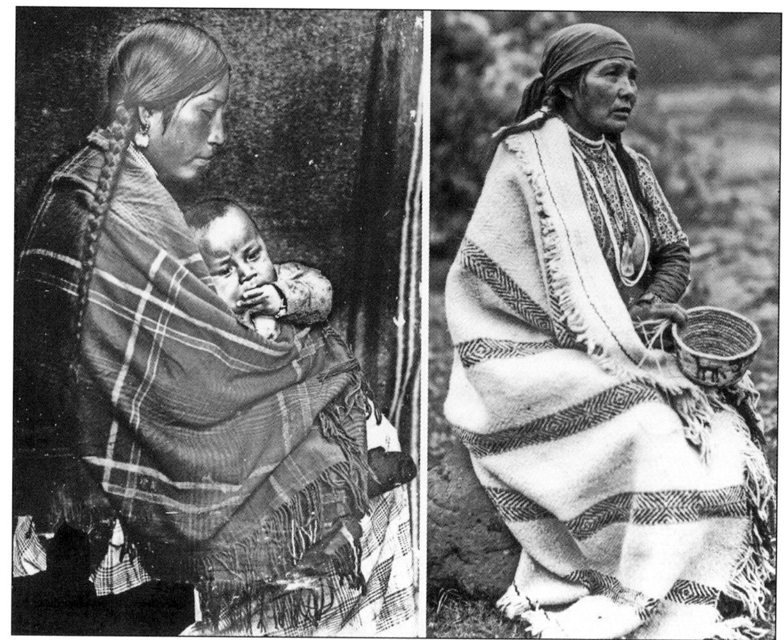

Lily E. White took these photographs of Native American women near Portland around 1902–1904. On the right is Sally Waukuaquas from the Klickitat tribe. (Doug Magedanz.)

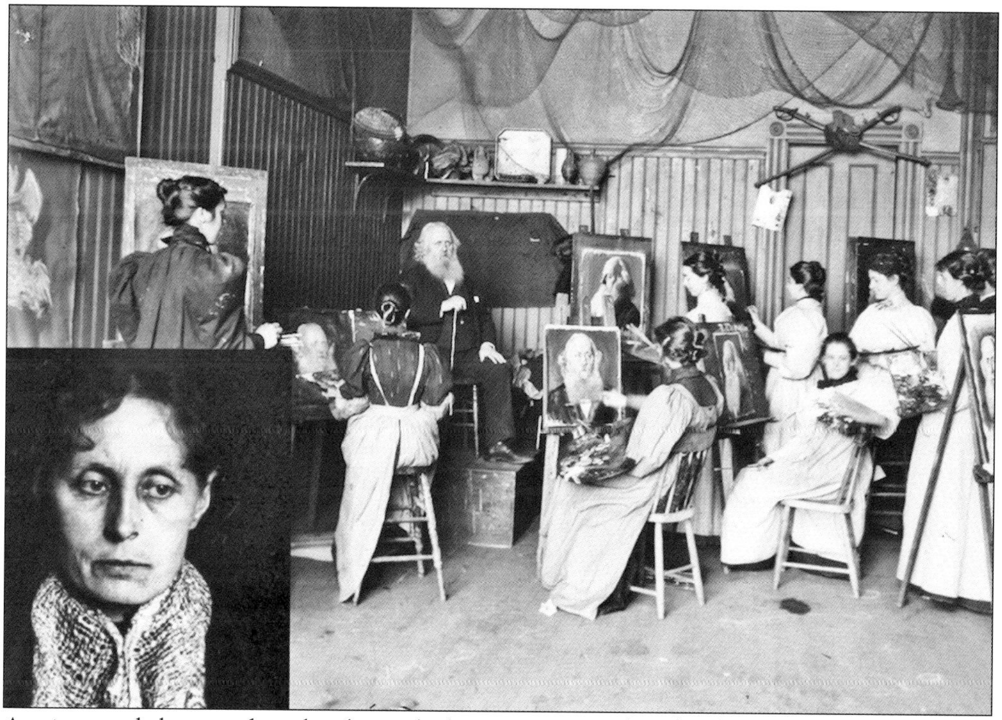

A painter and photographer who also worked in ceramic, metal, and sculpting, Julia E. Christianson Hoffman (1856–1934) founded the Arts and Crafts Society in 1907, now the Oregon College of Art and Craft. Hoffman also helped found the Museum Art School and was a strong supporter of the Portland Garden Club and the Portland Symphony (now the Oregon Symphony). Her daughter, Marjorie Hoffman Smith, is featured on page 106.

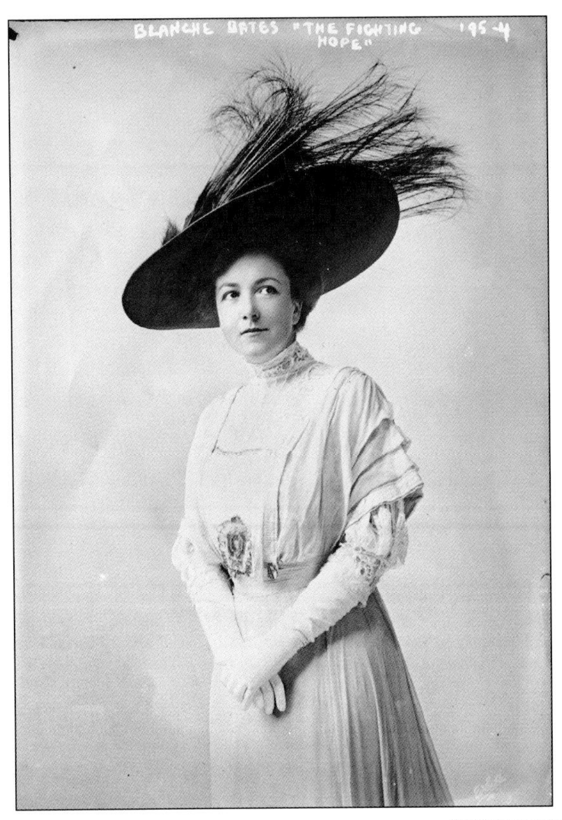

Born in Portland, Blanche Bates (1873–1941), who acted from 1898 to 1934, starred in many Broadway plays including *The Darling of the Gods* (1902), *The Girl of the Golden West* (1905), and *The Famous Mrs. Fair* (1919) as well as in silent films such as *The Border Legion* (1918) and *Tom's Little Star* (1919). A well-known stage actress, she was a favorite of legendary theatrical producer David Belasco, who featured her in his plays. Blanche starred in his one-act adaptation of *Madame Butterfly* (1900), which Puccini saw and then created his 1904 opera. She is pictured in an image from a Broadway play, *The Fighting Hope* (1909). (W.)

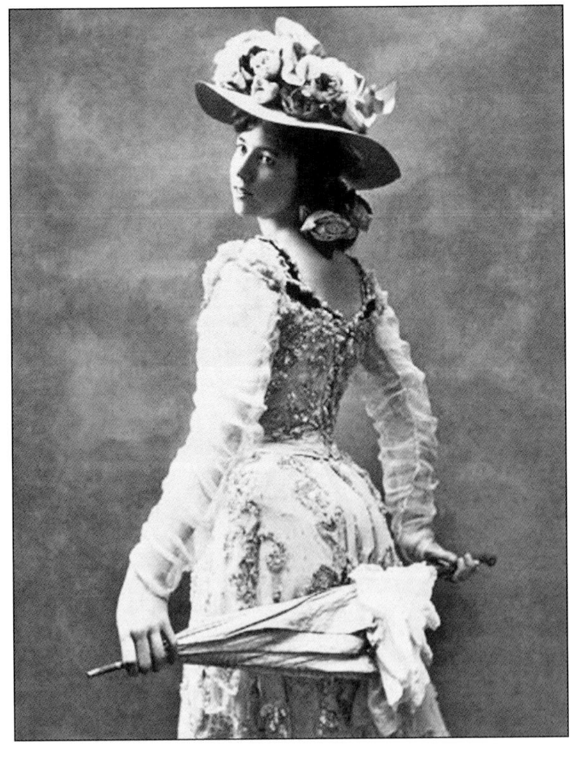

Kathleen Rockwell (1876–1957) was a vaudeville star best known as Klondike Kate. While living in New York City, Rockwell heard about the Klondike gold rush. She moved to Canada's Yukon in 1899 and was a dancer in Dawson City, where she developed her signature "Flame Dance." She wore a red dress with 200 feet of trailing chiffon, and her racy dance titillated gold miners. She toured West Coast saloons and theaters with her act. After retiring from dancing, she homesteaded 320 acres in central Oregon, doing the hard labor of proving up the land while wearing fancy gowns and dance shoes. She lived in Oregon for 45 years, many of them in the Willamette Valley. (W.)

From 1930 to 1938, singer and actress Bernice Claire (1906–2003) appeared in 13 films, including *Spring is Here* (1930), *Moonlight and Pretzels* (1933), and *No, No, Nanette* (1930). Born Bernice Jahnigen, she lived in Portland for many years during her retirement. (W.)

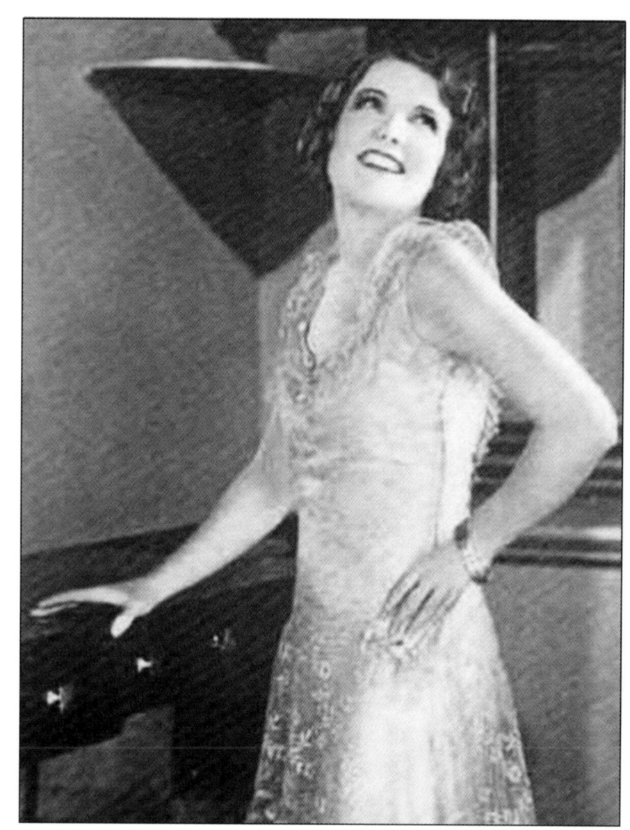

Colista Dowling (1881–1968) was an original officer of the Oregon Society of Artists in 1929, which named a memorial gallery in her honor at 2185 Southwest Park Place. Known for her watercolors and book illustrations (below) and *Pacific Monthly* illustrations, Dowling trained at the Art Students League of New York. Her works were exhibited at the Portland Art Museum and the Seattle Art Museum and are in the Oregon Historical Society collection.

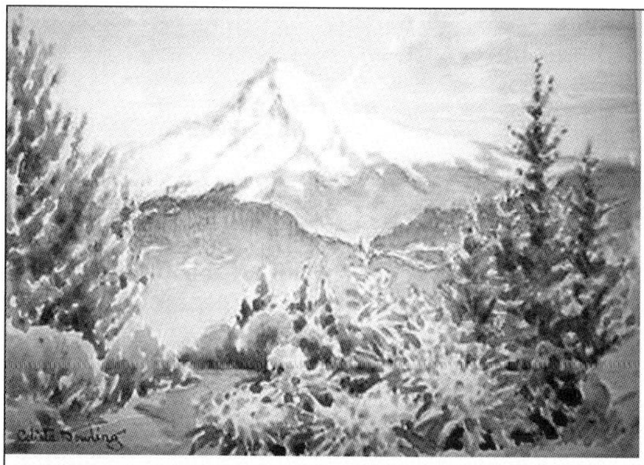

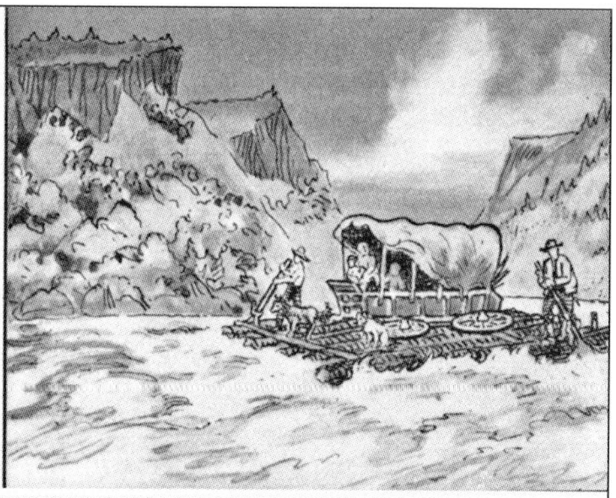

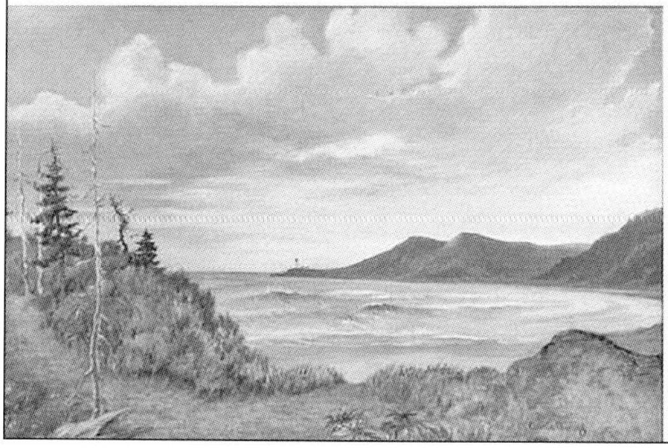

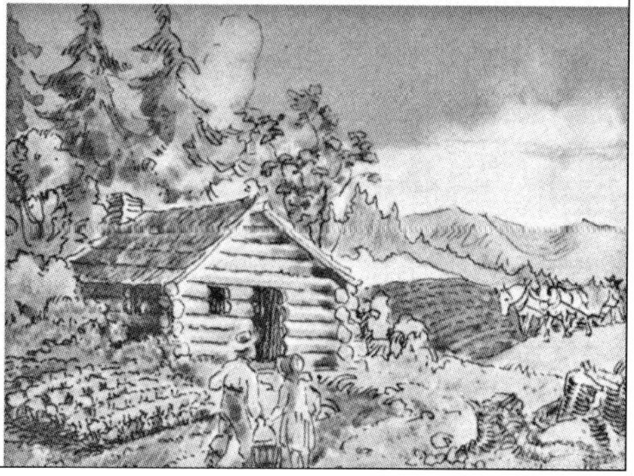

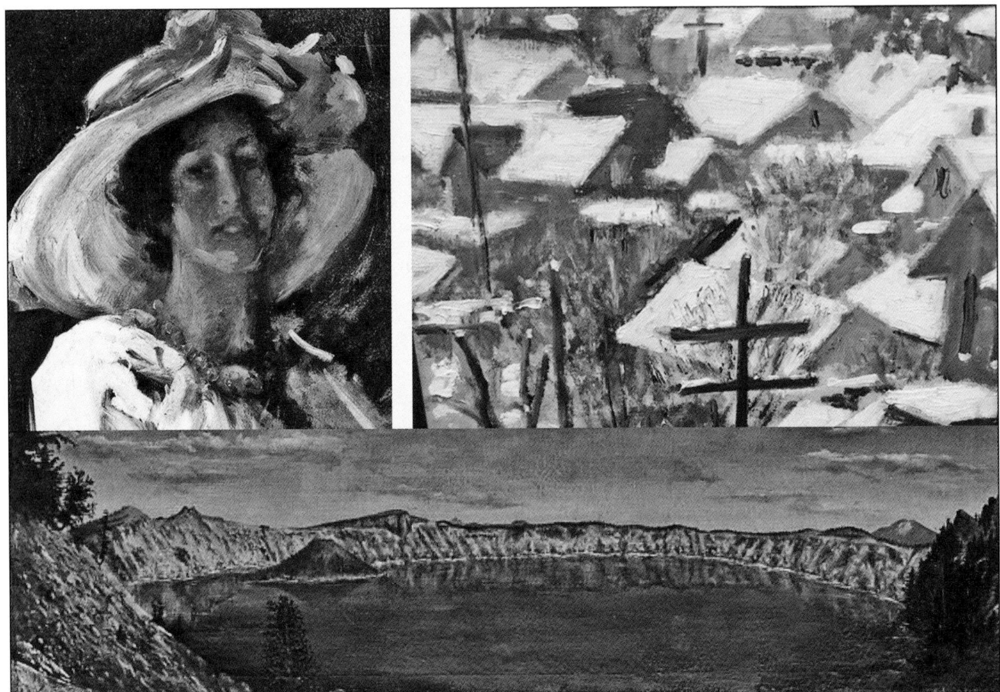

Born in England, artist Clara Jane Stephens (1877-1952) moved to Portland in 1894 and was a Portland Museum Art School instructor. She studied in France and Italy with William Merritt Chase, who painted her portrait (left), and in New York with Kenyon Cox and Frank DuMond. She exhibited her paintings at the 1905 Lewis and Clark Expo, the 1915 Panama-Pacific International Exposition, and in San Francisco, Seattle, Oakland, Hollywood, and New York. Her paintings above are of Crater Lake and a cityscape. Below, three St. Mary's students play harps in the 1950s. The oldest continually operating secondary school in Oregon, St. Mary's Academy has been an all-girls school with interfaith students since its start in 1859. (Below, Sisters.)

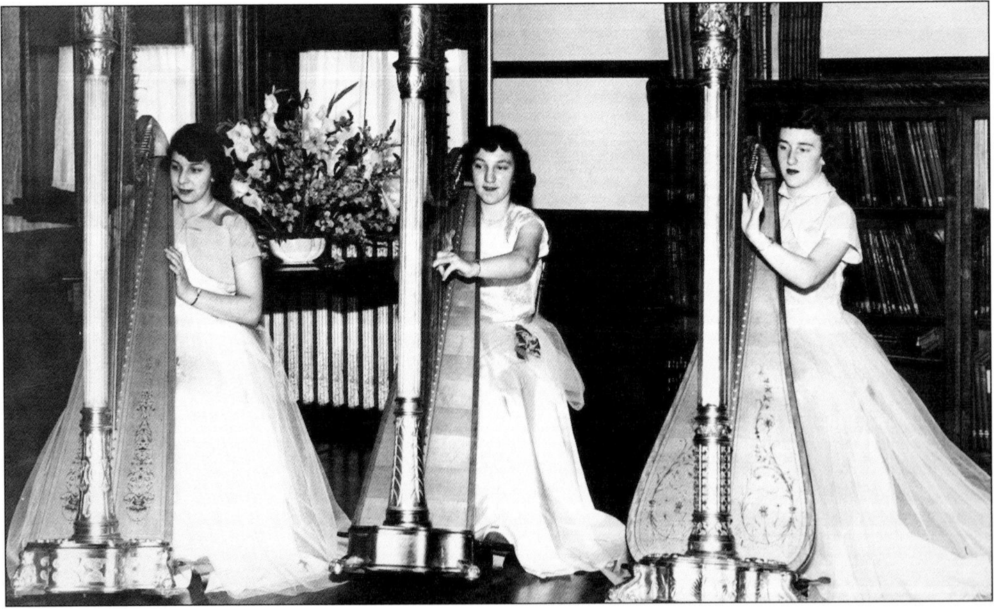

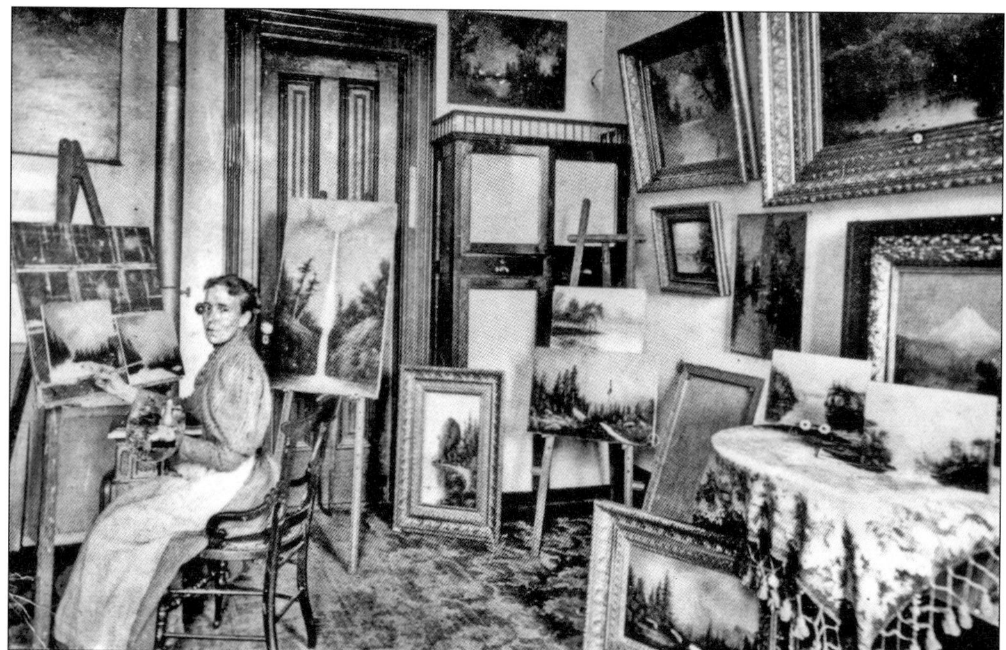

Well-known Oregon landscape artist Eliza R. Lamb Barchus (1857–1959) moved to Portland in 1880 with her husband, John. Eliza Barchus took art lessons from William Parrott, was active in the Mutual Art Association, and exhibited her paintings frequently, including in 1890 at the National Academy of Design in New York City. In 1905, her paintings were prominently featured at the Lewis and Clark Exposition and still grace many Portland homes. (OHS bb006440.)

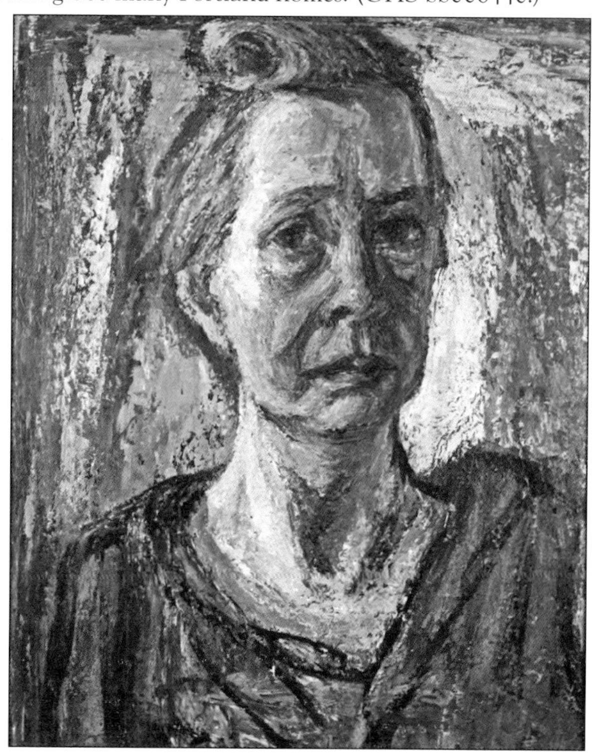

Known for her abstracted painting style with elements of Impressionism and Expressionism, Amanda Tester Snyder (1894–1980) attended the Portland Art Museum School in 1917 and was influenced by fellow Works Progress Administration (WPA) artists C.S. Price and Charles Heaney. In 1964, the Portland Art Museum exhibited *Amanda Snyder, Paintings and Collages*. Her works are held by the Oregon Historical Society, the Portland Art Museum, the Seattle Art Museum, Reed College, the Jordan Schnitzer Museum of Art, and the Hallie Ford Museum of Art, which owns this 1948 *Self-Portrait*.

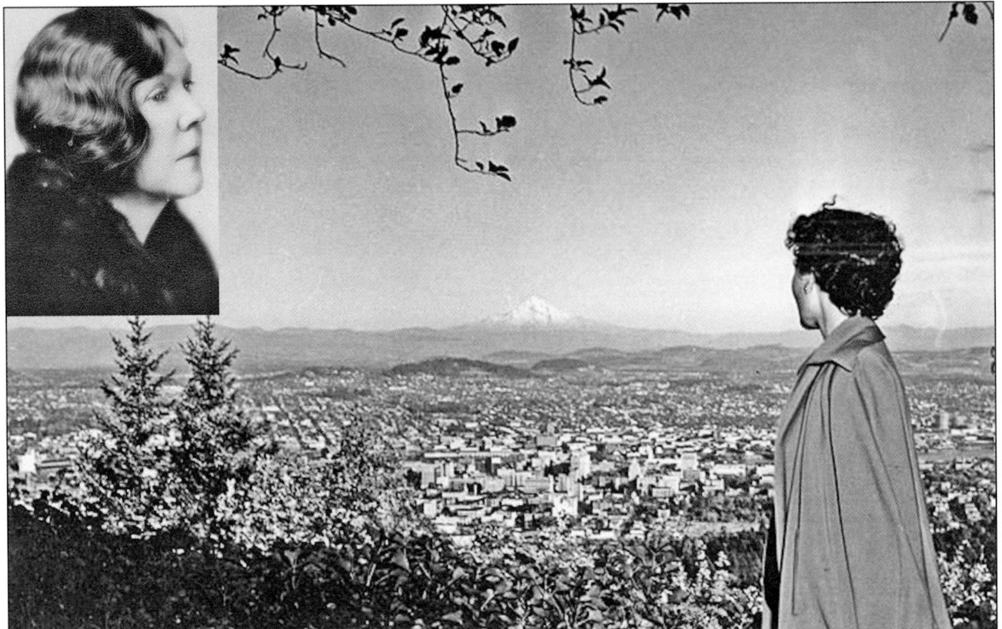

Ada Hasting Hedges (1884–1980) was WPA supervising editor of production for the Oregon State Guide. It includes this photograph of Portland. Hedges is likely the woman in the foreground. She was also assistant editor at Binfords and Mort Publishers. Her main interest was in poetry, and her poems appeared in the *Nation*, *Poetry* magazine, the *New York Times*, *London Mercury*, *American Mercury*, and various other magazines and newspapers.

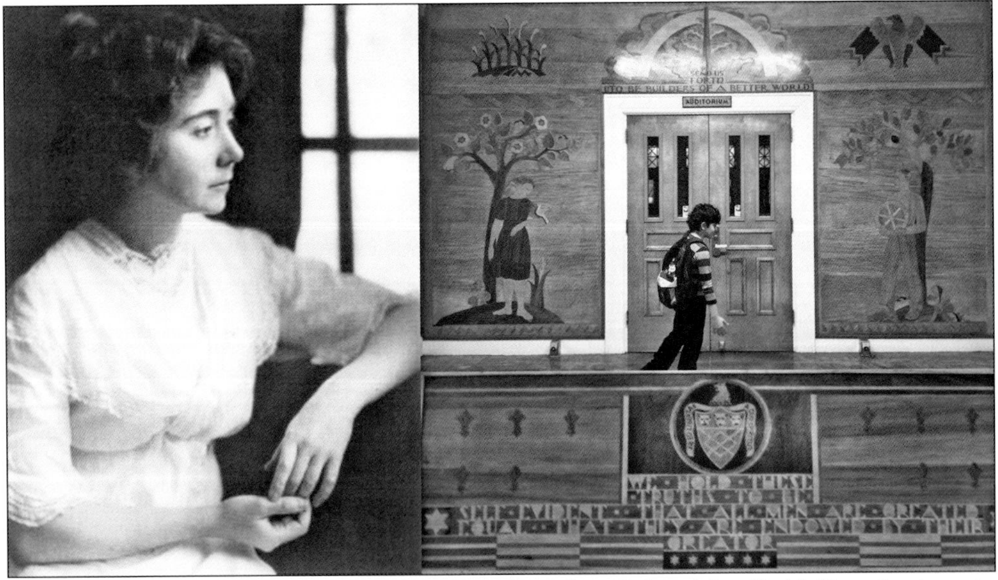

WPA artist Aimee Spencer Gorham (1883–1973) graduated from New York's Pratt Institute in 1913, taught art for Portland schools and Portland Art Museum and worked in marquetry, stained glass, paintings, sculptures, and illustrations. Gorham's marquetry murals are at Timberline Lodge, Oregon State University, the Portland Art Museum, and Portland schools Ainsworth, Alameda, Chapman (top), Irvington, Jefferson (bottom), Riverdale, and Roseway Heights. She lived at 2187 Southwest Market Street Drive and then at 1830 Northwest Everett Street. (OCHC.)

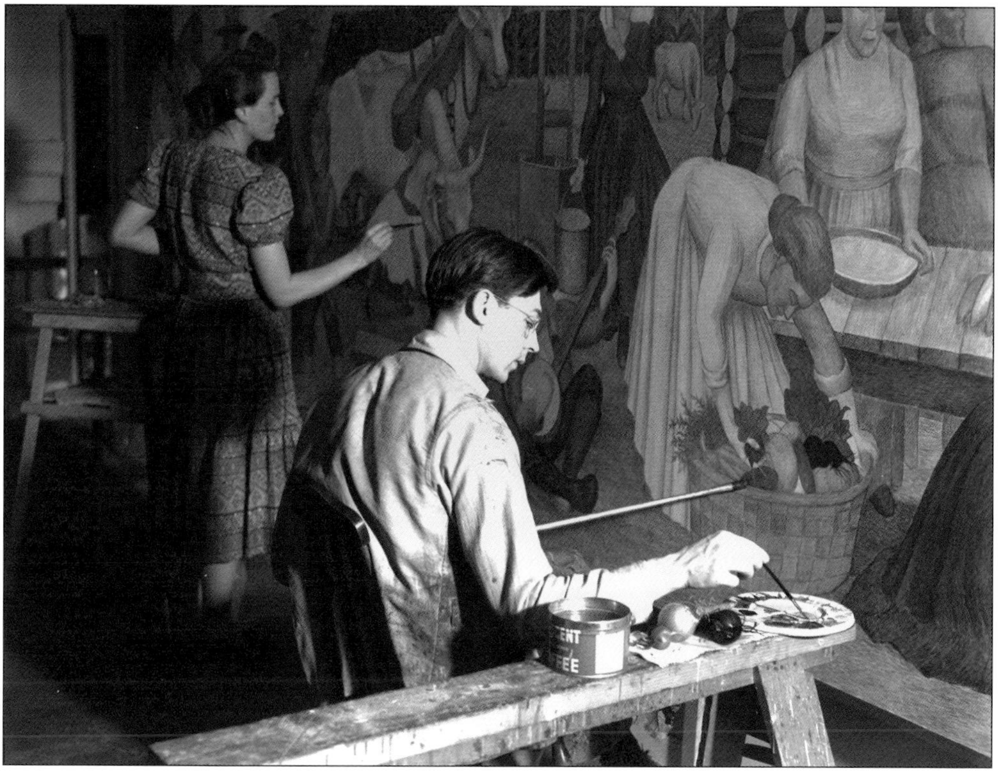

WPA artist Martina Gangle Curl (1906–1994) attended the Museum Art School and was a painter, printmaker, woodcarver and artist at Timberline Lodge. During World War II, she worked at Kaiser shipyards and painted coworkers. She exhibited at the Portland Art Museum, the 1939 New York World's Fair, and Seattle's Northwest Printmakers Exhibits. Her Portland murals are on page 16. This 1940 Minor White photograph is of Martina Gangle and Walter Pritchard painting an Arthur Renquist mural in Pendleton. (PAM 4960.)

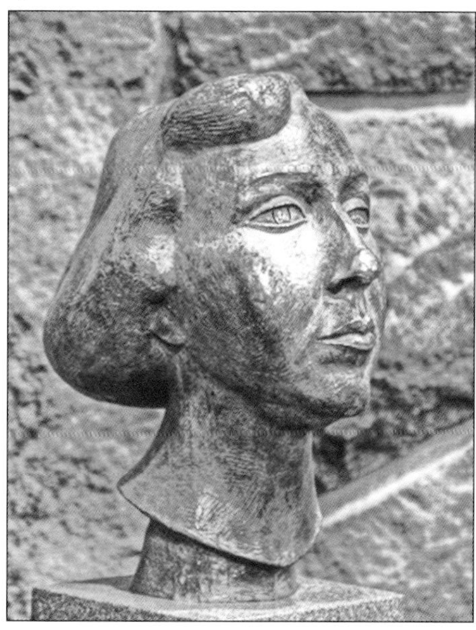

Portland Art Museum curator from 1960 to 1974, Rachael Griffin (1906–1983) developed art programs for Portland schools and advocated for Oregon artists. She was a member of the Albina Arts Center, the Contemporary Crafts Association, the Portland Dance Theater, the Boys and Girls Aid Society, and the Oregon Committee for Art in Public Places. A former WPA artist, she was a 1975 founding member of Friends of Timberline, who honored her with this bronze statue at Timberline Lodge.

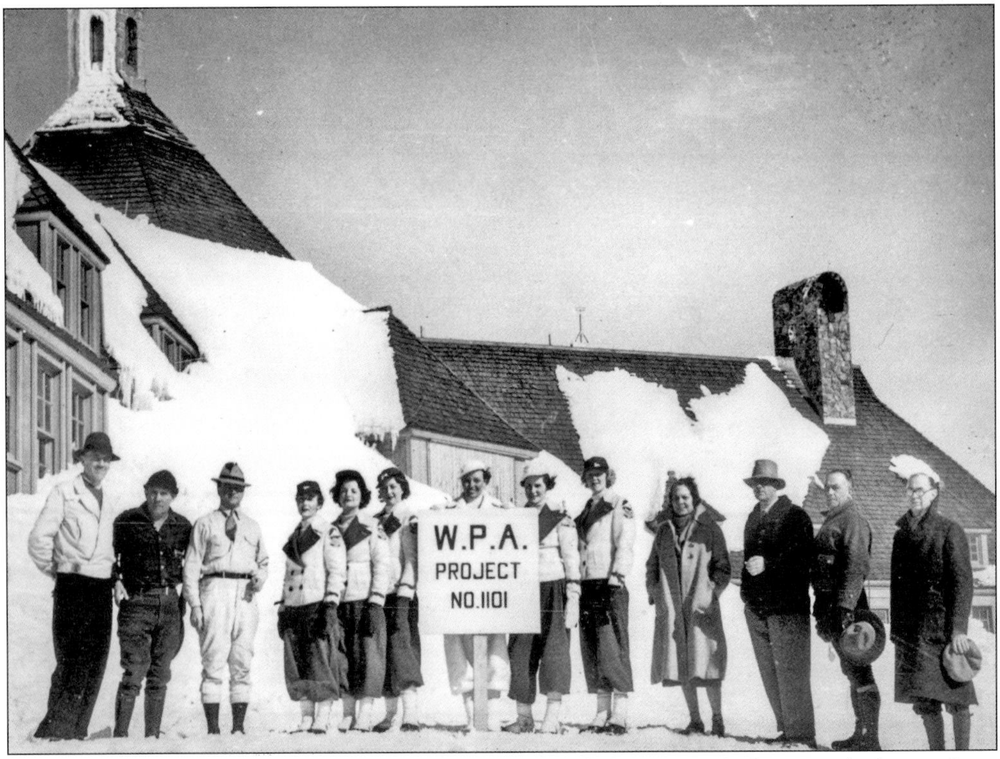

Standing fourth from the right, Margery Hoffman Smith (1888–1981), the "grande dame of arts and crafts," was assistant state director of the Federal Art Project, in charge of Works Progress Administration project No. 1101—Timberline Lodge on Mount Hood. She worked with artists on handcrafted furnishings, paintings, lithographs, and murals to decorate the lodge—art admired by generations of Oregonians. (OHS 013026.)

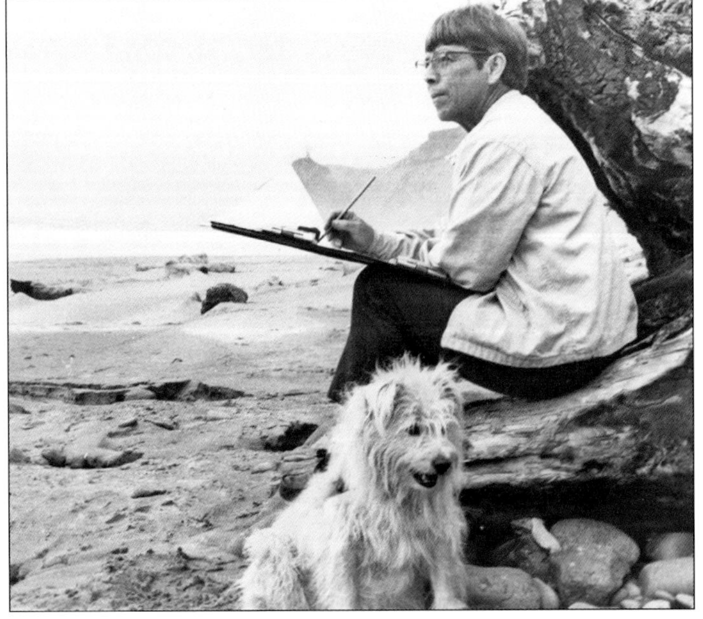

Born in Portland, artist Ruth Dennis Grover (1912–2003) promoted Oregon arts on the coast. A watercolorist known for depictions of beaches and coastal architecture, she was founder/director of Cascade Artists collective from 1952 to 1978. Grover helped develop the Lincoln County Art Center, taught classes, and exhibited there. Her works are in the collections of the Coos Art Museum, the Hallie Ford Museum of Art, the University of Oregon, and the Oregon Historical Society. (WU.)

Opera singer Mona Paulee was born Minnie Berg (1911–1995) in Canada. She was discovered while singing during silent movies at her father's South Portland theater. She changed her name and became an internationally known mezzo-soprano for the Metropolitan Opera and throughout Europe. She graduated from Lincoln High School in 1930 and grew up at 2075 Northwest Thurman Street in the Slabtown neighborhood.

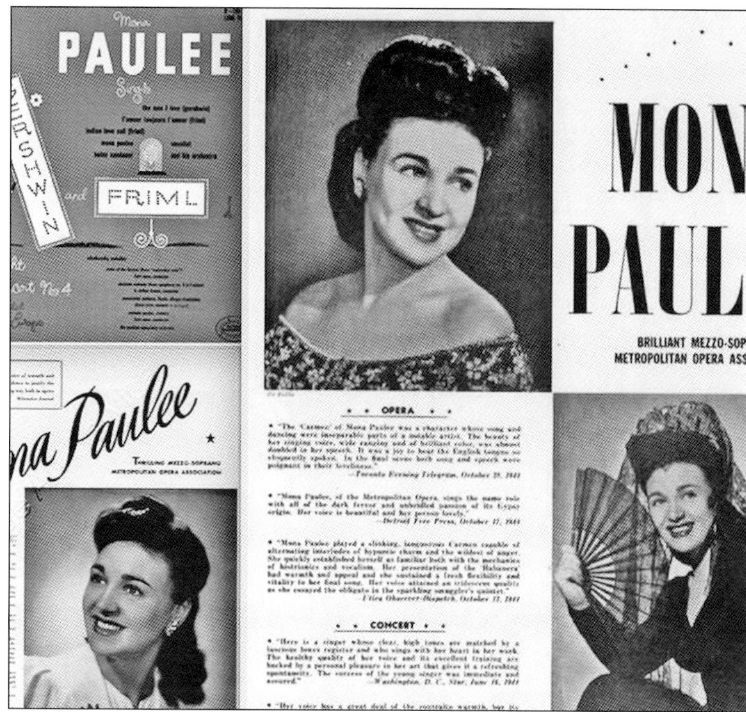

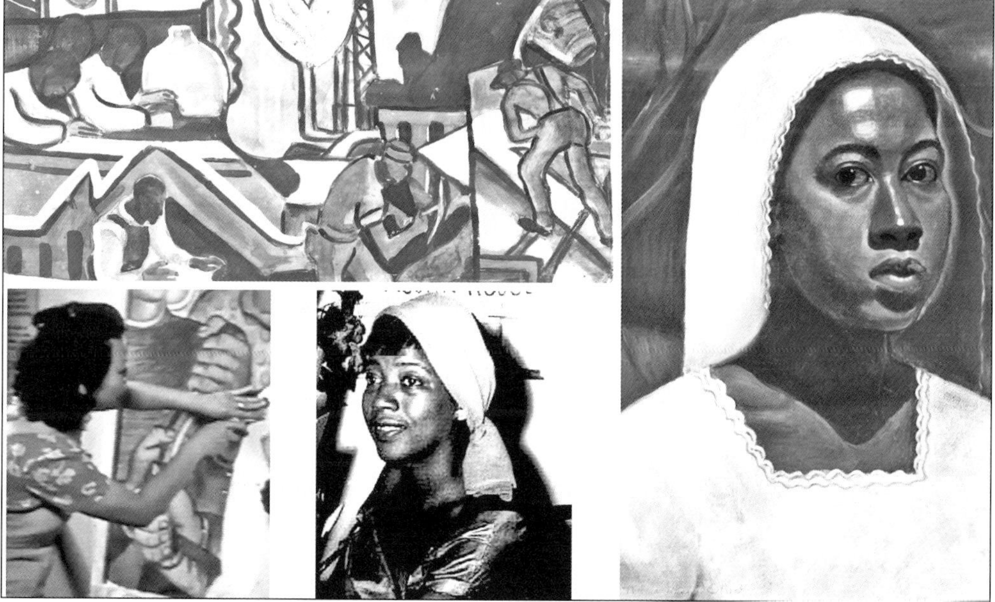

Thelma Johnson Streat (1911–1959), was a dancer and artist. Her mural *Death of a Black Sailor* drew Ku Klux Klan threats. She assisted Diego Rivera on his San Francisco WPA mural *Pan American Unity*. Her works are in the collections of the Smithsonian's National Museum of African American History & Culture (upper left), Reed College (right), Mills College, the Honolulu Museum of Art, and the San Francisco Museum of Art; she was also the first African American woman exhibited at the Museum of Modern Art in New York. (Lower left, SFBATA).

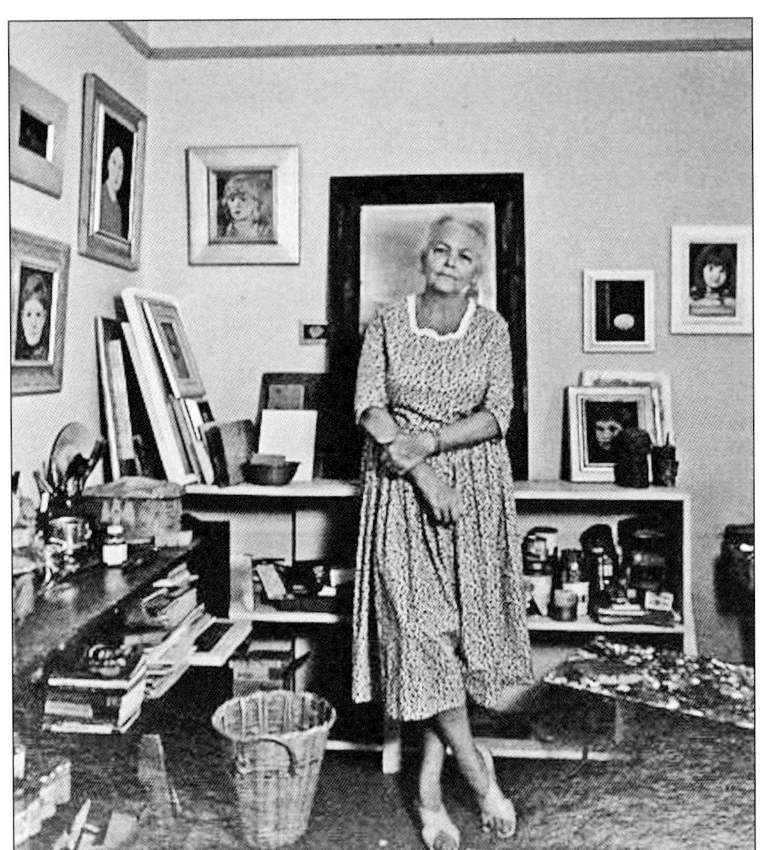

Sally Haley (1908–2007) moved to Portland in 1947 with her husband, artist Michele Russo. Her work has been exhibited throughout the Northwest, with retrospectives by the Portland Art Museum in 1975 and Marylhurst College in 1993, and is in the collections of the Tacoma Art Museum, the Hallie Ford Museum of Art, and many private and corporate collections. (PAM.)

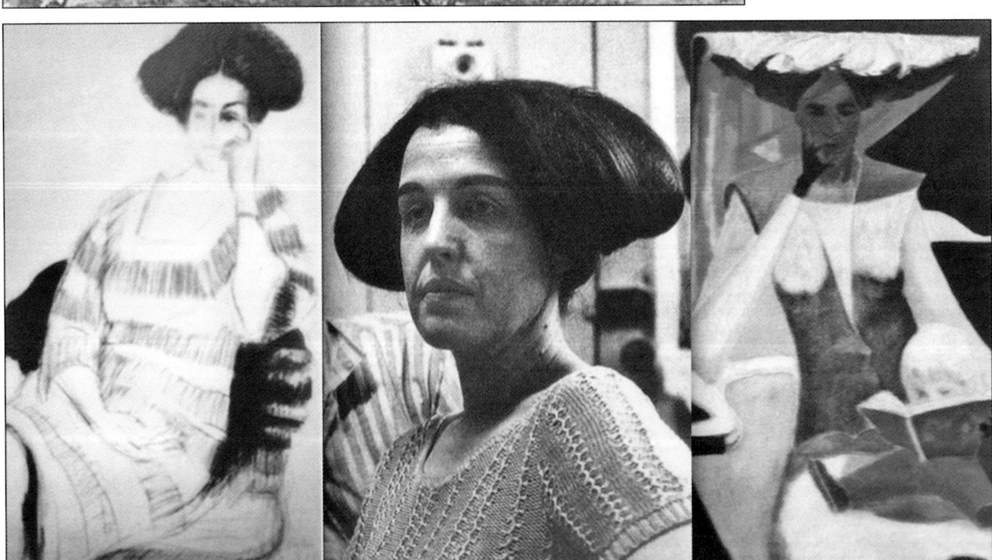

Barbara McLarty (born 1919) published and edited many art books, including those of her husband, Jack, such as *Charles Heaney: Master of the Oregon Scene* (1980), *Lillie Helvi Lauha: An Oregon Collection* (2001), and *Worldwatcher: Jack McLarty* (1995). Barbara and Jack opened the Image Gallery, in operation from 1961 to 1986, promoting artists such as Charles Heaney, George Johanson, and Harry Widman.

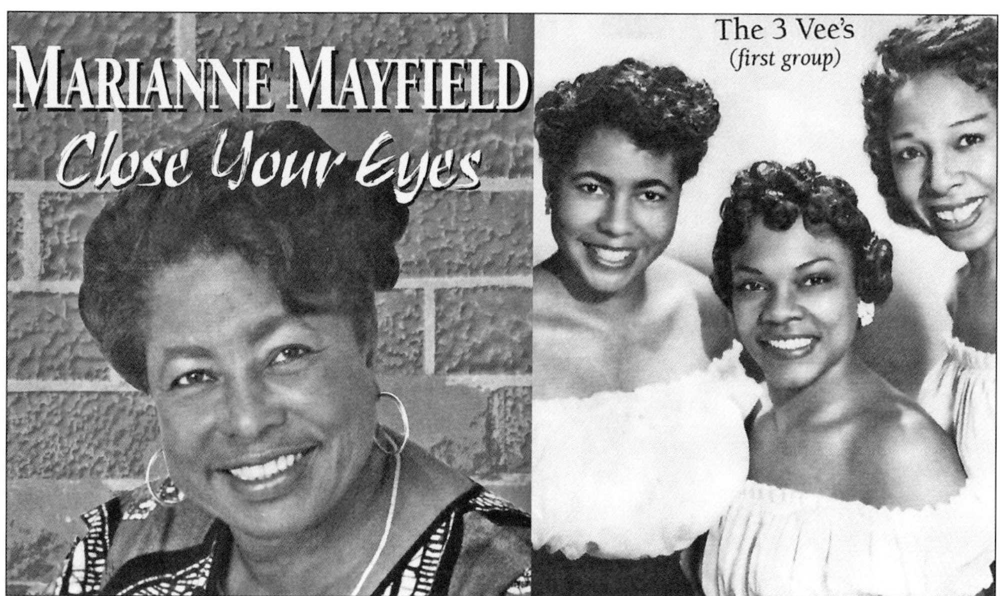

Marianne Mayfield Hill (1936–2004), a singer and bassist, was beloved in the Portland jazz scene for decades. Her performances drew diverse crowds, and she played many jazz and blues festivals. She released several albums, including *Close Your Eyes* in 1994. Beginning in the late 1970s, Mayfield led groups in Portland nightclubs—Parchman Farm, the Prima Donna, the Jazz Quarry, and the Village Jazz. Her first group was the 3 Vee's.

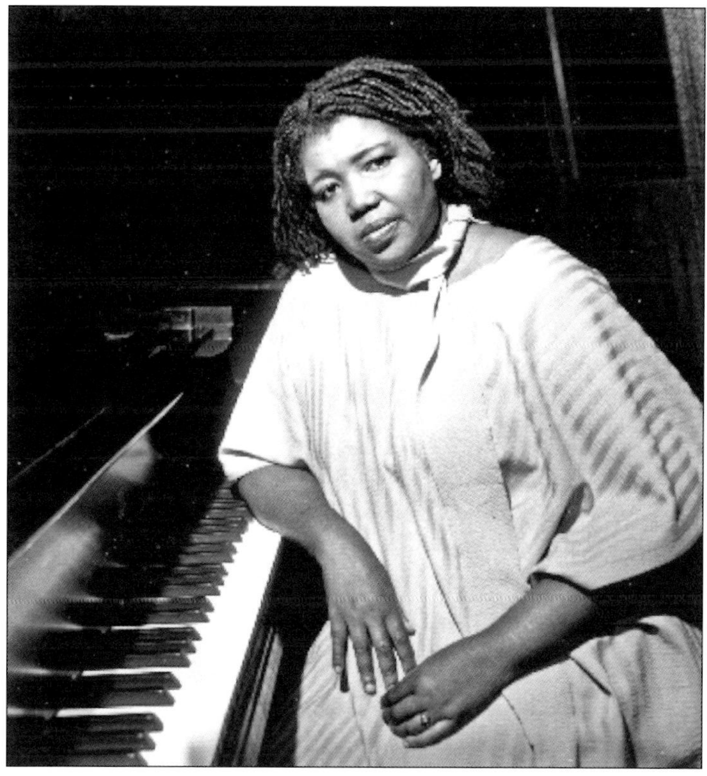

Janice Scroggins (1955–2014), a pianist, music director, and composer, was a huge part of Portland's blues, gospel, and jazz communities. She contributed to many critically acclaimed albums, including *Janice Scroggins Plays Scott Joplin* (1987) and *Piano Love* (2014) and is featured on a Grammy-winning album by former student Esperanza Spalding. She performed with Thara Memory, Curtis Salgado, Obo Addy, and Linda Hornbuckle and at the Portland Jazz Festival and Waterfront Blues Festival. She was inducted into the Oregon Music Hall of Fame in 2013.

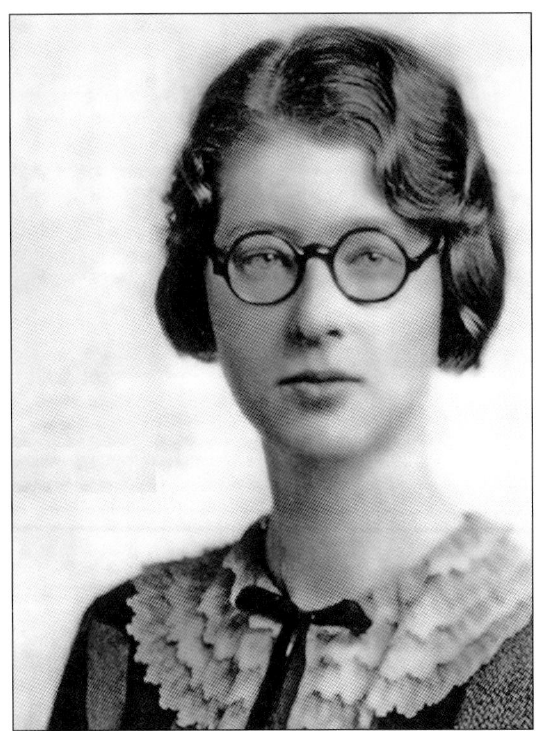

Mary Barnard (1909–2001), a poet and classicist, was a frequently anthologized poet, including her works "Cool Country" and "The Trestle." She won the Levinson Award, Elliston Award, Western States Book Award, Washington State Governor's Award, and May Sarton Award for Poetry. She was mentored by Ezra Pound and William Carlos Williams.

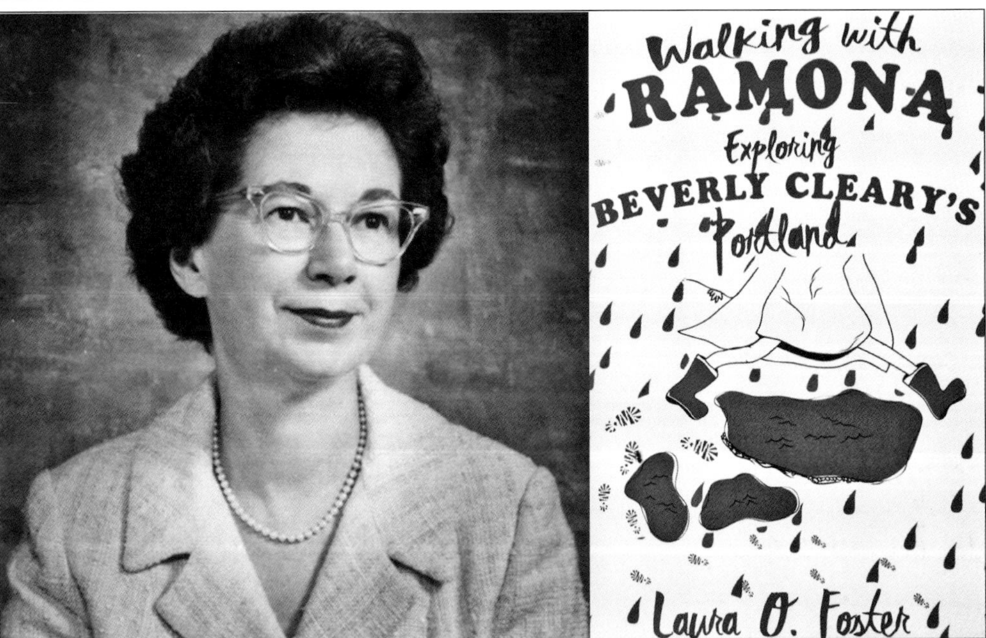

With 91 million books sold, Library of Congress "Living Legend" Beverly Bunn Cleary (born 1916) poured her childhood memories of Northeast Portland into over 40 endearing children's books such as *Henry Huggins* (1950), *Ribsy* (1964), and *Ramona the Pest* (1968)—characters memorialized in the 1995 Grant Park Sculpture Garden. Cleary received the Newbery Award, National Book Award, and the National Medal of Arts. Laura Foster's book *Walking with Ramona* explores the Portland neighborhoods Cleary lovingly wrote about. (W.)

Library of Congress "Living Legend" Ursula K. Le Guin (born 1929) is beloved for children's books, poetry, essays, short stories like "The One Who Walk Away from Omelas" and 20 novels—including *The Left Hand of Darkness* (1969) and *The Wizard of Earthsea* (1968). She has received PEN, Pushcart, Newbery, Hugo, Nebula, Locus, and National Book Awards. Le Guin is revered by fellow writers for railing against Amazon's control over the publishing industry at the 2014 National Book Awards and against Google's hegemony over scanned books by resigning from the Author's Guild. Born Ursula Kroeber in Berkeley, California, she and her husband, Charles, have lived in Portland since 1959. (PAM.)

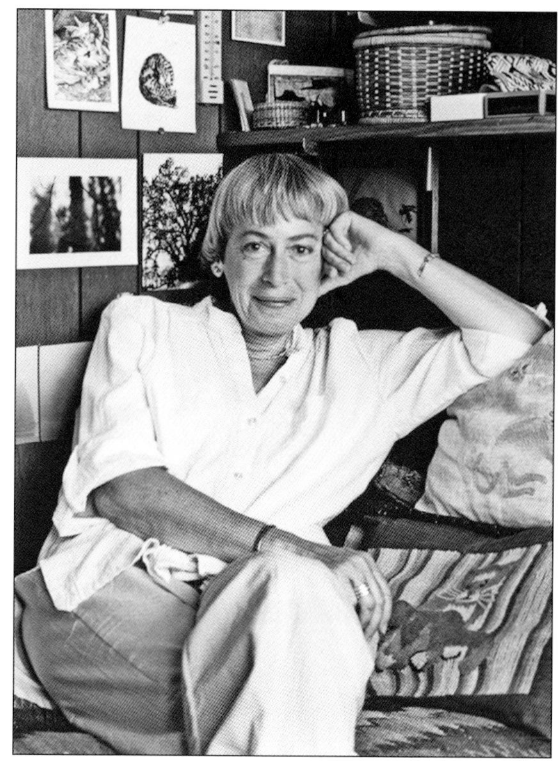

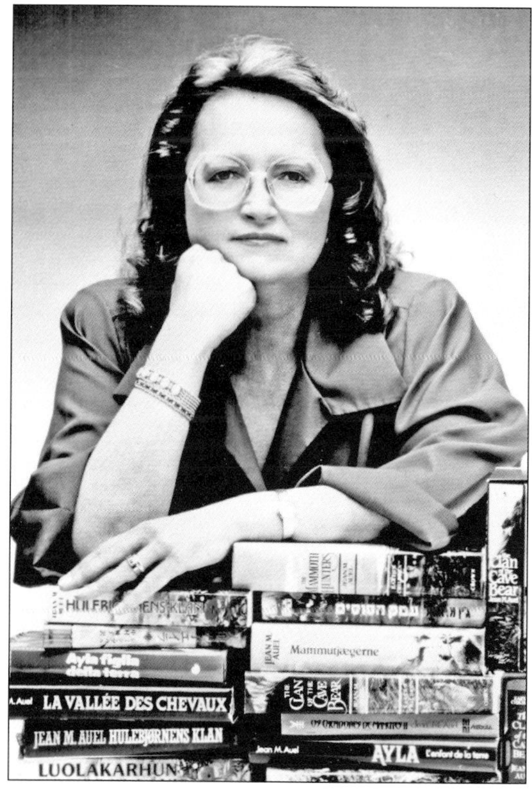

Internationally renowned author Jean M. Auel (born 1936) has sold over 45 million books. All six of the Earth's Children series have been New York Times Best Sellers—*The Clan of the Cave Bear* (1980), *The Valley of Horses* (1982), The Mammoth Hunters (1985), *The Plains of Passage* (1990), *The Shelters of Stone* (2002), and *The Land of Painted Caves* (2011). Her research on prehistoric Europe, Cro-Magnon people, and Neanderthals is respected by anthropologists and archeologists around the world. Born Jean Marie Untinen to Finnish immigrants in Chicago, Auel and her husband Ray have lived in Portland for many decades, where they raised five children. In 2008, France named Auel an Officer of the Ordre des Arts et des Lettres. (Auel.)

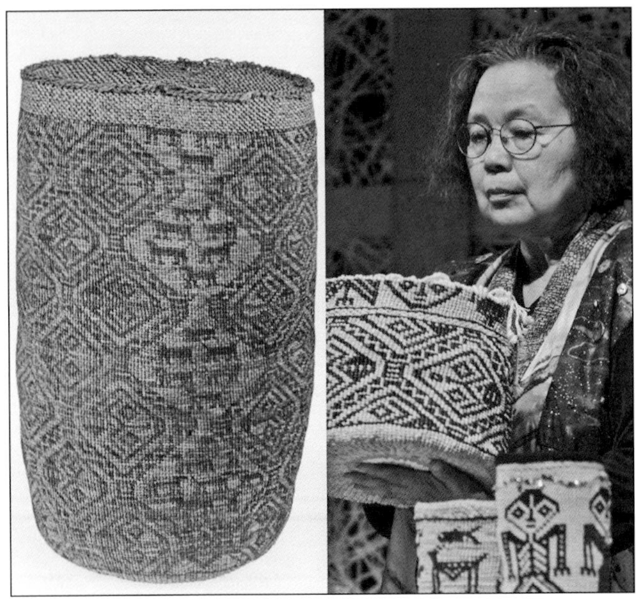

Pat Courtney Gold (born 1939) is a Wasco Native American (a branch of the Chinook people) and was raised on Warm Springs Reservation. An internationally acclaimed artist, she studied a Wasco basket collected by Lewis and Clark along the Columbia River in 1805 (left), now at Harvard University's Peabody Museum. She analyzed the weaving patterns, noticing that the design seemed inspired by petroglyphs like *She Who Watches*. Gold's basketry designs honor her Wasco history, and she teaches basket weaving throughout the region. (Left, Peabody Museum; right, OSU.)

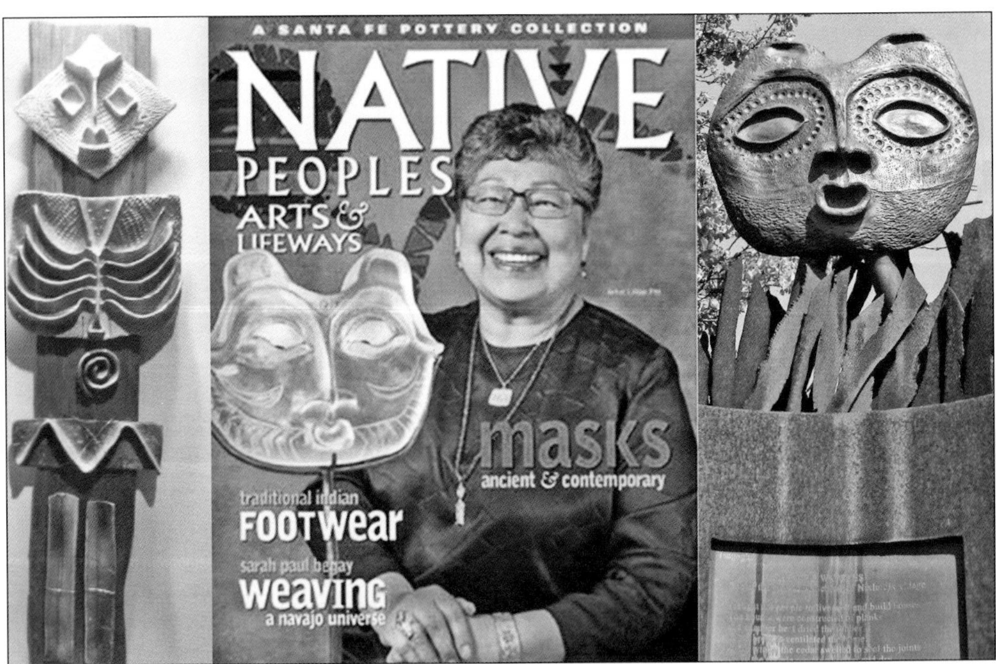

Internationally known Wasco, Yakama, and Warm Springs artist Lillian Pitt was born in 1943 on Warm Springs Reservation, moving to Portland in the 1960s. Inspired by 12,000 years of Native history along the Columbia River, she has won numerous awards, and her works are in many museums. Her art honoring Chinook women is part of the Vancouver Land Bridge installation of Maya Lin's Confluence Project. At right is *Wasco Totem* at the Portland Art Museum, and left is *She Who Watches* at North Interstate and Ainsworth Streets.

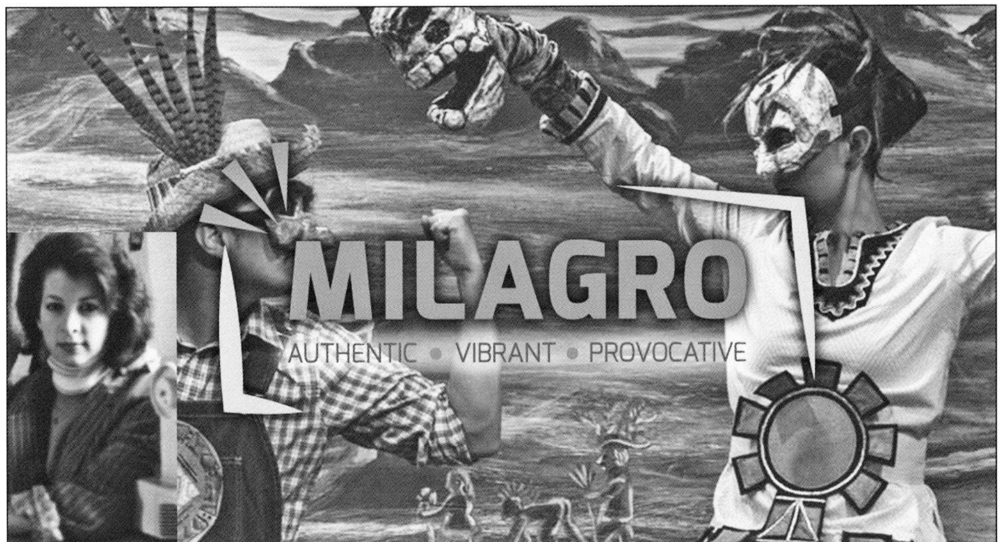

Dañel Malán cofounded the Milagro Theatre with her husband, José Eduardo González, and she created the bilingual national touring program Teatro Milagro. She has written several bilingual scripts for Teatro Milagro, which include *Cuéntame Coyote* (2005 and 2014) and *FRIDA, un retablo* (2006 and 2013) and designed residencies, workshops, and school curricula. Milagro Theatre promotes Spanish-language theater.

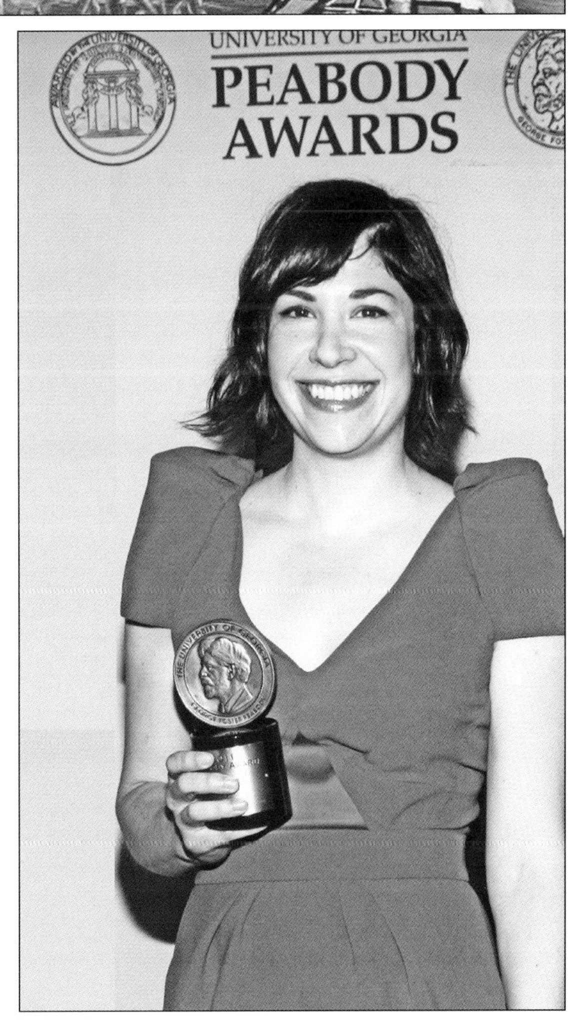

Carrie Brownstein (born 1974), a musician, actress, writer, and comedian, wrote and appeared in the smash hit *Portlandia*, an Emmy- and Peabody Award–winning TV series with absurdist spoofs of the types of characters who make Portland weird. In college, she formed the band *Excuse 17* and toured with the band *Heavens to Betsy*. The bands combined to create the highly regarded *Sleater-Kinney*, releasing nine albums. Brownstein is the only woman in *Rolling Stone*'s 25 "Most Underrated Guitarists of All Time" list for 2006. (W.)

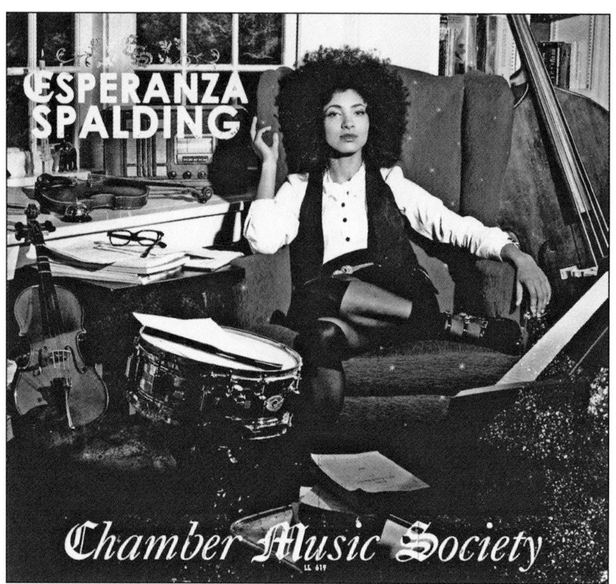

Singer, bassist, violinist, pianist, and Grammy winner (in 2011, 2013, and 2014), Esperanza Spalding (born 1984) played in clubs around Portland as a teen and learned from her time in the Chamber Music Society of Oregon's youth programs and with Portland greats Thara Memory, Janice Scroggins, Darrell Grant, and many others. Starting at Portland State University's music program, she graduated from Berklee School of Music in 2002. Her albums *Junjo* (2005), *Esperanza* (2008), and *Chamber Music Society* (2010) have received great acclaim.

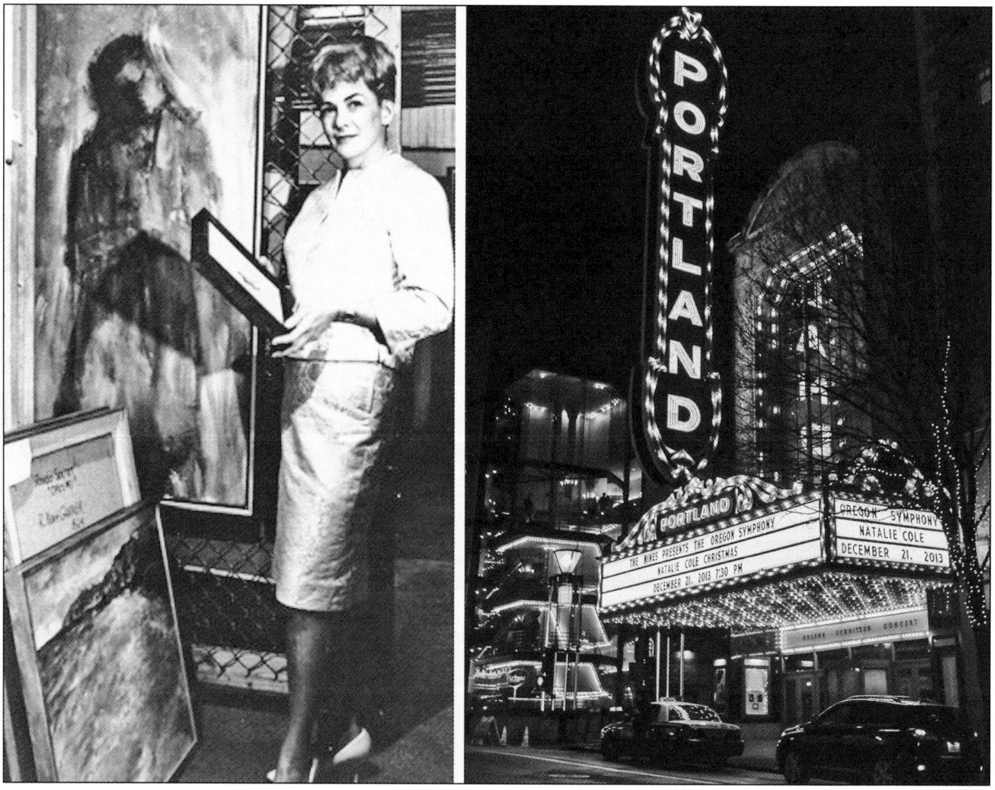

Arlene Director Schnitzer (born 1929) promoted Pacific Northwest artists for decades at her Fountain Gallery, pictured here. She and her husband, Harold, have given millions to universities and museums. But perhaps her most visible Portland legacy is the Arlene Schnitzer Concert Hall, a gloriously restored 1927 Italianate-ish theater. Generations of Portlanders reminisce about nights at "the Schnitz," thanks to Arlene Schnitzer's devotion to the arts in Portland. (Harold & Arlene Schnitzer CARE Foundation, W.)

Six

Women in Politics 1920s to Present

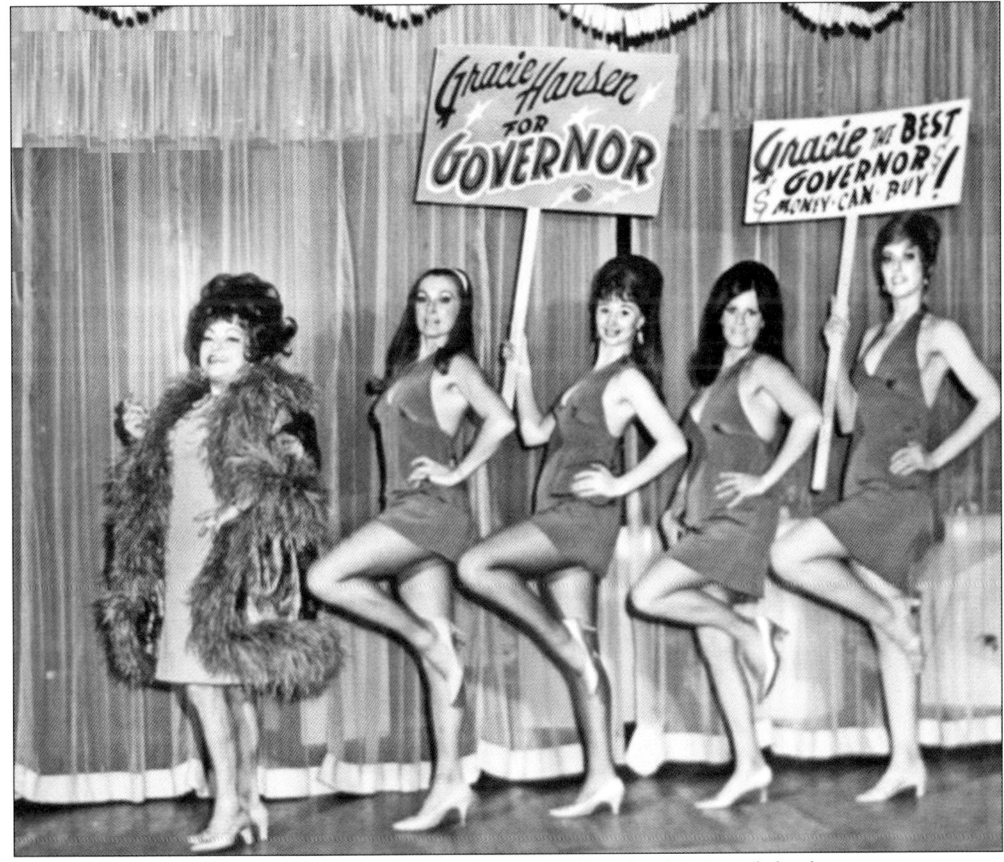

Portland women have made their marks on state and national politics, with both women governors coming from Portland and a lot of firsts as women pushed boundaries to seek political equality. Gracie Hansen was the most colorful candidate and the first woman to run for governor, in 1970 (see page 89). Outrageous as always, she declared herself "The Best Governor Money can buy!" and said, "I've had my eye on [Gov.] Tom McCall's seat for a long time."

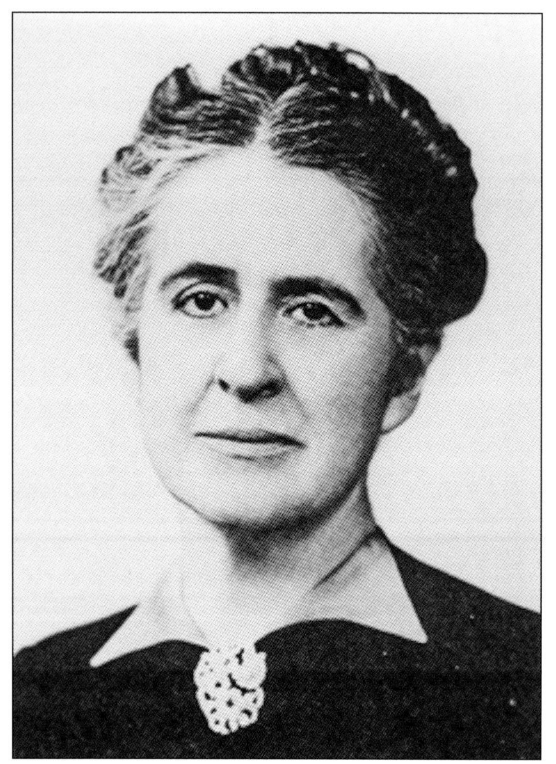

Nan Wood Honeyman (1881–1970) was Oregon's first congresswoman, serving from 1937 to 1939. She served in the Oregon House of Representatives from 1935 to 1937 and in the Oregon Senate from 1941 to 1942. Her parents were Charles Erskine Scott Wood and Nanny Moale Wood, who lived at 1132 Southwest Vista Avenue, now the site of the Portland Garden Club. Congresswoman Honeyman was president of the League of Women Voters, committeewoman of Oregon's Democratic Party, president of the Woman's National Organization for Prohibition Reform (lobbying to repeal Prohibition), and a strong supporter of the Bonneville Dam and Roosevelt's New Deal. (W.)

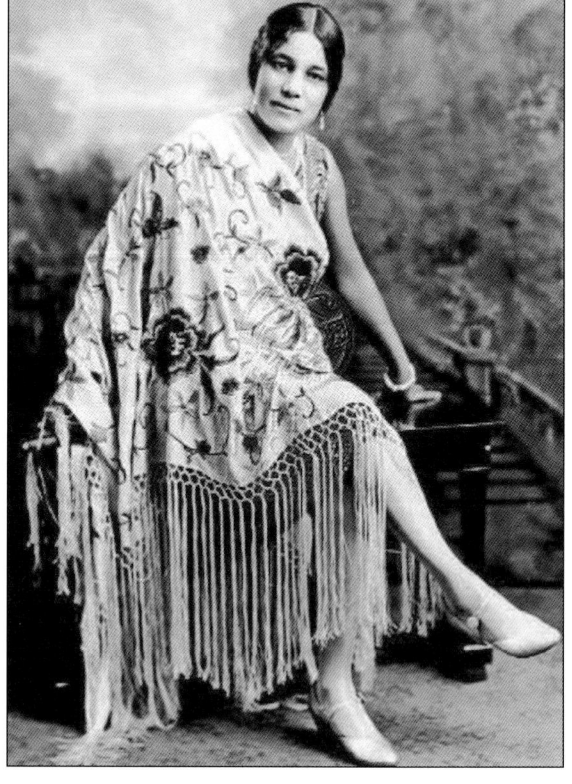

Influential civil rights activist Beatrice Morrow Cannady (1889–1974) was the first African American woman to graduate from an Oregon law school in 1922 and the first African American to run for office in Oregon in 1932, though her campaign was unsuccessful. She was co-founder and vice president of the Portland chapter of the National Association for the Advancement Colored People (in 1914). She was editor and publisher of the *Advocate*, a newspaper cofounded in 1903 by her husband Edward. She challenged racial discrimination such as public schools excluding black children, Oregon's notorious "black laws," the KKK, and the racist film *The Birth of a Nation*. (PSU.)

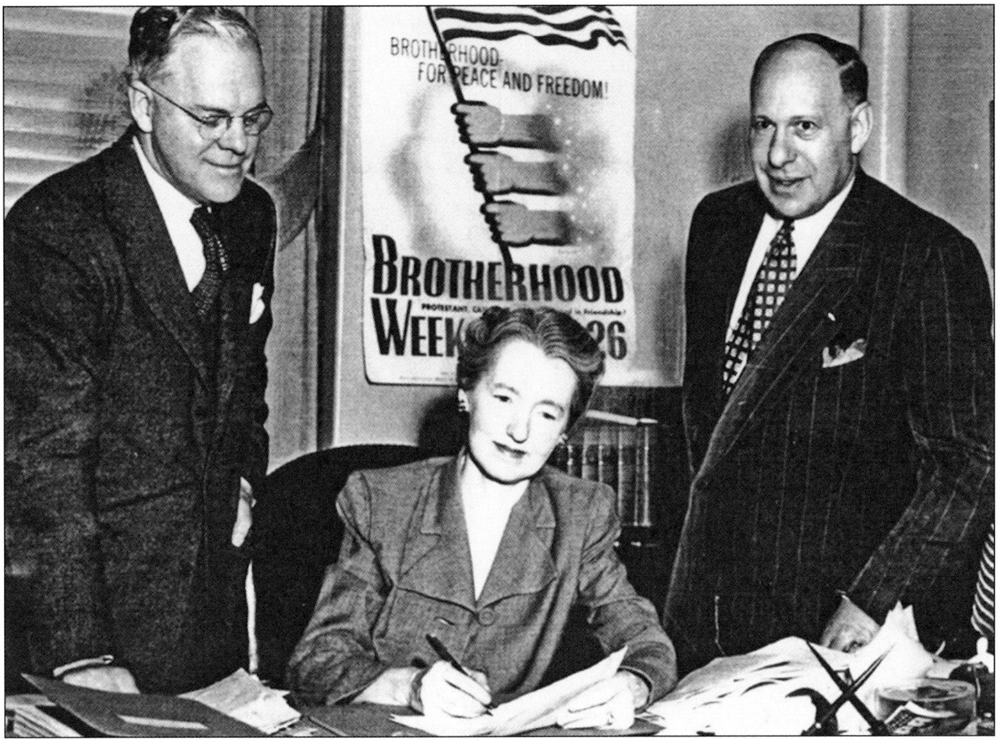

A lawyer and politician, Dorothy McCullough Lee (1901–1981) moved to Portland in 1924 and opened the first all-female law practice in Oregon. Lee also served in the Oregon House of Representatives and Senate and as city commissioner. In 1948, she became the first female mayor of Portland and came to be known as "No Sin Lee," as she cracked down on Portland's notorious vice industry: gambling, burlesque houses, brothels, and organized crime. (PSU.)

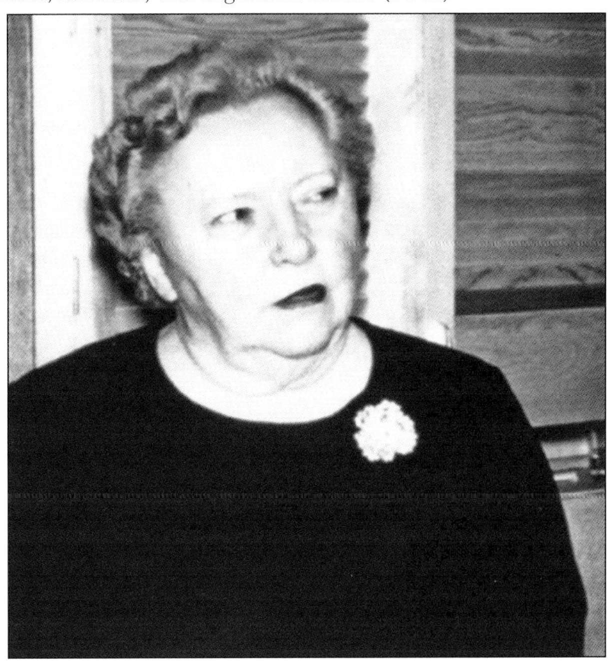

Although she did not run for office, Margaret Goodin Fritsch (1899–1993) held an important position with the State Board of Architectural Examiners. She was the first women graduate from the University of Oregon's School of Architecture, in 1923, and the first woman licensed as an architect in Oregon. She opened her own practice and later served as a city planner in Alaska. Secretary of the Oregon State Board of Architectural Examiners (1926–1936), she was elected to the American Institute of Architects in 1935.

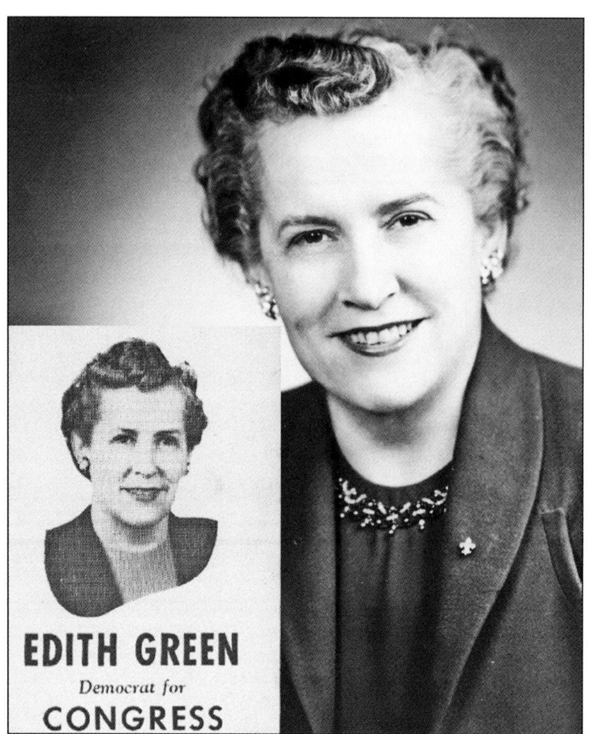

Edith Starrett Green (1910–1987), was the second Oregonian woman to be elected to the US House of Representatives. She served for 10 terms, from 1955 to 1974. She proposed the 1955 Equal Pay Act that became law eight years later, requiring men and women to be paid equal pay for equal work. Rep. Edith Green played an instrumental role in passing the 1972 Equal Opportunity in Education Act, known as Title IX, requiring gender equity in higher education. The Federal Building at 1220 Southwest Third Avenue is named after Green. (Inset, OHS 011170; larger image, PSU.)

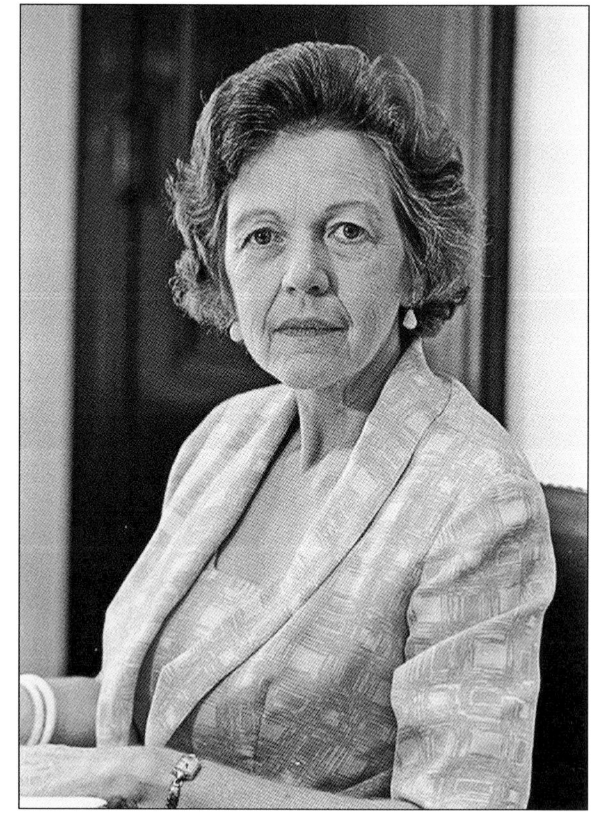

Maurine Brown Neuberger (1907–2000) was the first and only Oregon woman as a United States senator, serving from 1961 to 1967. She was the fourth woman elected and tenth woman to serve in the Oregon Senate. She also served in the Oregon House of Representatives from 1950 to 1955. Sen. Neuberger advocated for consumer rights, women's rights, and environmental and health laws. She promoted legislation that would have given women equal rights, but her efforts were not supported by her predominantly male colleagues. In 1961, President Kennedy appointed her to the Presidential Commission on the Status of Women. (W.)

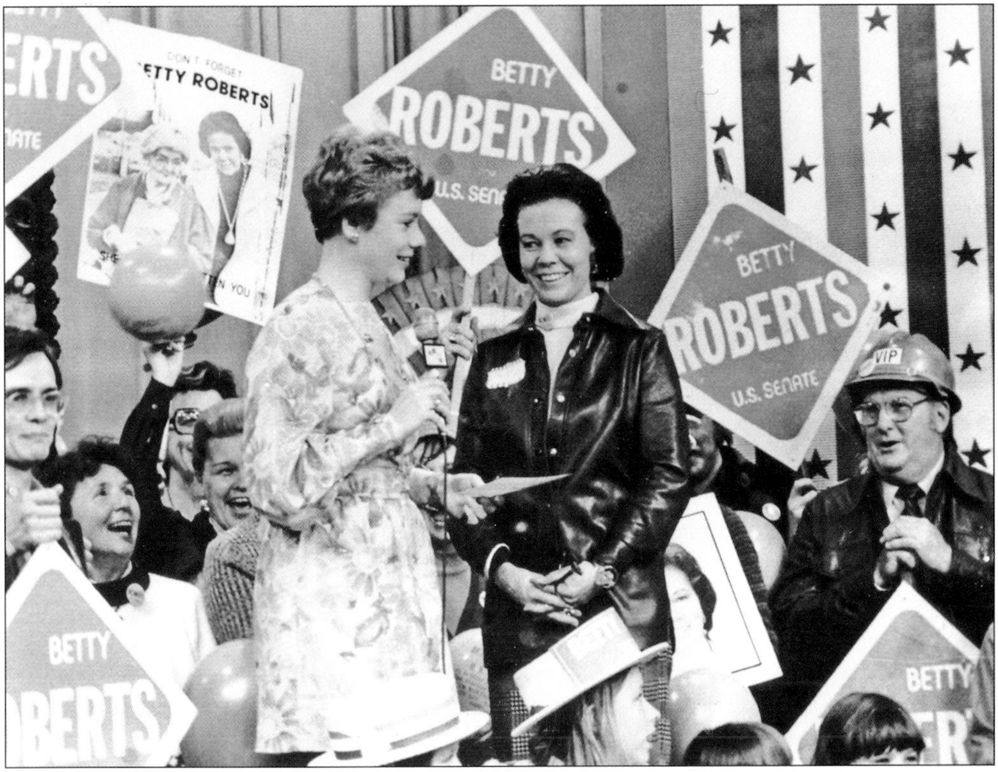

The first woman on the Oregon Supreme Court, Betty Cantrell Roberts (1923–2011) worked to change laws that discriminated against women and ethnic minorities. She was also the first woman on the Oregon Court of Appeals. Betty Roberts served in the Oregon House of Representatives from 1964 to 1968 and the Oregon Senate from 1968 to 1976, where she was cosponsor of the nation's first Bottle Bill. She ran, unsuccessfully, for governor and for the US Senate. She was the recipient of many awards, including the Oregon State Bar Association's Award of Merit, the Woman of the Year for the Oregon Women's Political Caucus, and the Education Citizen of the Year by the Oregon Education Association. In 2008, Roberts published her autobiography, *With Wit and Grace*. (OSA.)

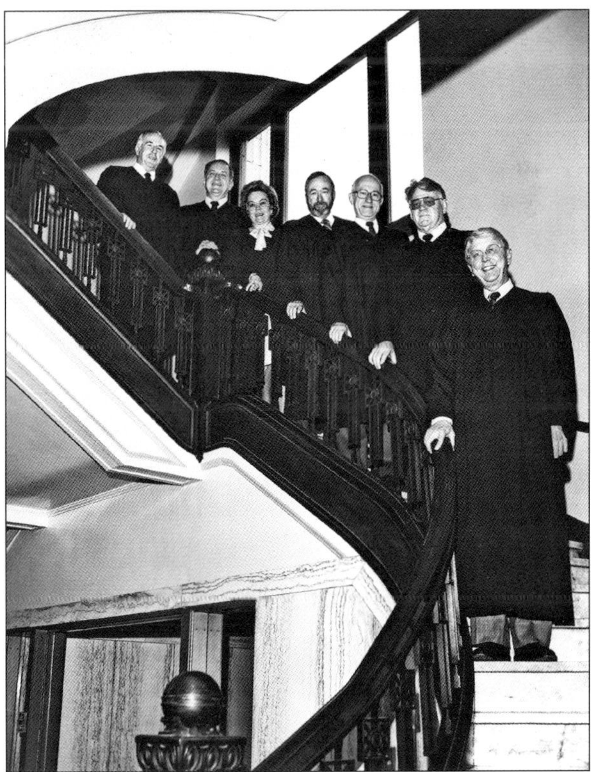

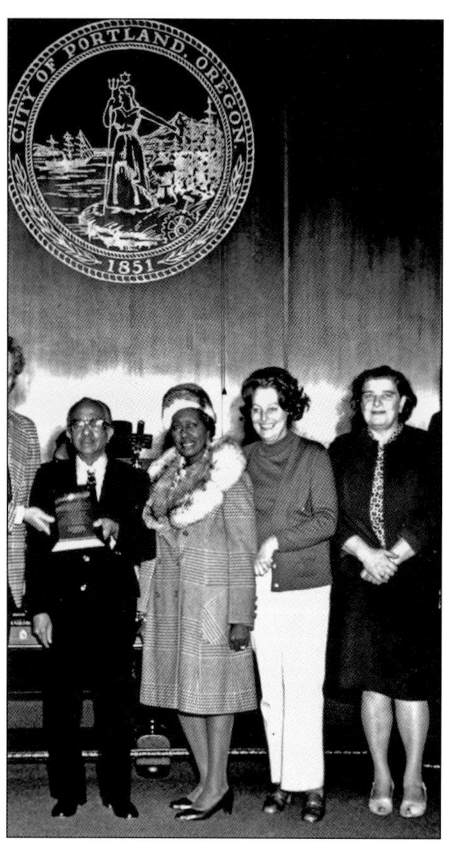

Pictured in 1974, Connie Averill McCready (second from right) and Mildred Schwab (far right) stand with honorees at Portland City Hall. Connie McCready (1921–2000) served in the Oregon House of Representatives (1967–1969); was appointed Portland commissioner (1970–1978) to replace Stanley Earl who had died; and was appointed Portland mayor (1979–1980) to replace Neil Goldschmidt, who became United States transportation secretary. Mildred Schwab (1917–1999) served as Portland commissioner (1973–1986). In 1939, when there were few women lawyers, she graduated from Northwestern College of Law and practiced law in Portland until she entered politics in 1973. In the 1970s, she worked to end the practice of some restaurants and City Club not allowing women. (CoPA.)

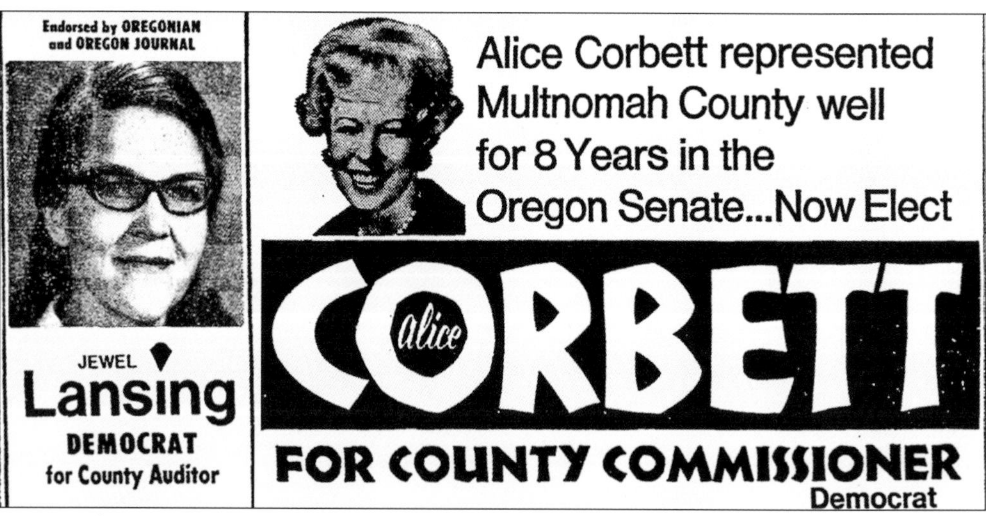

In 1974, the first women ever elected to office in Multnomah County were Jewel Lansing (born 1930) as auditor and Alice Reckard Corbett (1921–2010) as county commissioner. Lansing was Portland auditor from 1983 to 1986 and ran, unsuccessfully, for state treasurer in 1976 and 1980. She is co-author, with Fred Leeson, of *Multnomah: The Tumultuous Story of Oregon's Most Populous County* and the author of *Portland: People, Politics, and Power, 1851–2001*. Alice Corbett served in the Oregon Senate from 1958 to 1966 and as national Democratic committeewoman for 16 years.

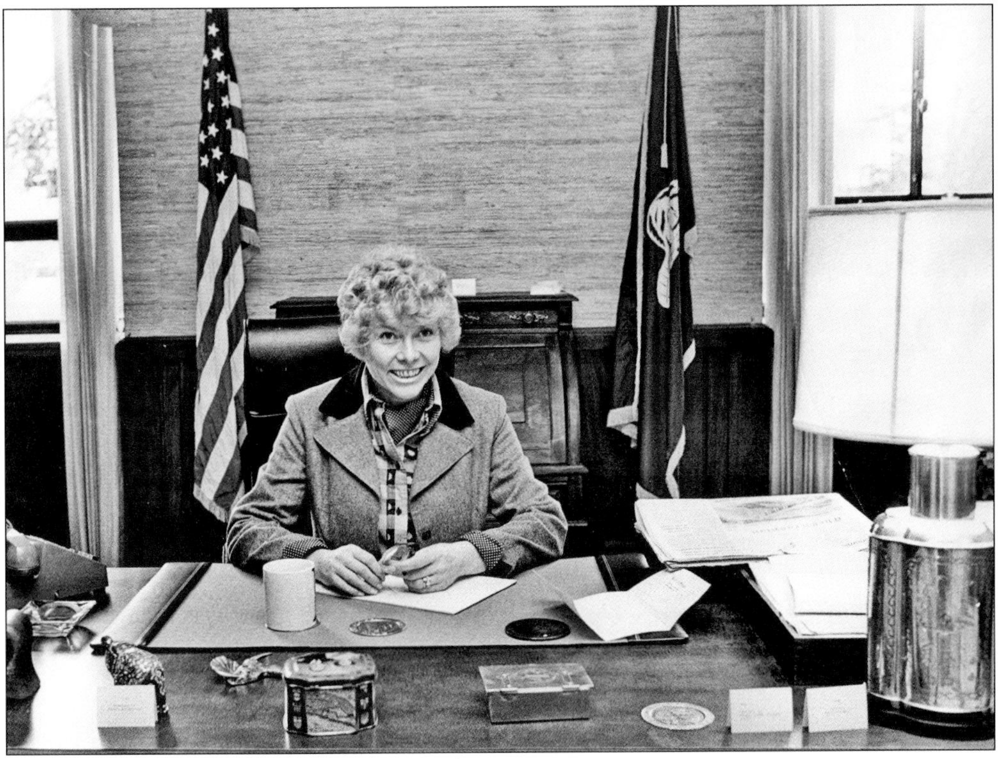

In 1977, Norma Peterson Paulus (born 1933) was the first woman elected to a statewide public office in Oregon when she became secretary of state. Norma Paulus served in the Oregon House of Representatives from 1970 to 1975 and was superintendent of public instruction. She ran, unsuccessfully, for governor and a US Senate seat. A founding member of the Oregon Women's Political Caucus, she was instrumental in efforts to pass the Equal Rights Amendment in Oregon in 1973 and 1977. Living in Portland, she remains politically active.

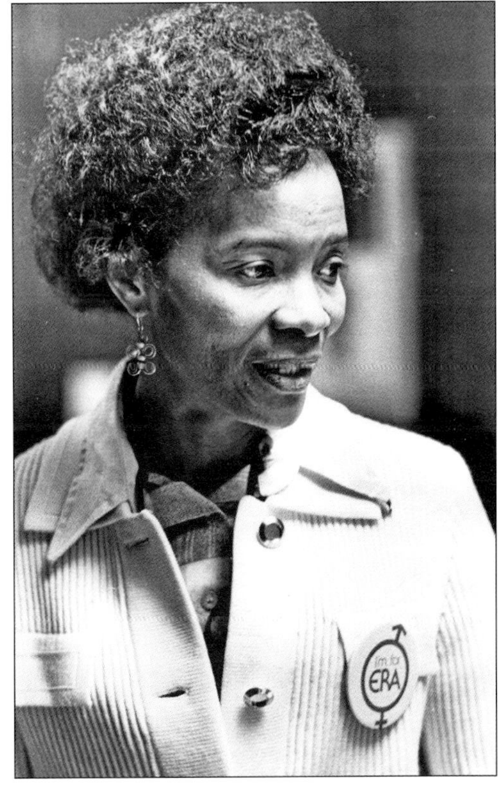

A graduate of Alabama's Talladega College, Gladys McCoy (1928–1993) was the first African American elected to public office in the state of Oregon. McCoy was elected to the Portland Public Schools Board in 1970, the Multnomah County Board of Commissioners in 1978 (resigning in 1984), and the Multnomah County Chair in 1986, serving until her death in 1993. Portland's McCoy Park is named after Gladys and her husband, Bill. She is pictured wearing an ERA (Equal Rights Amendment) button.

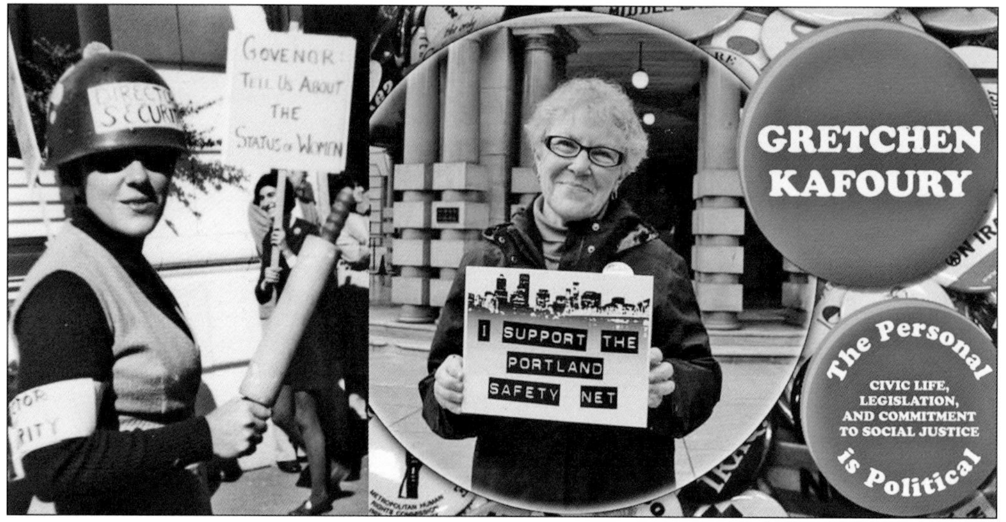

Gretchen Miller Kafoury (1942–2015) holds a rolling pin in a 1972 City Club protest, fighting against its ban on women members. She fought for the Equal Rights Amendment for women, the homeless, and affordable housing as a member of the Oregon House of Representatives (1977–1982), Multnomah County commissioner (1985–1991), and Portland commissioner (1991–1998). She cofounded Oregon's National Organization for Women chapter in 1970 and Oregon Women's Political Caucus in 1971 and taught at Portland State University. (Left, City Club; right, PSU.)

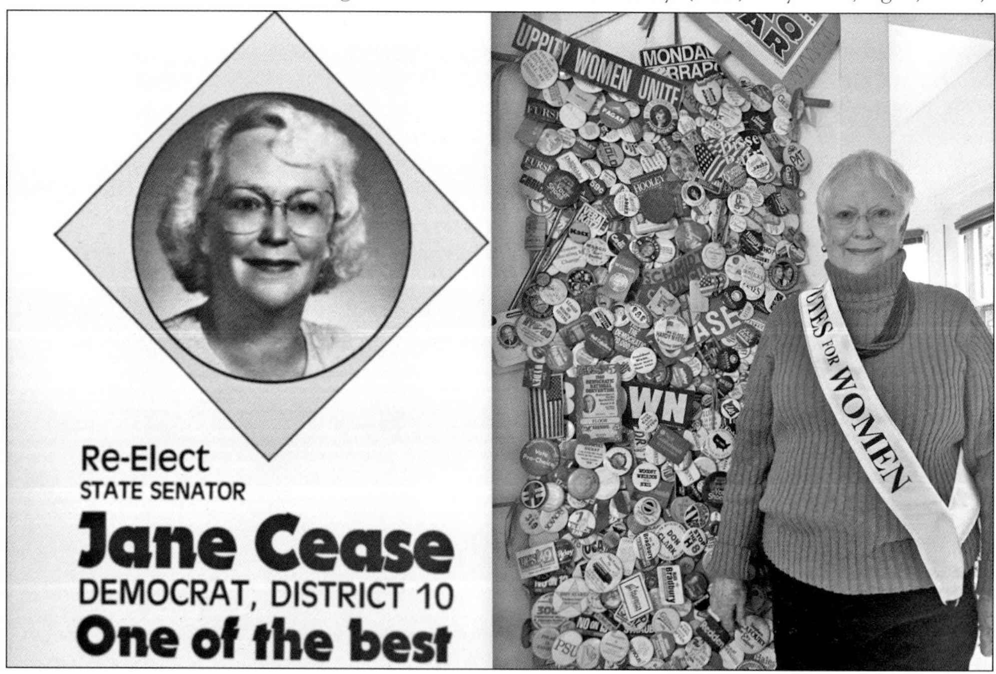

Jane Hardy Cease (born 1936) was in the Oregon House of Representatives (1979–1985), in the Oregon Senate (1985–1991), president of the League of Women Voters, the first woman to chair an Oregon legislative revenue committee, and the first women to lead the Driver and Motor Vehicle Services Division. On the boards of the Women's Investment Network PAC and the Center for Women's Leadership, she is pictured with her collection of 400 campaign buttons, wearing the Votes for Women sash from *Century of Action: Oregon Women Vote 1912–2012*.

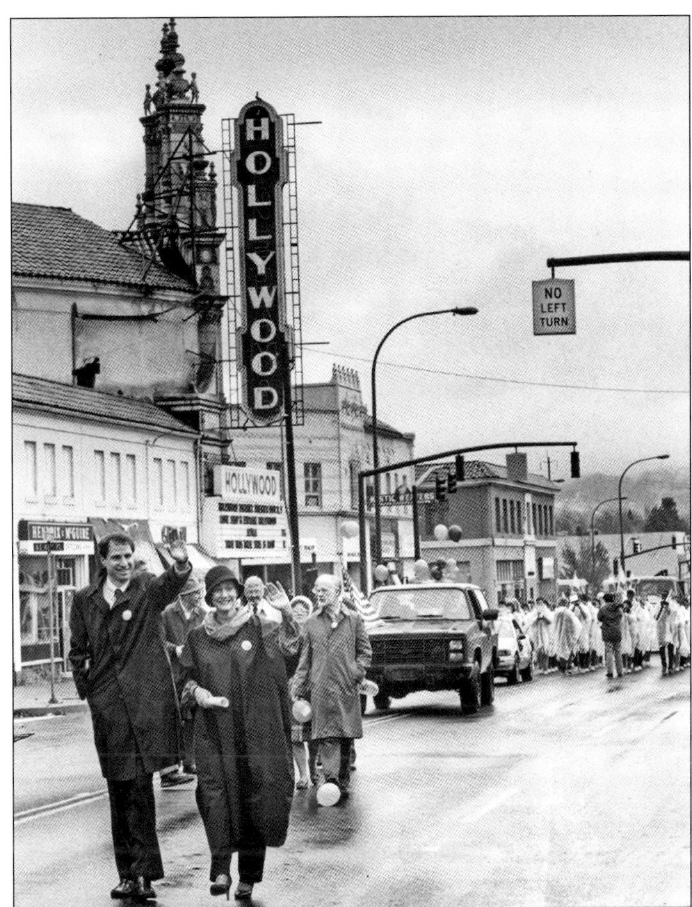

A 1985 photograph shows US representative Ron Wyden and City Commissioner Margaret Strachan marching in a parade on Southeast Sandy Boulevard, passing by the Hollywood Theater. Strachan was a Portland city commissioner from 1981 to 1986. She was the first woman elected—not appointed—to that office. She was the commissioner in charge of planning, transportation, and housing. In 1988, she was honored with a Distinguished Leadership Award from the American Planning Association.

The first African American woman elected to the Oregon Legislature, Margaret Hunter Carter (born 1935) served in the Oregon House of Representatives from 1985 to 1999 and in the Oregon Senate from 2001 to 2009. She served as president pro tempore of the senate and vice chair for Ways and Means. In 2009, she was deputy director for human service programs at the Oregon Department of Human Services. While a legislator, she fought against apartheid and helped commemorate Martin Luther King Jr.'s birthday as a state holiday and advocated for skills training centers and summer programs for kids. She was Urban League president from 1999 to 2002. (OSA.)

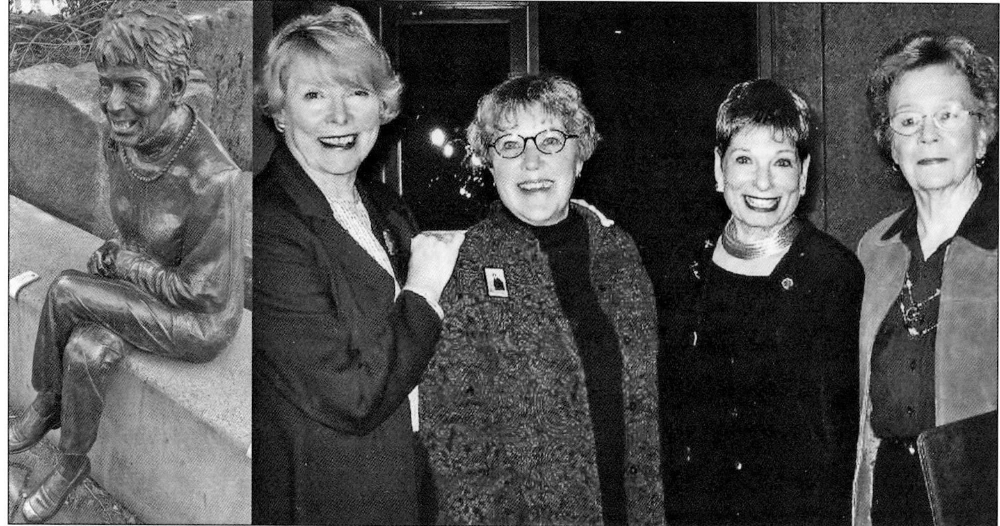

Vera Pistrak Katz (born 1933) fled Hitler during World War II to emigrate to America. She was mayor of Portland (1993–2005) and the first women to serve as the Speaker of the Oregon House of Representatives (serving in the House from 1973 to 1990). In the 1970s, she and other women protested City Club's exclusion of women. Portland honored her championship of the Eastbank Esplanade with this bronze statue. Pictured, from left to right, are Norma Paulus, Gretchen Kafoury, Vera Katz, and Betty Roberts. (PSU.)

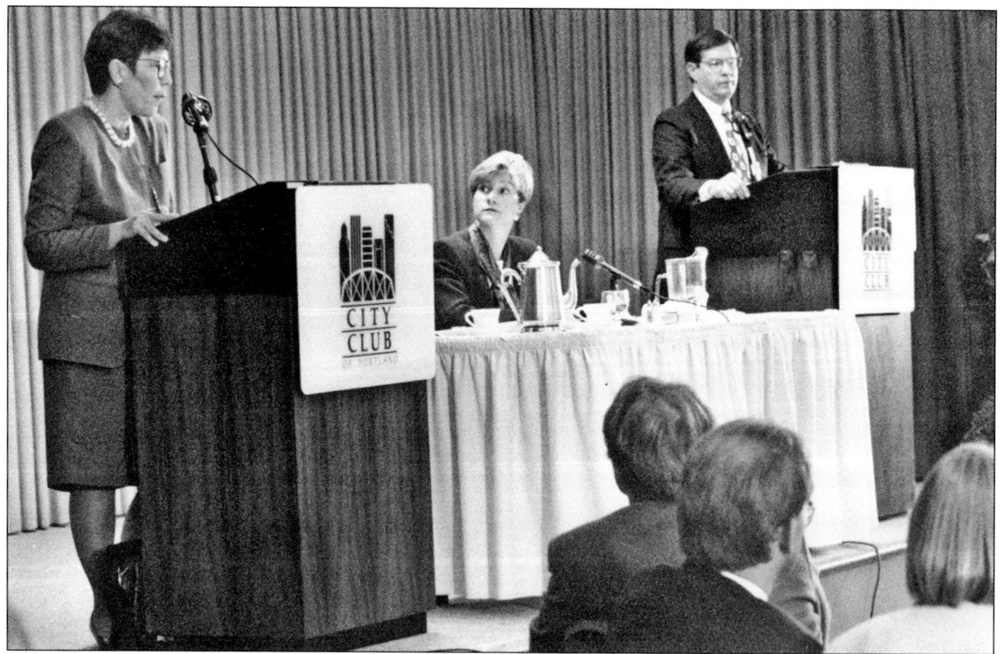

Representing Oregon's 1st Congressional District from 1993 to 1999, Elizabeth Furse (born 1936) was the first person born in Africa to be elected to the US Congress; she is pictured here at a 1992 City Club debate against opponent Tony Meeker. Furse supported Oregon tribal struggles to win federal recognition, successfully lobbying Congress to grant federal recognition to the Coquille, Klamath, and Grand Ronde tribes. She also founded and served as director of the Institute for Tribal Government at Portland State University.

Avel Gordly (born 1947), the first African American woman elected to the Oregon State Senate, served from 1992 to 2009 and in the Oregon House from 1991 to 1996. She led efforts for Oregon's 1995 minimum wage law and Measure 14, removing racist language from Oregon's constitution. Gordly grew up going to women's club meetings with her mother and grandmother and worked with the Black United Front handling media and coordinating African American history programs. She published her memoir, *Remembering the Power of Words*, with Dr. Patricia Schechter. (PSU.)

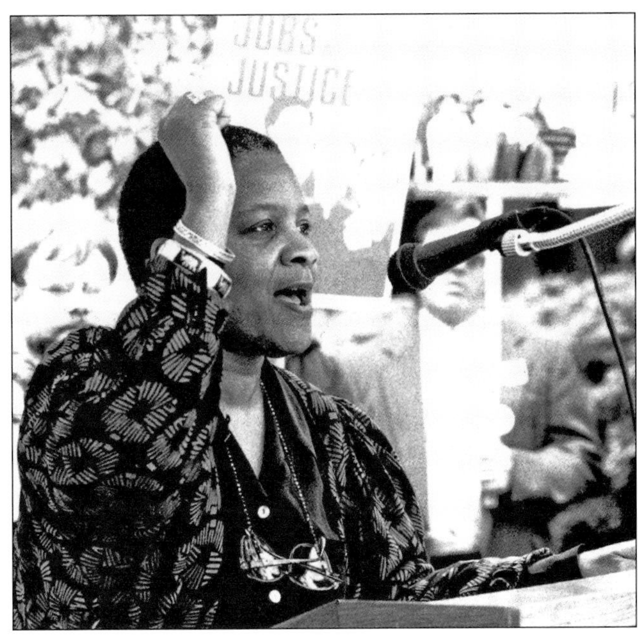

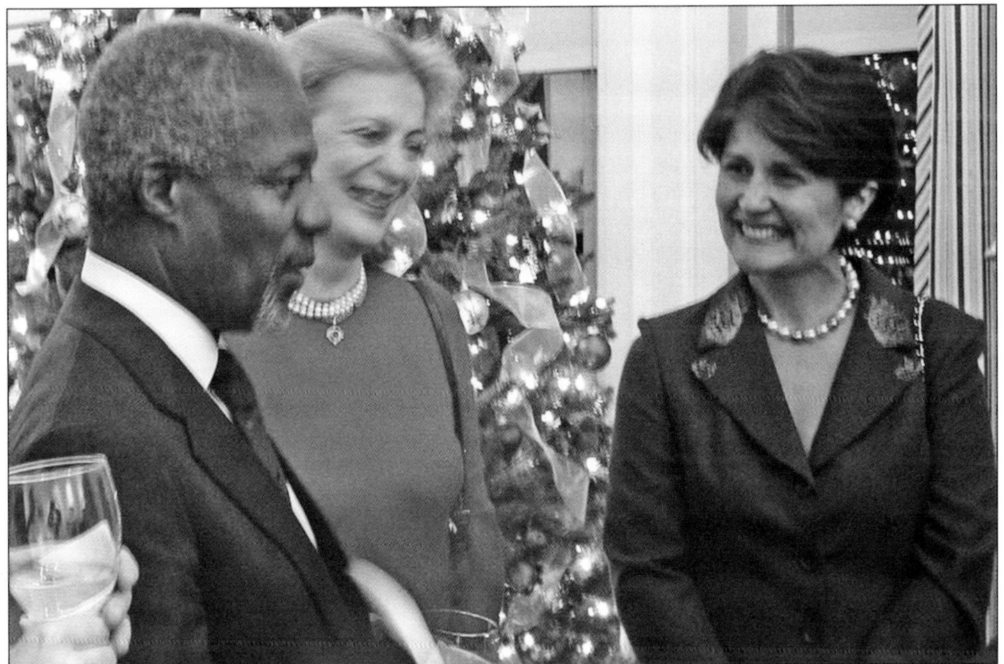

A diplomat and Portland businesswoman, Goli Yazdi Ameri (born 1956) is the president and CEO of the Center for Global Engagement. She was under-secretary-general for the International Federation of Red Cross and Red Crescent Societies from 2010 to 2012, US assistant secretary of state for educational and cultural affairs in 2008 and 2009, and representative to the United Nations in 2005. She ran for the US House of Representatives as a Republican in 2004. (W.)

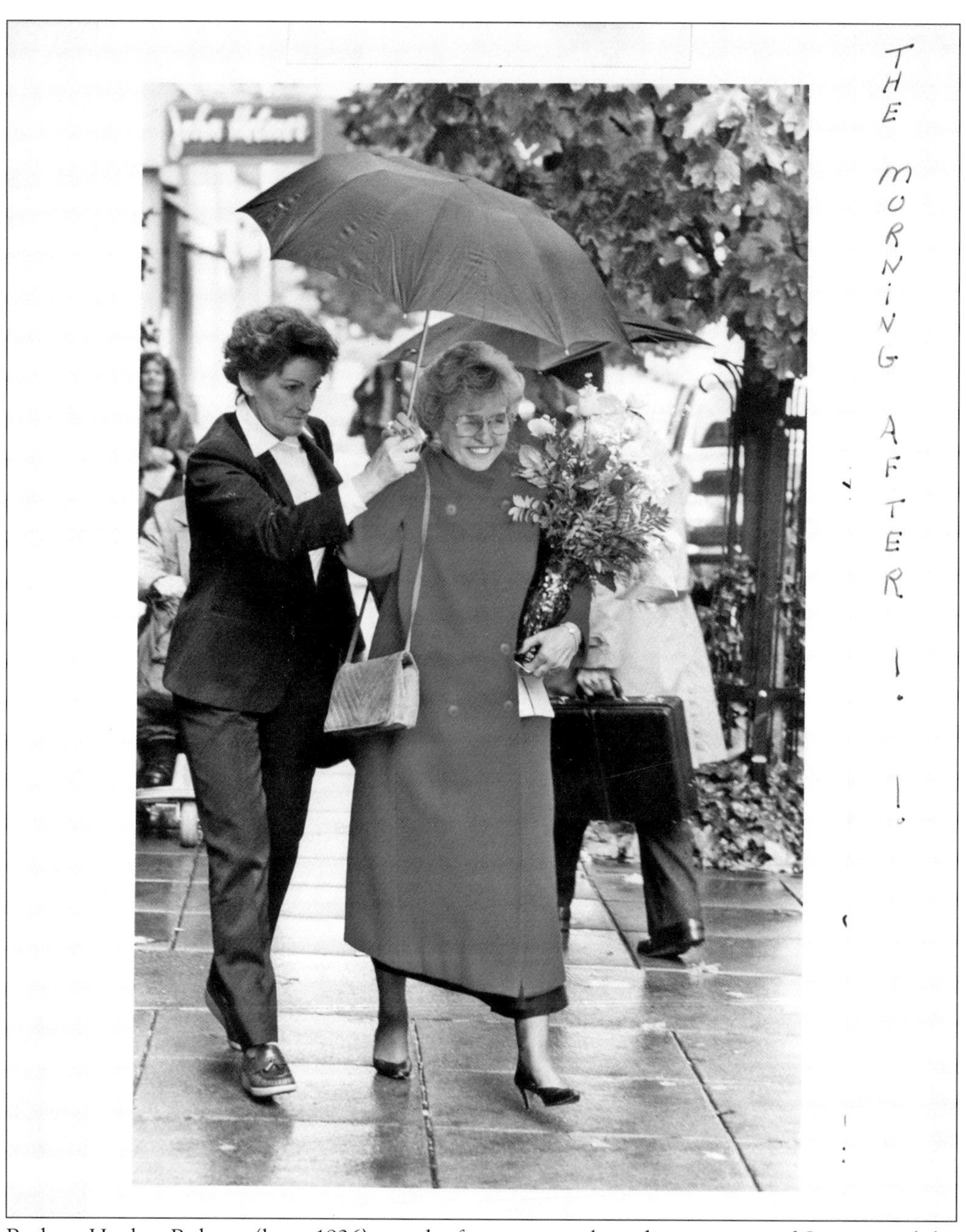

Barbara Hughey Roberts (born 1936) was the first woman elected as governor of Oregon and the 34th governor of Oregon, from 1991 to 1995. Prior to that, she served as Oregon secretary of state and was the first woman to serve as a majority leader in the Oregon House of Representatives. She was a member of the Oregon House from 1981 to 1985 and a metro commissioner from 2011 to 2013. In her time as governor, Roberts helped to secure federal waivers and funding for the Oregon Health Plan. Gov. Barbara Roberts also helped expand the Head Start Program and increased financing for affordable housing. (PSU.)

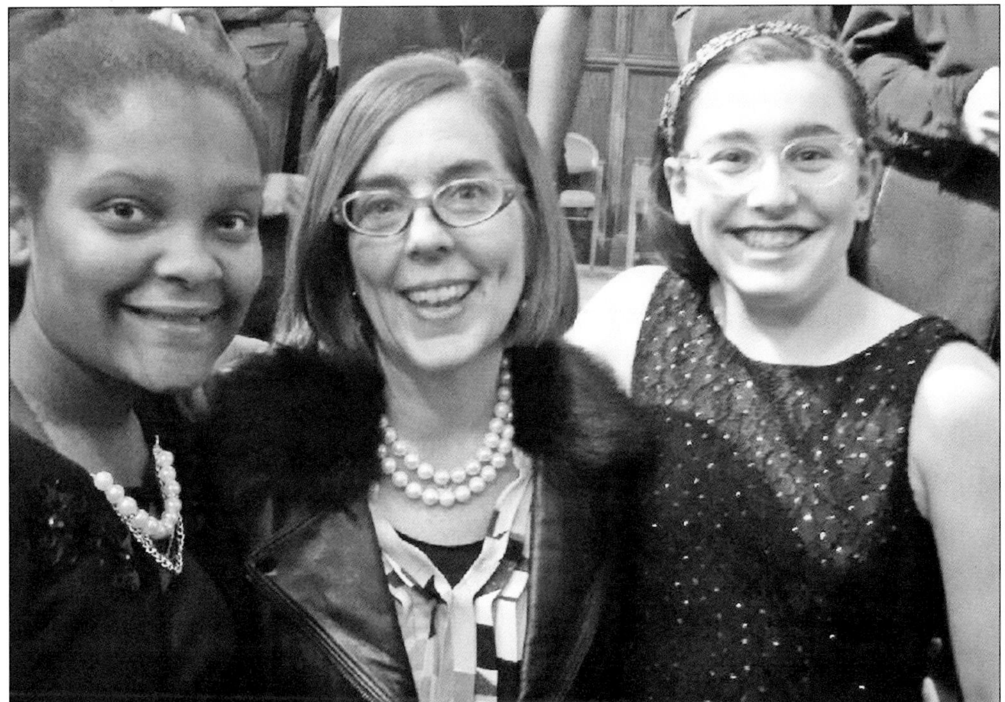

THE AUTHORS: Co-author Zadie Schaffer (right) poses in her younger days with Gov. Kate Brown (born 1960) and friend Karina Talton (left). Governor Brown is the second female governor of Oregon. Becoming governor in 2015, Brown was earlier Oregon secretary of state and majority leader of the Oregon State Senate.

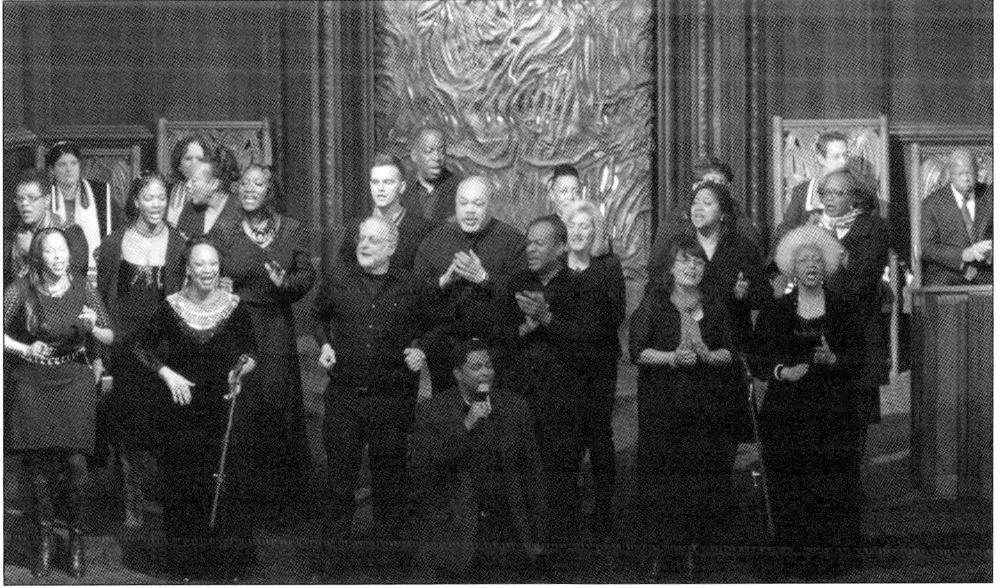

Co-author Dr. Tracy Prince (front row, second from right) is pictured singing with the Northwest Freedom Singers (an interfaith gospel choir that teaches songs from the civil rights movement) at the 2014 Dr. Martin Luther King Jr. service at Congregation Beth Israel. Special speaker civil rights leader Congressman John Lewis sits behind the choir to the right.

Consistent with our mission to preserve history on a local level, this book was printed in South Carolina on American-made paper and manufactured entirely in the United States. Products carrying the accredited Forest Stewardship Council (FSC) label are printed on 100 percent FSC-certified paper.

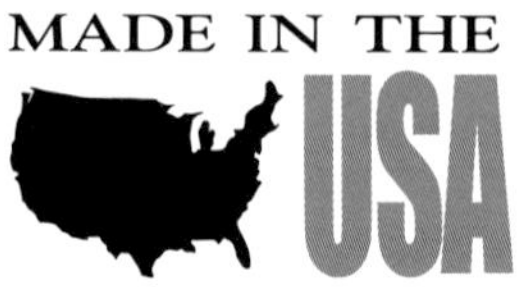

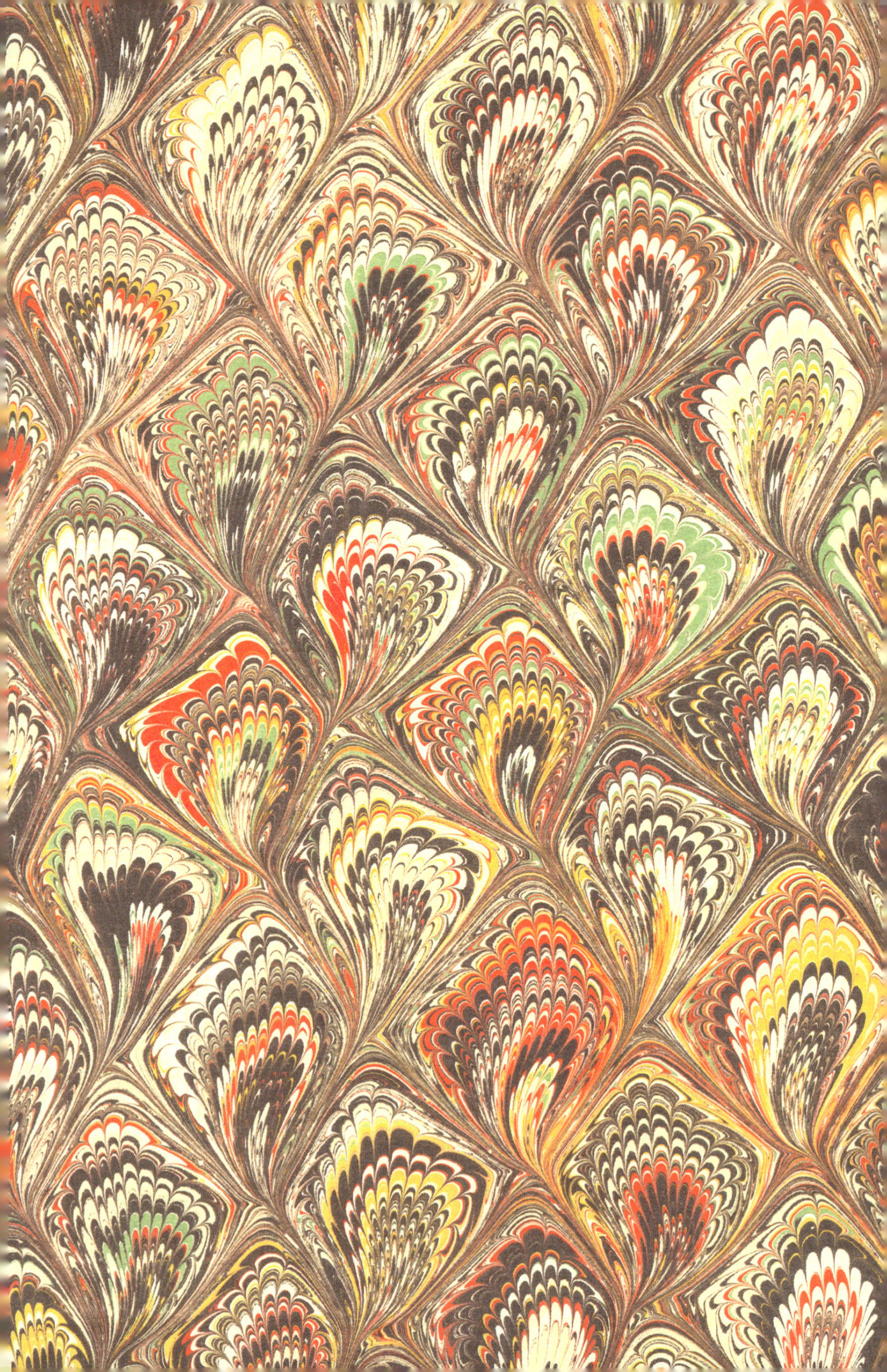